AF412042

Robert Louis Stevenson and theories of reading

Robert Louis Stevenson and theories of reading

The reader as vagabond

GLENDA NORQUAY

Manchester University Press

Manchester and New York

distributed exclusively in the USA by Palgrave

Published by Manchester University Press
Oxford Road, Manchester M13 9NR, UK
and Room 400, 175 Fifth Avenue, New York, NY 10010, USA
www.manchesteruniversitypress.co.uk

Distributed exclusively in the USA by
Palgrave, 175 Fifth Avenue, New York,
NY 10010, USA

Distributed exclusively in Canada by
UBC Press, University of British Columbia, 2029 West Mall,
Vancouver, BC, Canada V6T 1Z2

British Library Cataloguing-in-Publication Data
A catalogue record for this book is available from the British Library

Library of Congress Cataloging-in-Publication Data applied for

ISBN 0 7190 7386 3 *hardback*
EAN 978 0 7190 7386 1

First published 2007

16 15 14 13 12 11 10 09 08 07   10 9 8 7 6 5 4 3 2 1

Typeset in Sabon and Gill Sans Display by
Koinonia, Manchester
Printed in Great Britain
by Bell & Bain Ltd, Glasgow

For Robert Norquay (1923–2004)

Contents

Acknowledgements

This book was completed through the support of the Arts and Humanities Research Council Research Leave Scheme. Early research was supported by a grant from the Carnegie Trust for the Universities in Scotland and facilitated by a Research Fellowship at the Institute for Advanced Studies in the Humanities, University of Edinburgh. I am grateful to all of the above and to Liverpool John Moores University and colleagues there who supported sabbatical leave.

The scholarship of two Stevensonians, Roger G. Swearingen and Neil Macara Brown, has made this book possible; their courtesy, enthusiasm and interest also made working on it a pleasure. The Biennial International Stevenson Conference also led to fruitful comments and pleasant companions: conversations with and the support of Richard Ambrosini, Stephen Arata, Daniel Balderston, Dennis Denisoff, Linda Dryden, Richard Dury, Liz Farr, Morgan Holmes, Wendy Katz, Catherine Kerrigan, Katherine Linehan, Eric Massie, Barry Menikoff, Ralph Parfect and Julia Reid have been important in developing ideas. I am also grateful to Janette Currie for sharing her insights on Covenanting literature. Carol Anderson, Cairns Craig, Douglas Gifford and Alastair Fowler were all influential in earlier stages of my thinking about Stevenson. Colleagues in the Department of English Literature and Cultural History at Liverpool John Moores continue to inspire, advise and encourage; I thank them all for creating such a good research and teaching environment. I am extremely grateful to Timothy Ashplant, for his consistently helpful, detailed and perceptive comments on the book, and to Joe Moran and Elspeth Graham for reading draft chapters. I would like to thank library staff at Liverpool John Moores (Sheena Streather in particular), at the Sidney Jones Library, Liverpool University, at the British Library, the Beinecke Collection, Yale University Library and, of course, the excellent staff at the National Library of Scotland. Pryce Roberts at LJMU was most helpful in technical matters. I am also grateful to all staff at Manchester University Press. Aileen Christianson, Christine and Allan McKenzie, Joanna Price, Fiona and Keith Pringle, Sarah McLennan, Trevor Long and Jayne Rollinson were all supportive friends in difficult times. Patience, fortitude and loving support have also been consistently demonstrated by my family: Jessie and Robert Norquay and Roger, Annie and Duncan Webster.

I

Introduction: the vagabonding reader

I do not know if reading is not, constitutively, a plural field of scattered practices, of irreducible effects, and if, consequently, the reading of reading, meta-reading, is not itself merely a burst of ideas, of fears, of desires, of delights, of oppressions about which we should speak in fits and starts, blow by blow.

Roland Barthes, 'On Reading'[1]

Writing from Paris to his mother in 1876, Robert Louis Stevenson admitted, 'I have been engaged in a wild hunt for books – all forenoon, all afternoon, with occasional returns to Rue Racine with an armful.'[2] Novelist, essayist, poet, Stevenson was also a compulsive reader. Even in an age when the value of fiction was hotly debated and the nature of the ever-increasing reading public a matter of concern, his interest in both the processes of reading and himself as a reader was extreme in its intensity. 'I kept always two books in my pocket, one to read, one to write in', he noted: this awareness of a duality of roles, consumer and producer, dominates Stevenson's critical writing and shapes his fiction.[3] It also makes this figure, who was raised in the environment of a Scottish home with powerfully held (if not always consistent views) on 'the Word' and lived through a period of significant changes in both aesthetics and the professionalisation of authorship, a particularly rich 'case' in which to examine the writer as reader.

In the development of reading theory in the twentieth century, initial interest in reading-oriented criticism – as concerned either with a psychological understanding of the responses patterned out by the individual reader, as in the work of Norman Holland and David Bleich, or with the 'construction' of various kinds of reader response in terms of 'implied readers' (Wolfgang Iser), 'super-readers' (Michel Riffaterre) or 'reading communities' (Stanley Fish) – was increasingly challenged and complicated. Impelled by a recognition that readers are historically or socially produced, rather than abstract, universal or eternal essences, there has been a movement towards greater specificity in identifying reading processes. The understanding that not only are readers very different from one another but that any individual reader is multiple and any single reading experience determined by difference has further problematised essentialising concepts of 'the reader'.[4] The framework for understanding Stevenson's theorisation of reading in this book is to a large extent determined by that interest in cultural, geographical and historical specificity, in terms of both the social forces which might determine the reader and the extent to which the responses of the 'individual' reader are themselves part of wider discursive formations. As a novelist aiming for both critical acclaim and commercial success, Stevenson was very much a participant in the literary debates and discourses of his time. But this writer, born in 1850 into a 'family of engineers' of professional prestige, bourgeois comfort and strict beliefs, and exposed in his early years to reading material shaped by Calvinism, the traditions of Scottish literature and the popular productions of an expanding publishing industry, also presents a very particular play of ideas and influences. Stevenson's travelling – that 'vagabonding' which will emerge as a key term in understanding his position – produced, moreover, an increasing distance from the dominant literary milieu, and led to those years in Samoa prior to his death in 1894 when his experiments in writing emerged from his own and unusual anxieties and experiences, to the disquiet of friends still centred in metropolitan culture. Much of this book is therefore concerned with tracing the historical, cultural and psychological formation of Stevenson as a reader and with mapping on to this the specifics of his represented reading experiences but it is also directed towards a broader examination of the dynamic between his reading matter and his activities as a writer, both fictional and critical, produced through dialogue with those formations.

The image of Robert Louis Stevenson as a restless traveller is a familiar one. Born in Edinburgh in 1850, this sickly child was first encouraged by his parents to improve his health through travel to the south of France; it was also through his father's profession of lighthouse engineer that he journeyed as a young man in the less kindly climate of Scotland's northern coast. His search for locations that would induce good health led him not only to continental resorts such as Davos but also in later life to the South Seas, where he died in 1894. His pursuit of love was also played out in romantic journeys in North America, first to California and later to a stay in the Adirondack mountains. His darkest moments came when he was forced to remain in one place, denied opportunities for exploration: during his stay in bourgeois Bournemouth, for example, he wrote *Strange Case of Dr Jekyll and Mr Hyde*, published in 1886. But the pleasure of travel was not confined to journeys across or between continents; as a youth he was happy tramping around the Pentland Hills, as a landowner in Samoa always keen to traverse his estate. In one of the many biographical celebrations of his life, Elsie Caldwell, describing his wanderings around the Scottish countryside and animated conversations with the locals, comments: 'He was merely vagabonding, consciously or unconsciously seeking health in the open air because of that insistent call of starving lungs.'[5]

Stevenson's wanderings also acquired a literary resonance. Most obviously titles of works such as *An Inland* Voyage (1878), *Travels with a Donkey* (1879), *The Amateur Emigrant* (1879) and *Across the Plains* (1892) drew attention to his peripatetic existence, but as both writer and reader Stevenson emphasised the wandering and undirected nature of his activities: as he wrote in the 1882 preface to *Familiar Studies of Men and Books*: 'In truth, these are but the readings of a literary vagrant.'[6] Indeed, after his death such self-definitions lingered on, used as both praise and condemnation: the *Saturday Review* was typical in tone: 'And in truth, he was always that, a literary vagrant; it is the secret of much of his charm and much of his weakness. He wandered, a literary vagrant, over the world, across life and across literature, an adventurous figure, with all the irresponsible and irresistible charm of the vagabond.'[7] This book adopts the figure of the 'literary vagabond' as a point of entry into the particular dynamics between Stevenson's reading and writing practices, by drawing on three aspects of his vagrancy: his wandering amongst books as a particularly eclectic reader; his ability as a writer to move across a wide range of genres; and his textual excursions in essays and letters in which he shifts between the roles of reader and writer. It also, however, scrutinises the cultural formations which encouraged the adoption of this specific trope of self-representation.

The vagabonding reader

Stevenson loved reading: as he travelled further and further from Scotland, his letters constantly demanded reading material, new and familiar; he commented on the books he had read, offered advice to aspiring writers, theorised on current literary developments. He was always keen to lift his pen and express readerly enthusiasm, and recipients of his effusions included not only Henry James and George Meredith but also Mary Braddon, Rudyard Kipling, S. R. Crockett and the once-popular Stanley J. Weyman. Even Mrs Humphry Ward, whose book he loathed, received a letter from this fervent reader who particularly enjoyed, he said, her discriminating morality. In much of his writing Stevenson stressed the undirected, wandering, nature of his reading activities. Consuming

Covenanting histories, the classics, sea-faring tales, military histories, geography and travel writing, he presents himself as roaming through the widest range of genres imaginable. 'What a boy turns out for himself, as he rummages the bookshelves, is the real test and pleasure,' he notes and from an early age the unsystematic acquisition of reading experiences was a personal imperative.[8] Although his father's library was 'a spot of some austerity', he nevertheless discovered, 'in holes and corners', the excitements of Scott, Defoe, Ainsworth and – 'how came it in that grave assembly!' – George Sand.[9] Even his ability to read is presented as fortuitous: 'I learned to read when I was seven, looking over the pages in illustrated papers while recovering from a gastric fever. It was thus done at a blow; all previous efforts to teach me having been defeated by my active idleness and remarkable inconsequence of mind.'[10] In his student days he again viewed himself as being at the mercy of whomever he had read most recently:

> Whenever I read a book or a passage that particularly pleased me, in which a thing was said or an effect rendered with propriety, in which there was either some conspicuous force or some happy distinction in the style, I must sit down at once and set myself to ape that quality … I have thus played the sedulous ape to Hazlitt, to Lamb, to Wordsworth, to Sir Thomas Browne, to Defoe, to Hawthorne, to Montaigne, to Baudelaire and to Obermann.[11]

Reading, in Stevenson, is thus consistently represented in terms of itinerancy, a random journey among books.

The vagabonding writer

Stevenson was also highly flexible as a writer over a range of forms; happy to produce 'busters', he was also criticised by contemporaries for his mannered indulgence in belles-lettres. A novelist who began writing history, he produced one of the best-loved adventures for children in *Treasure Island*, imprinted *Dr Jekyll and Mr Hyde* upon the world's imagination, mapped out Scotland in three major novels, created a series of memorable short stories and, after the extravagances of *The New Arabian Nights* and *Prince Otto*, developed his own grim analyses of colonialism in *The Ebb-Tide* and 'The Beach of Falesá'. His desire to adapt, imitate, experiment in different genres, to play – in that unfortunate phrase that returned to haunt, 'the sedulous ape' – in itself became an opportunity for analysis: as he wrote to the critic George Saintsbury, 'I never feel that I know a writer till I have tried to imitate him.'[12] For both Stevenson and his critics this quality suggested a certain lack of rootedness: while as a writer he drew upon a range of different genres his flexibility was at times perceived, and internalised, as a weakness, an absence of direction. 'The truth is,' he wrote to Edmund Gosse, 'I have a little lost my way, and stand bemused at the crossroads. A subject? Aye, I have dozens, I have at least four novels begun, they are none good enough.'[13] Although Stevenson may have thought of himself as a 'fictitious article', and complained towards the end of his life that his appeal to so many different groups meant he couldn't take himself seriously as an artist,[14] a more positive reading of this desire to imitate emerges in Italo Calvino's suggestion that Stevenson tried to write 'the kinds of books he would have liked to read'.[15] This powerful awareness of himself as a reader was ever present for Stevenson, certainly as dominant as that concern with the role and responsibilities of the writer more characteristic of his contemporaries. Indeed, fuelled by the keenness of his readerly desires, Stevenson at times despaired that no other writer would be able to meet his needs: 'But I do desire a book of adventure – a romance – and no man will get or write me one. Dumas I have read and re-read too often; Scott, too, and I am short. I want to hear swords clash. I want a book to begin in a good way.'[16] Stevenson's complaint in this letter to W. E. Henley reveals how, while often expressing anxieties common to writers of his time about the doubtful nature of popularity and the tension between consumers' acclaim and aesthetic success, he still saw pleasure and the fulfilment of a reader's wants as key to understanding the nature of literary activity.

This duality of focus, seeing himself simultaneously and with equal emphasis, as both reader and writer characterised all Stevenson's critical writing as well as determining the nature of much of his fiction. Calvino's perceptive comment, embodied by the letter to Henley, suggests that for Stevenson his role as reader was always a dominant factor in his thinking; shaping the fiction he produced to gratify the demands of a perceived audience which included himself, it also propelled him into the complex analyses of textual pleasure, the role of the writer and the relationship between commercial and aesthetic economies, which dominated his critical writing. In this body of work, neglected until relatively recently, Stevenson's delight in writing as a reader is evident.[17] His critical oeuvre, indeed, can be understood as an extended and performative analysis of the activity of reading. Although his terms differ from those used by phenomenologists and reader theorists of the late twentieth century, the areas of interest are often similar. In essays written for a variety of British and American literary magazines, he explored the pleasures inherent in the reading event, the nature of the imagination, and the relationship between the delights of reading and the pressures of writing in a commercial context. The reader, performing acts of reading and rereading, thus takes centre stage in his critical writing. Garrett Stewart has suggested that the figure of 'the reader' becomes less explicit, less apostrophised in nineteenth-century fiction, and the reading event increasingly extrapolated in parabolic mode, but Stevenson's critical writing directly represented the figure of the reader, playing out a variety of roles through remembered scene or anecdote.[18] At times this readerly figure may be that of RLS as a child, as in 'Penny Plain and Twopence Coloured' in which he recreated his excitement at the purchase, perusal and creation of Skelt's toy theatre and considered the way in which Skelt's narratives shaped his imagination; or, in 'The Lantern-Bearers', revisiting scenes of childhood games and boyhood imagination. In other essays Stevenson presented himself both synchronically and diachronically as a reader; we are shown the various 'Robert Louis Stevensons' growing, changing, reinterpreting, then remapping his relationship with certain fictions which transported him when young: 'it was for this last pleasure that we read so closely, and loved our books so dearly, in the bright, troubled period of boyhood.'[19] Such is the dynamic expressed in 'A Gossip on a Novel of Dumas's', in which he described returning again and again to his favourite Dumas novel, the *Vicomte de Bragelonne*. At other times Stevenson identified himself with a community of readers, such as the group of boys finding discarded romances among the ruins at Neidpath Castle and 'in the shade of a contiguous fir-wood, lying on blaeberries' becoming acquainted with the popular works of Viles and Errym.[20] His essays are characterised by the absolute specificity of those reading scenes: the moment one summer evening when he first discovered he loves reading, perusing fairy-tales while walking into the village on an errand; or reading Dumas on a winter's night in the Pentland hills.[21]

Through narratives which construct a variety of readers he played out the complicated relationships between different reading positions. In 'Popular Authors', for example, he appeared at some points to occupy the literary high ground in comparison with a gullible populace whose life ambitions are shaped by their reading of popular fiction, yet in other parts of the same essay he identified with the enthusiastic consumer of such material. In 'My First Book, *Treasure Island*' he claimed his own critical distance and expertise as a writer, gently chiding an earlier, naively influenced, reading self for plagiarism used by his writing self, then critiqued himself in the manner of a literary critic tracking down influences.[22] His letters too constructed differing versions of himself as reader for his range of correspondents: gloating over adventure stories was reserved almost exclusively for Henley, his buccaneering model of Silver; he pondered his reading of Scottish material with fellow novelists Crockett and Barrie; the morality of reading was debated with his father, and he became a more 'professional' reader when arguing aesthetics with two men: his cousin Bob Stevenson, whose perspective as a painter often provided a useful platform for discussion, and, most famously, fellow-novelist and friend Henry James. With American artist W. H. Low he maintained his quarrel over the profession of letters, but the critic Richard Le Gallienne became a worthy combatant in this debate too.

In general, however, Stevenson's insights on reading emerged not through careful and measured debate or authoritative analysis but through what he often termed 'gossip': vivid stories, small cameos, always circulating around different versions of his reading self, both object and vehicle of his speculations. Although he may have told Low that one day he would produce an 'arid' treatise on literature, his essays were filled with living readers and lively self-representations.[23] In this respect Stevenson's non-fictional writings were driven as much by the sense of himself as a consuming and public reader as by a self-image of the writer fated to meet the demands of 'the beast whom we feed'.[24] In *The Pleasure of the Text* Roland Barthes asks 'How can we take pleasure in a *reported* pleasure …? How can we read criticism? Only one way: since I am here a second-degree reader, I must shift my position: instead of agreeing to be the confidant of this critical pleasure – a sure way to miss it – I can make myself its voyeur: I observe clandestinely the pleasure of others.'[25] In his active engagement with the reading process, Stevenson observed himself, re-enacting his pleasures rather than passively reporting them. As a result, his readers are also forced into performances of pleasure: in consuming his essays we may begin as voyeuristic observers but are rarely allowed to remain so as the essays themselves lead us into imitative engagement with the reading process. In 'A Gossip on a Novel of Dumas's', for example, his itemisation and analysis of the delights of the Musketeers saga, demanding dramatic recounting of key episodes and framed in an equally compelling history of Stevenson's own encounters with the text, produces two powerful narratives for the reader. The more rapidly he moves between the roles of author, critic and reader, the more the readers of his essays also experience a blurring of established textual relationships.

That a similar movement may have been experienced by Stevenson's correspondents is evidenced by a letter to Henley, in which reflections on *Treasure Island* become a discussion of highwayman adventure fiction then slide into the beginning of such a tale:

> I propose to follow up *The Sea Cook* at proper intervals by
> Jerry Abershaw: *A Tale of Putney Heath* (which or its site I must visit.)
> *The Leading Light: A Tale of the Coast*
> *The Squaw Men; or the Wild West.*

and other instructive and entertaining works. ....
I love writing boy's books. This first is only an experiment: wait till you see
what I can make 'em with my hand in.

> > > > I'll
> > > > > be
> > > > > > the
> > > > > Harrison
> > > > > > > > Ainsworth
> > > > > of
> > > > > > > > the
> > > > > > > > > > > Future.

> > > > > ...

Jerry Abershaw – O what a title! ... Jerry Abershaw: d—n it, sir, it's a
poem. The two most lovely words in English: and what a sentiment. Hark
you, how the hoofs ring! Is this a blacksmith's. No, it's a wayside inn. Jerry
Abershaw.
  'It was a clear frost evening, not 100 miles from Putney etc.'
  Jerry Abershaw.
... Jerry Abershaw. Jerry Abershaw. Jerry Abershaw. *The Sea Cook* is now
in its XVIth chapter, and bids for well up in the thirties.[26]

As Henley read, the work must have unfolded, the words acquiring a
resonance beyond that of an authorial outline of future plans or a critic's
speculations on form. Stevenson's own fiction, experimenting with such a
wide range of literary genres, demonstrated a similarly conscious engagement with the nature of readerly activity that was explicitly addressed
in his essays. The letter to Henley, shifting from analysis of narrative to
its enactment, offers a key to understanding the relationship between
Stevenson's interest in reading and his activities as a writer; in both
fiction and criticism he was rarely content to remain in a fixed position,
preferring to maintain a wandering guise.

Approaching reading

It is this highly developed consciousness of himself as a reader, figured in
the vagabonding trope, which makes Stevenson not only interesting as
a literary theorist but also as a strange and fruitful 'case' for developing
a more nuanced understanding both of the broader network of cultural
and historical pressures shaping literary consumption at the end of the
nineteenth century and of the specific complexities which contribute to
the formation of a 'reader'.

  In calling for a new kind of literary history, which would further
advance the understand of reading processes, the cultural historian
Robert Darnton advocates a number of different strategies involving

both historicisation and theorisation. In addition to the 'macroanalytical' approach, which attempts to establish large-scale social histories of reading habits, he also stresses the value of a 'microanalytical' approach: 'most of us would agree that a catalogue of a private library can serve as a profile of a reader; even though we don't read all the books we own and we do read many books that we never purchase'.[27] The project of constructing a reader, as Darnton acknowledges, is fraught with problems but should be possible – though not easy: 'for the documents rarely show readers at work, fashioning meaning from texts, and the documents are texts themselves, which also require interpretation'.[28] The deployment of literary theory can be helpful in revealing 'the range of potential responses to a text'.[29] Through combining different kinds of research, he suggests, we can move towards a knowledge, necessary for understanding changes in reading within our own culture, of 'the ideals and assumptions underlying readings in the past' – which books were valued, how they were treated, the ways in which reading was learned and what reading meant'.[30]

From his letters, from the accounts of his library and from biographies, the patterns of Stevenson's reading can be identified; representations of the 'reader at work' are, moreover, at the heart of several key essays. This book is not, however, simply about the reconstruction of Stevenson as a reader: rather it aims to consider, using the detailed information available, the highly complex relationship between his representation of himself as a reader, his production of fiction as a writer and the location of both within contemporary critical and cultural contexts. While aiming for this historical specificity in reconstruction of Stevenson's self-presentation of himself as a reader through detailed tracing of his attitudes and experiences would appear to meet some of the requirements of Darnton's project, the problems around essentialising an abstract reader or fixing single readers remain. As Steven Mailloux has argued in *Interpretive Conventions*, there is a tendency to separate out the figures of ideal or implied reader and the 'actual' reader, and to act as if there was an absolute distinction between these figures. He suggests, however, that 'Such a move is misleading insofar as it suggests a distinction between real and hypothetical readers and one between neutrally described and critically constructed reading experiences. In fact, all readers are hypothetical and all reading experiences critically constructed.'[31] Rather than oversimplified translation of readers into what he calls 'identity themes', he argues that 'all reading must be seen through some interpretive framework that in fact constitutes the reading experience described'.[32] In examining Stevenson's essays, letters, borrowings and fiction we begin to get some sense of what reading meant to him and how he articulated his understanding of it, within a specific literary context, but while Stevenson existed and read, and therefore was in a sense a 'real' reader', the 'reader' that emerges in these pages is in itself always a hypothetical and textual construction, both on his part and on our part as interpreters. Moreover, readers obviously exist in relation to what they read and, as Darnton reminds us, any relational understanding of readers and books must take into account the relationship between changing readerships and their construction of shifting texts.[33] Just as Stevenson's self-representation as a reader was consciously motivated by his engagement with particular texts, arenas of cultural debate and individual memory, so that image (and the textual strategies used to articulate it) can be understood also as the product of certain personal, cultural, geographical and historical determinants.

In seeking to offer a highly specific account of one reader emerging from a particular historical moment, place and structure of feeling, but also to relate the insights emerging from this analysis back to a wider understanding of the reading process, the figure of the vagabond gains further significance. Alerting us to the undirected, at times apparently uncritical, nature of his reading activities, the 'vagrancy' of Stevenson's reading permits, indeed encourages, his construction as a 'representa-tive', rather than literary or critical, reader. His emphasis on an absence of textual mastery, a lack of direction, combined with a deep interest in pleasure, made him unusual among his contemporaries, creating a position from which he could, as a writer, work within a range of genres, but also, as a reader, negotiate a series of different reading roles. Indeed this image of 'literary vagrant' prefigures a later projection of 'reader as traveller' deployed by the cultural theorist Michel de Certeau in his important exploration of reading as consumption, *The Practice of Everyday Life*.[34] In an attempt to avoid overemphasis on the activities of an intellectual elite, de Certeau focuses on the practices of might be called the 'general', rather than the 'literary', reader and challenges notions of passivity hitherto associated with reading activity within popular culture.[35] Questioning the dominant idea that 'the use of the book made by privileged readers constitutes it as a secret of which they are the "true" interpreters', de Certeau draws on the image of 'reading as poaching', to suggest that the reader is not simply the passive recipient of the written word. Instead he calls for a model of reading in which the reader

> insinuates into another person's text the ruses of pleasure and appropria-tion: he poaches on it, is transported into it, pluralises himself into it like the internal rumblings of one's body ... Words become the outlet or product of silent histories. The readable transforms itself into the memorable: Barthes reads Proust in Stendhal's text, the viewer reads the landscape

of his childhood in the evening news. The thin film of writing becomes a
movement of strata, a play of spaces. A different world (the reader's) slips
into the author's place.
    This mutation makes the text habitable, like a rented apartment.[36]

This model of writing, with its dual play of pleasure and appropriation,
attractively avoids fixity of the text or of the reading process, allowing
the reader agency without mastery.
De Certeau's images of reading as travelling and poaching resonate
with Stevenson's trope of the vagabonding reader in significant ways.
Firstly, the image draws attention to Stevenson's unusual position within
nineteenth-century literary debates: his self-identification with the idea
of a literary vagrant suggests that he constructed a role for himself which
was much closer to that of a 'general reader' than that of a literary
'master'. While Stevenson, of course, was undoubtedly a 'literary' reader
in many respects, part of that elite which debated and constructed the
aesthetic systems of its time and, by virtue of his class, education and
milieu, undoubtedly in a position of privilege, his self-proclaimed interests – as expressed in both his essays and his fiction – are with reading as
understood in terms close to de Certeau's image: undirected, eclectic and
unconcerned with mastery. In consciously presenting himself as 'reader'
rather than 'privileged interpreter' in his essays, in exploring his own
readerly responses to a range of texts from classics to the popular, and
in admitting the pleasures which all these texts bring to him, Stevenson
avoided that mode of analysis which 'interposes a frontier between the
text and its readers that can be crossed only if one has a passport delivered by these official interpreters'.[37] Although he often wrote from a
position of literary knowingness, this was rarely deployed in interpretative mastery, and he took equal interest in constructing himself as a
child (and therefore unformed) reader, or as a reader lost in books to
such an extent that his responses cannot be consciously articulated and
analysed. Indeed, at times Stevenson's representation of himself as reader
was not dissimilar to the image of nineteenth-century autodidact readers
for, as Jonathan Rose notes (reinforcing Bourdieu's point that autodidact
culture was often mocked for its lack of organisation or systems of
acquisition), 'a promiscuous mix of high and low was a common pattern
among working-class readers of all regions, generations, and economic
strata. Their approach to literature was a random walk.'[38]
    In its construction of reading as itinerancy, *The Practice of Everyday
Life* complicates this concept of a 'random walk', by suggesting that
'readers are travellers; they move across lands belonging to someone
else, like nomads poaching their way across fields they did not write'.[39]
This concept of the reader as poacher, as traveller, engaging in a process

of bricolage, collecting bits and pieces, which are then transformed in use and function, suggests a second appealing resonance in relation to Stevenson's writing. In working within a range of popular genres in his fiction, at times to the disappointment of his reviewers, critical of his desire to please too wide a readership, he likewise moved in a different direction to that of the contemporary literary elite, however much he might also have been representative, in garb and lifestyle at least, of what Bourdieu describes as the commodification of the artist. Rather he travelled across a range of literary forms, experimenting and moving on, motivated not only by what he desired to say but by what he desired to write. In this pattern Stevenson was not engaging in political strategy, the simple valorisation of the popular as a denial of bourgeois value, but was refusing to occupy a fixed place within existing critical paradigms.[40] Emphasising his own reading experiences, avoiding positions of interpretative mastery, the notion of reader as vagabond also freed Stevenson into phenomenological dissection of reading as an activity.

Michel de Certeau's idea of textual 'exchanges' thus offers a more appropriate model for understanding Stevenson as reader and critic, alerting us to the tactical significance of his self-representation. In this study of the dynamic between the reading and writing process, de Certeau's work is also of methodological use because the idea of reading as poaching represents a model of textual relations which avoids oversimplified identification of 'sources and influences'. Exploring the relationship between Stevenson's reading and writing, this book focuses also on the activity of bricolage. Rather than seeing 'consumption-as-receptacle', it is interested in the 'ruses of pleasures and appropriation' which obtain between the books Stevenson most enjoyed and the books he himself produced. In this context de Certeau's model offers an alternative to the straightforward notion of 'literary influence' or the model of 'misprision' advanced by Harold Bloom, in which the 'strong' poet swerves from or kills his forefathers.[41] On a practical level, this combative image of the 'intellectual' reader appears inappropriate to Stevenson who presented himself as eclectic, if not indiscriminate, in his reading tastes. de Certeau's images of the reader engaged in a process of bricolage gestures towards the complicated and nuanced relationship Stevenson has with his own reading activities. Translating this concept into a methodological framework, therefore, the second part of this book operates through case-study analysis of the relationships between key texts in Stevenson's literary consumption which provoke him into identification of specific theoretical concerns and the further addressing of such concerns in his fiction.

Illuminating as de Certeau's concept of the reader as poacher is, when read alongside Stevenson's notion of literary vagrancy, the relationship between the two tropes also raises questions, especially set against the important points made by both the cultural historian Darnton and the literary theorist Mailloux. While Stevenson may be read as an 'undirected' and possibly 'representative' reader, these elements of self-representation indicate the terms in which he *constructs* himself as a reader. If we accept the idea that all readers are in fact hypothetical and textually produced, then such an explicit strategy of representing oneself as 'vagrant' or 'gossip' demands interrogation. In examining Stevenson's personal identity formation and cultural milieu it becomes clear that this representation is in itself a response to existing perceptions of the nature and value of reading and has to be understood within that discursive context. He did not arrive by chance at the figure of vagabond. Moreover, in addition to identifying the cultural inflection of this particular textual strategy, Stevenson's deployment of this image has to be situated alongside other figures of reading which emerge from his writing. 'Vagabonding' may be a dominant image in Stevenson's self-representation as reader but it is not the only one. A second image, which he used frequently, was that of the 'transgressive' reader. This trope also has implications for recontextualising the 'reader as vagabond', suggesting that, while the presentation of himself as a literary vagrant liberated Stevenson into new and exciting areas of speculation on the nature of reading, propelling him towards areas of debate more commonly found in the work of twentieth-century phenomenologists, that image was also a direct response to older and influential perceptions of literary consumption in his own background.

The transgressive reader

Less explicit, more contradictory, this second dominant construction of the reader in Stevenson's writing sits less easily with the framework offered by de Certeau. The origins of the 'transgressive' reader, as manifested through a consistent concern with the tension between guilt and pleasure associated with reading as an activity, are very clearly located in Stevenson's upbringing. In *Memoirs of Himself*, he revealed what he saw as the religious, but also literary, influence of one of the 'Songstries' he heard his Nurse reciting just as he fell asleep:

> It dealt summarily with the Fall of Man, taking a view most inimical to Satan; but what is truly odd, it fell into a loose irregular measure with a tendency toward the ten-syllable heroic line. This, as I am sure I can then have heard little or nothing but hymn metres, seems to show a leaning in the very constitution of the language to that form of verse; or was it but a trick of the ear, inherited from eighteenth-century ancestors? It was

certainly marked when taken in connection with my high-strung religious ecstasies and terrors.[42]

The emotional impact of this experience was, from the outset, marked by guilt on a number of levels. Firstly, as Stevenson recognised, there was the dangerous thrill of being confronted with sinfulness, which should intimidate but instead excited: 'The idea of sin, attached to particular actions absolutely, far from repelling, soon exerts an attraction on young minds ... I can never again take so much interest in anything, as I took, in childhood, in doing for its own sake what I believed to be sinful.'[43] Secondly, there was a level of guilt induced by the recognition that the intensity of the experience itself, although 'religious', was also transgressive in its depth and not universally viewed as improving:

> It is to my nurse that I owe these last [religious ... terrors]: my mother was shocked when, in days long after, she heard what I had suffered. I would not only lie awake to weep for Jesus, which I have done many a time, but I would fear to trust myself to slumber lest I was not accepted and should slip, ere I awoke, into eternal ruin.[44]

Finally, there is guilt at the fact that he is excited by a pleasure in the language as much as by the notions of sin: a specifically literary guilt. Stevenson's account of such early linguistic thrills is typical in both the association of pleasure with guilt and in its discriminating sense of different kinds of readings and their associative values. Both characteristics are evident again in his description of an early encounter with the serialised version of J. F. Smith's popular novel *The Soldier of Fortune* to which he attributed, 'as my leading "worldliness" of the moment', night pains and terrors, but are present too in his account of the attractions of *The Pilgrim's Progress*.[45] Although much has been written about the impact of this text on Stevenson as a child in the context of his religious upbringing, Stevenson himself emphasises the power it had over his imagination, glorying in the way in which Great-heart could, with no apparent justification in relation to the allegory, be presented as 'a stout, honest, big-busted ancient, adjusting his shoulder-belts, twirling his long moustaches as he speaks'.[46] When reviewing the particularly fine illustrated edition of 'Bagster's *Pilgrim's Progress*' his emphasis was again on the literary qualities of the text: Bunyan's style is like 'the talk of strong uneducated men, when it does not impress by its force, still charms by its simplicity' and while 'the mere story and the allegorical design enjoyed perhaps his equal favour', Bunyan too can become immersed in the tale itself: at times, 'his characters become so real to him that he forgets the end of their creation'.[47]

The evident tensions in his writing between guilt and enjoyment, expressed as a dichotomy between the ethical and the aesthetic import of literature, are further exacerbated when the economics of literary production are brought into play. As we shall see, Stevenson's negotiations of his own regret at not following the worthy career his father had envisaged for him, combined with guilt either at his commercial success – 'There must be something wrong in me, or I would not be popular' – or his lack of it, further complicated the pleasures of both reading and writing.[48] The distinctive nature of this complex of sinfulness emerges from the particular context of his own upbringing, one dominated by Scottish Calvinism. As subsequent chapters argue, Calvinism, which appears to perform such a powerful role in shaping this particular reader, also emerged as a highly dominant force in the formation of his specific aesthetic concerns.

This configuration of a 'transgressive reader' therefore complicates understanding of the 'literary vagrant': one suggests a struggle against constraint while the other celebrates an image of freedom. Nevertheless, their apparently polarised connotations can both be read as self-projections emerging from and in response to the cultural and historical context in which Stevenson developed as a writer. Just as 'the transgressive reader' is marked by both a defiant assertion of pleasure and the internalisation of guilt, so the 'vagabonding reader', attractively free from fixity, offers an alternative to both mastery by the text and mastery of the text – again problematic concepts with the dynamics of Scottish Calvinism. Stevenson's interest in the role of 'literary vagrant', his deployment of tactics similar to those of 'reader as poacher', can therefore be understood as emerging from a highly specific cultural-historical context, determined not only by his geographically marginal and romantically bohemian relationship with the nineteenth-century literary establishment but also by his upbringing within a powerful religious tradition which inflected both his aesthetics and his self-representation in complicated and contradictory ways.

The very specificity of this dynamic in turn calls for a reappraisal of any over-simplified deployment of de Certeau's image of the 'general' reader. While Stevenson's role within an intellectual elite already raises some practical questions about his occupancy of such a position, the detailed determinants shaping his own theories of reading also lead to questioning of the relatively un-constructed model offered by de Certeau. The model for cultural consumption offered in *The Practice of Everyday Life* has been criticised from a political perspective, most notably by John Frow, who argues that both Bourdieu and de Certeau 'tend to fix an emotional domain of the popular, without every specifying its institutional characteristics'.[49] Noting that theoretical accounts of popular culture become caught in a tension between the 'widespread and historically hard-learned perception of the need to recognise the specificity of textual transactions' and the importance of defining 'the systematic constraints within which textual choice is possible', Frow points to the work of Stuart Hall as a significant negotiation of the 'theoretical middle ground' in that it recognises that 'The meaning of a cultural form and its place or position in the cultural field is not inscribed inside its form. Nor is its position fixed once and forever ... The meaning of a cultural symbol is given in part by the social field in which it is incorporated, the practices with which it articulates and is made to resonate.'[50] De Certeau's nuanced representation of 'general' reading, as both active and complicated, is useful in challenging established notions of passive consumption while the image of 'reader as vagabond/traveller or poacher' has a particular resonance in relation to the ways in which Robert Louis Stevenson represented and understood his own reading activities. However, as Frow suggests, 'the analysis of cultural texts must be set in relation to the institutionalised regimes of value that sustain them and that organise them in relations of difference and distinction'.[51] In Stevenson's case, at least, that powerful trope of vagrancy emerges from cultural and historical specifics, serving to define a particular response from Stevenson to such determinants, but also freighted with wider value. While in its structure this book draws upon de Certeau's more flexible understanding of the dynamics between general reader and text, adopting a bricolage model of literary relationships rather than a high culture structure of influence, it also acknowledges, following Darnton's call for a microanalytic approach to readers, that Stevenson's concerns and self-representation as reader need to be understood within a national and historical formation.

The first part of the book therefore maps out the influence of Stevenson's Calvinist inheritance on his explicit engagement with theories of reading and on the implicit negotiations of his role as writer and reader, then locates this within the context of late nineteenth-century literary debates over pleasure, realism and the public. The second part of the book addresses the ways in which key theoretical issues identified in the first part are translated into the intertextual play of reader, matter, critical analysis and fiction. The book presents, therefore, a series of detailed analyses of specific key texts, which have a particular resonance for Stevenson's interest in reading and in writing. This is traced out through 'influences' in a conventional sense but also explored through the cross-connections between letters, essays, reading patterns and fiction. Barthes, in *The Pleasure of the Text*, talks of reading Proust in a text cited by Stendhal and in Flaubert: 'I recognize that Proust's work, for myself at least, is *the* reference work, the general *mathesis*, the *mandala* of the entire literary cosmogony ... Proust is what comes to me, not what I summon up; not an "authority", simply a *circular memory*.[52] So, for Stevenson, the novels of Dumas or Scottish Covenanting histories or sea-faring yarns are part of a 'circular memory', texts central to his own reading history but also works whose dynamics inflect the literary strategies and concerns of his fiction. The book moves therefore towards an assertion that, while Stevenson maintained an unusually intense link with, and understanding of, the 'general' reader, that position in itself was the product of specific circumstances which combined to make him both a sophisticated and an idiosyncratic theorist of reading.

Stevenson's reading

Stevenson's textual self-construction as both writer and reader nevertheless emerged from identifiable reading activities. In terms of Stevenson's 'real' reading there is a considerable amount of evidence in letters, essays, memoirs, descriptions of his library and catalogues of book sales of a lifetime's engagement with a wide body of literature. Interest in the figure of Stevenson prompted avid collecting and cataloguing of books he owned, both by private individual and by libraries, and his letters, now fully annotated in the Booth and Mehew edition, provide detailed accounts of requests for books to be sent to his various locations.[53] The second volume of Roger G. Swearingen's PhD dissertation *The Early Literary Career of Robert Louis Stevenson 1850–1881: A Biographical Study* offers a penetrating account of his early reading.[54] Neil Macara Brown also published a series of articles in *Scottish Book Collector* in the mid-1990s, which helpfully trace Stevenson's reading according to particular themes within his library.[55] Through the sources available and such scholarship a Stevensonian reading map can be constructed.[56]

Well-versed in the study of those books characterised by 'intensive reading', such as the Bible and classical epics, Stevenson had also read extensively in writers such as Bunyan and Milton who constituted the backbone of British Protestant literary culture, in eighteenth-century fiction, and in French literature (read in French). He was a keen reader of history, both for its own sake and for accuracy of detail when preparing any piece of fiction or non-fiction with a specific historical background. He can also be seen, however, as part of a developing literary culture of the mass, with a taste for excitement and sensation: he knew well the material to be found in the *London Journal*, had encountered Penny Dreadfuls at fairly early age and wrote vividly about his less salubrious boyhood forays into popular literature. Through the encouragement of his nurse, Alison Cunningham, he became familiar with a rather different form of literature for popular consumption: the family periodical, as exemplified by *Cassell's Family Paper* with its improving fiction, entertainment and advice which, by presupposing the family as a sounding board for literature, occupied a significant place in the transformation of public and private spheres. He was also, of course, familiar with a range of writers from his Scottish background: not only religious writings and histories but also the works of Scott, Hogg, Burns and Fergusson and, in later life, with the fiction of Scottish contemporaries such as Crockett and Barrie. Although from his own account, he learned to read when he was seven,[57] he had already been exposed to a wide range of literary material from the reading aloud of Cummy, who liked both extreme accounts of religious martyrdom and serialised adventures such as *The Soldier of Fortune*, that of his mother, who favoured equally pious but rather less extreme religious works, and the stories told to him by his father which took him into the world of pirates and highwaymen that he always loved: his father would sit by his bedside 'and feign conversations with guards or coachmen or innkeepers'.[58]

In his analysis of early reading Swearingen emphasises the importance of the religious material Stevenson was encouraged to consume, by his nurse, and to a lesser extent by his family, but also notes the ways in which readings in the lives of martyrs sat alongside avid consumption of adventure tales: 'piety and romance coexisted happily in the Stevenson household'.[59] As he convincingly argues, for Stevenson both secular romances and Christian literature offered imaginative excitement and emotional colour; they also structured his thinking around a series of moral polarities which continued to shape his fiction. Swearingen notes in particular the impact of both *Pilgrim's Progress* (1678) and Harriet Beecher Stowe's *Uncle Tom's Cabin* (1852) as texts in which the 'monstrous, powerful and hideously consuming' nature of evil is emphasised in the confrontation between light and darkness.[60] Defoe provides another example of that powerful mixture of spiritual autobiography and adventure romance which so captured Stevenson's imagination.[61]

An enthusiastic essayist, Stevenson's shorter pieces also provide key evidence of his reading activities, in terms of both background reading for projects which required considerable research – such as his work on John Knox – and reading for pleasure. A number of essays offered meditations drawing directly upon personal experiences and recollections: in the *Cornhill, Fortnightly Review, Longman's, The Magazine of Art, The Academy*, Stevenson described his readerly and writerly self. Key to his approach to reading are essays written for the American *Scribner's Magazine*, providing what he felt was a very generous commission when enduring the cold and isolation of life at Saranac Lake in the Adirondack mountains in 1887–88. Audiences clearly determined some of the content of his prose; the religious and moral bias of *The British Weekly*, for example, may account for the particularly serious selection of texts in 'Books Which Have Influenced Me', contrasting with the rather more exciting consumption of penny thrillers detailed in 'The Lantern-Bearers' and 'Popular Authors'; *The Magazine of Art* had earlier provided an appropriate home for the aesthetic speculations of 'On Realism'.[62]

The letters offer a rather different perspective on Stevenson as reader. In the magnificent eight-volume edition of the letters, Ernest Mehew agrees with their first editor, Colvin, that Stevenson made little effort to polish or redraft his letters; in them, Colvin states, 'Stevenson the deliberate artist is scarcely forthcoming at all'.[63] The letters are energetic, warm, open in their opinions, even at the risk of offending authors whose work Stevenson feels would benefit from his own candid advice. The letters are also, at times, contradictory and need to be read against each other: the enthusiastic praise addressed to Mrs Humphry Ward in description of the 'art – or is it the virtue – by which you seem to have touched on all these burning matters with equal justice and discretion' is not supported by his comments to Sidney Colvin: 'Mrs Humphry Ward has sent me, with a very handsome dedication, three volumes of a work ... which I cannot peruse for the life of me. It is the most invertebrate languid twaddle.'[64]

On a more practical level, books in his possession also indicate his reading patterns. The contents of his library, even after their dispersal, have been the subject of more meticulous attention than most writer's. Neil Macara Brown's essays, working towards a reconstruction of Stevenson's library, usefully divide his reading material into categories. Building on information from the Yale edition of the letters, catalogues from auctions of effects following Stevenson's death, the holdings of Stevenson collections, including titles from Stevenson's library at Yale, Princeton and private records of sales, he pieces together a remarkably detailed analysis of books Stevenson had in his library at Vailima in Samoa – 'not more than 500 volumes'.[65]

As Brown notes, the library was described by Graham Balfour as divided into shelves allotted to the history of Scotland, French books, either modern or relating to the fifteenth century, military books and books relating to the Pacific. The library also contained, according to H. J. Moors, an American living in Samoa, the many volumes of magazines Stevenson had sent out to him and, as all commentators note, a wealth of books on history and South Seas travel.[66] As his letters suggest, French literature was well represented but a visitor, Arthur Mahaffy, noted that although there were some yellow-back volumes there were only a few:

'nor did I see … much trash of any description'. He was, however, disappointed at Stevenson's use of Bohn's translations of the classics 'while on the shelf beneath lay the originals uncut!'[67] Both Balfour and Moors comment on the amount of Scottish material, mainly historical but also literary and travel texts, supplemented by a range of religious material passed down from his father: 'From Thomas Stevenson, a master imbiber of bibles, undoubtedly descended the vast bulk of these "black books", associated prayeriana, hymnaries and such-like – numbering no fewer than thirty-eight items out of about seventy religious works, give or take a catechism or two'.[68] Brown's research also led to a useful assembly of readings in military history, a topic on which Stevenson remained enthusiastic, including a large collection of material on the Duke of Wellington with which he had planned a contribution to English Worthies series edited by Longman, and first brought to his attention by Andrew Lang.[69] Once again, as with Knox, he had perhaps read too much for, although he was 'neck-deep in Wellington' in 1885, he never completed the project.[70] With French literature his taste was again determined by research and enthusiasm: he perused much history, in particular of the fifteenth century – describing his collection, 'really pretty large and almost all paper-bound', as being treated as 'waste-paper' at Vailima.[71] As Brown notes, apart from Dumas and Montaigne, both long-standing favourites for different reasons, he was also a strong proclaimer of the quite distinctive values of the popular romance writer Barbey d'Aurevilly and the more experimental Paul Bourget. Daudet he also admired, but was critical of Zola throughout his essays and letters.[72] Balzac was a recurring point of reference, frequently invoked in debates on realism; as one memoir noted of Stevenson in the 1870s: 'He was fascinated by Balzac; steeped in Balzac. It was as if he had left Balzac and all his books locked up in some room upstairs.'[73] Flaubert, Renan, Sand, Michelet, Molière and Baudelaire, were also all writers who reinforced his admiration of French literature.

Although Edinburgh University Library retains no records of Stevenson's borrowings from his student days, his brief and periodic use of the Advocate's Library in Edinburgh between 1875 and 1880 again reveals his determined practical research for specific projects – readings of history of the Cévennes for instance – and shows him returning to familiar favourite areas: French history, Scottish history, Scottish poetry and a range of fiction from Defoe through Meredith to the rather more popular *Edith the Captive*.[74] The literary activities of his student life are, however, recorded in various memoirs in which he describes a relatively unsurprising journey through English literature: Shakespeare, Browne, Bacon, Herrick, Massinger, Lamb, de Quincey, Wordsworth, Keats,

Hazlitt (a particular favourite), Tennyson, Browning, Arnold, Swinburne, Pater, Carlyle.[75] He also was well-read in the classics.

This map of Stevenson's reading offers a history of the single reader. To understand that reader's perceptions of the activity of reading, however, and to identify the factors that produce in Stevenson the author of a wide-ranging body of fiction and an anecdotally expressed but particularly sophisticated theorist of reading, this individual map needs to be placed in a wider context. The first three chapters of this book therefore explore the ways in Stevenson's ideas about reading were shaped by the cultural debates of his time but also located within a particular personal context of the determining influences of Scottish Calvinism. They suggest that this particular configuration led him to adopt a position of a 'general reader', emphasising textual pleasure but also scrutinising it; engaging with the dynamics of the word but also claiming little authority for it; writing in terms of debasement about the commercial world of public production and the demands it produced but also almost defiantly placing himself within that context – as means of avoiding making claims for his fiction. By locating the much-discussed biographical evidence of Stevenson's religious upbringing in relation to a wider historical and philosophical context this book therefore offers a fresh context for understanding Stevenson's Calvinist inheritance. In Chapter 2 it reappraises existing critical responses to this influence in Scottish literature, then maps out the relationship between a Calvinist way of thinking and Stevenson's theorisation of reading as an activity. In Chapter 3 the more historically specific effects of this determining influence are considered in relation to particular cultural developments towards the end of the nineteenth century, including Stevenson's contribution to aesthetic debates which were structured through the opposition between realism and romance. The formative effects of a 'Calvinist' imagination combined with the particularities of a personal history in a climate of literary anxiety are addressed further in Chapter 4, as Stevenson's difficult – but intellectually fruitful – engagement with the pleasures of reading is considered. By bringing together analysis of broader cultural debates and influences with detailed examination of one writer's personal literary dynamics these chapters move towards a form of microanalysis of the reader advocated by Darnton.

Subsequent chapters take the process further, unpicking Stevenson's relationship to three sources of reading pleasure which also provided opportunities for redefining his literary position: Covenanting histories; chivalric romance; popular sea-faring fiction. These chapters trace his vagabonding, showing how, in both his critical writing and his fiction, issues raised by this business of textual consumption – the relationship between the word and the world, the nature and validity of pleasure in reading and the role of the artist in the world of commercial production – are played out. Chapter 5 addresses the significance of Scottish Covenanting history for Stevenson, suggesting that the troubled relationship he identified between narrative and the historical event becomes evident in the different approaches taken by those who had related Scotland's religious past. These narrative problematics are then reconfigured by Stevenson in a quite different historical context in his novel *The Master of Ballantrae.* The relationship between reading and pleasure is further scrutinised in Chapter 6, which focuses on the play of love and loss discerned by Stevenson in adventure romance. It discusses his particular affection for the work of Dumas but also looks at his own unfinished adventure novel, *St Ives*, as representative of the increasingly problematic status of chivalric romance in the late nineteenth century. Beginning with a debate over the origins of *Treasure Island*, Chapter 7 considers further Stevenson's negotiation of the creative and commercial contexts in which the writer works through detailed analysis of his late fiction *The Wrecker.* In its structure the book replicates the emphasis of Stevenson's own reading patterns, with a concentration on religious history, romance and adventure. As a result a primary focus is on Stevenson's non-fictional writing as a significant contribution to reading theory. Works of fiction discussed in detail are those that might be understood as on the margins of Stevenson's oeuvre, in terms of critical attention. With the exception of *The Master of Ballantrae*, those novels that are most familiar both to Stevensonians and to a general reading public – *Treasure Island, Dr Jekyll and Mr Hyde, Weir of Hermiston* – appear only briefly. For this is not a critical analysis of Stevenson's fiction so much as an exploration of Stevenson as theorist of reading, situating his ideas within a highly specific context (that of Scottish Calvinism) and broader nineteenth-century cultural formations but also following the directions in which his wanderings took him.

Notes

1　R. Barthes, 'On Reading', *The Rustle of Language*, trans. R. Howard (Oxford: Basil Blackwell, 1986), p. 33.

2　20/9/76 to his mother, B. A. Booth and E. Mehew (eds), *The Letters of Robert Louis Stevenson* 8 vols (New Haven: Yale University Press, 1994–5), vol. 2, p. 191. All subsequent references are to *Letters*.

3　R. L. Stevenson: 'A College Magazine', *Memories and Portraits, The Works of Robert Louis Stevenson*, Tusitala edition, 35 vols (London: William Heinemann Ltd, 1923–24), vol. XXIX, p. 28. All references in this book are to the Tusitala edition.

4 A. Bennett, *Readers and Reading* (London and New York: Longman, 1995), p. 4.
5 E. N. Caldwell, *Last Witness for Robert Louis Stevenson* (Norman: University of Oklahoma Press, 1960), p. 74.
6 Tusitala XXVII, p. xii. (For the complicated publishing history of *The Amateur Emigrant* and *Across the Plains* see R. G. Swearingen, *The Prose Writings of Robert Louis Stevenson: A Guide* (London: Macmillan, 1980), pp. 42–5.)
7 'Robert Louis Stevenson', *Saturday Review*, 78:2043 (22 December 1894), 675–6, p. 675.
8 'Rosa Quo Locorum', Tusitala XXX, pp. 1–8, p. 6.
9 *Ibid.*, pp. 6–7.
10 *Memoirs of Himself*, Tusitala XXIX, p. 156.
11 'A College Magazine', *Memories and Portraits* (Tusitala XXIX), pp. 29–30. In other essays, however, he presents different versions of his own literary history: the piece written for the highly respectable *British Weekly*, 'Books Which Have Influenced Me', (1887) addresses the 'improvable reader' and defines 'influence' not as that which shapes style or produces pleasure but that which brings about a change in thinking. Amongst his first selection of books are Shakespeare, Dumas's *Vicomte de Bragelonne* (for the effect of the elderly D'Artagnan) and *The Pilgrim's Progress*; he also remarks upon the long-lasting influence of the essays of Montaigne, the New Testament, especially St Matthew's Gospel, Herbert Spencer and the *Life of Goethe* by Lewes. Martial, the meditations of Marcus Aurelius, Wordsworth and *The Egoist* ('It is art, if you like, but it belongs purely to didactic art, and from all the novels I have read (and I have read thousands) stands in a place by itself') are also seen as contributing to developments in his thinking. The effect of Whitman's *Leaves of Grass* – 'a book which tumbled the world upside down for me, blew into space a thousand cobwebs of genteel and ethical illusion' – is, however, 'only a book for those who have the gift of reading'. With its emphasis on moral influence, this essay focuses on the discriminating reader demanded by such weighty material: 'He who cannot judge had better stick to fiction and the daily papers.' The publishing context for this theorising is significant: this is one of the few essays in which Stevenson adopts a note of authority in describing the 'good' reader: 'The gift of reading ... consists, first of all, in a vast intellectual endowment ... by which a man rises to understand that he is not punctually right, nor those from whom he differs absolutely wrong.' *British Weekly*, 2:28 (13 May 1884), 17–19, *Essays Literary and Critical*, Tusitala XXVIII, pp. 62–8, p. 67.
Different books and authors are presented as key references in other essays: in 'The Morality of the Profession of Letters' (1881) (*Essays Literary and Critical*, Tusitala XXVIII), Carlyle performs this function, as do Boswell, Tacitus, Michelet, Macaulay, but in 'A Humble Remonstrance' (1884) references are much more contemporary – Meredith, Hardy, Charles Reade, Balzac (Tusitala XXIX). A wide range of authors (Thackeray, Trollope, Meredith, Defoe, Verne, Scott) is mentioned in 'A Gossip on Romance'

(1882) (Tusitala XXIX) and in 'A Note on Realism' (1883; Tusitala XXIX) Thackeray is set in opposition to Zola. In some essays, august groupings include a popular author – Clark Russell in 'A Gossip on Romance' – while in 'On Some Technical Elements of Style' (1885; Tusitala XXVIII) amongst references to Shakespeare, Victor Hugo, Macaulay and Milton is found 'that admired friend of my boyhood, Captain Reid'.

12 4/3/86, *Letters*, vol. 5, p. 218.

13 10/6/93, *Letters*, vol. 8, p. 103.

14 'But I am a fictitious article and have long known it … But I cannot take myself seriously as an artist; the limitations are so obvious.' 6/10/94 to Sidney Colvin, *Letters*, vol. 8, p. 372.

15 Italo Calvino, Introduction to *I nostri antenati* (*Our Ancestors*), trans. I. Quigley (London: Picador, 1980), pp. vi–vii.

16 ?/6/84 to W. E. Henley, *Letters*, vol. 4, p. 307.

17 J. C. Furnas in Appendix A, 'Dialectics of a Reputation', offers a useful early analysis of critical perceptions of Stevenson, *Voyage to Windward* (New York: William Sloane Associates, 1951), while David Daiches, *Stevenson and the Art of Fiction* (New York: privately printed, 1951), draws attention to his criticism, as does Kenneth Graham, 'Stevenson and Henry James: A Crossing', in A. Noble (ed.) *Robert Louis Stevenson* (London: Vision Press and Barnes and Noble, 1983). For more recent attention see G. Norquay, *R. L. Stevenson on Fiction* (Edinburgh: Edinburgh University Press, 1999); S. Arata, 'Stevenson Reading', *Journal of Stevenson Studies*, 1 (2004): 192–200; R. Ambrosini, 'The Art of Writing and the Pleasure of Reading: R. L. Stevenson as Theorist and Popular Author', in W. B. Jones (ed.), *Robert Louis Stevenson Reconsidered* (Jefferson, NC and London: McFarland and Company, 2003), pp. 21–36.

18 G. Stewart, *Dear Reader: The Conscripted Audience in Nineteenth-century British Fiction*, (Baltimore and London: Johns Hopkins University Press, 1996), p. 19.

19 'A Gossip on Romance', *Memories and Portraits*, Tusitala XXIX, pp. 119–31, p. 119.

20 'Popular Authors', *Essays Literary and Critical*, Tusitala XXVIII, pp. 20–32, p. 27.

21 '*Rosa Quo Locorum*', Tusitala XXX, pp. 4–5; 'A Gossip on a Novel of Dumas's', *Memories and Portraits*, Tusitala XXIX, pp. 110–18.

22 'My First Book, *Treasure Island*', Tusitala II, pp. xxiii–xxxi.

23 'my Treatise on the Art of Literature: a small, arid book that shall some day appear.' 13/3/85 to W. H. Low, *Letters*, vol. 5, p. 88.

24 'Let us tell each other sad stories of the bestiality of the beast whom we feed.' 2/1/86 to E. Gosse, *Letters*, vol. 5, p. 171.

25 R. Barthes, *The Pleasure of the Text*, trans. Richard Miller (New York: Hill and Wang, 1975), p. 17.

26 ?/9/81, *Letters*, vol. 3, p. 230.

27 R. Darnton, 'First Steps Towards a History of Reading', *The Kiss of Lamourette: Reflections in Cultural History* (London: Faber and Faber, 1990), p. 162.

28 *Ibid.*, p. 157.

29 *Ibid.*, p. 181.

30 *Ibid.*, p. 171.

31 S. Mailloux, *Interpretive Conventions* (Ithaca: Cornell University Press, 1982), p. 202.

32 *Ibid.*, p. 204.

33 Darnton, *The Kiss of Lamourette*, p. 187.

34 M. de Certeau, *The Practice of Everyday Life*, trans. S. Rendall (Berkeley and Los Angeles: University of California Press, 1984; 1988).

35 'But the mutation that caused the transition from educational archaeology to the technocracy of the media did not touch the assumption that consumption is essentially passive – an assumption that is precisely what should be examined ... The efficiency of production implies the inertia of consumption. It reproduces the ideology of consumption-as-a-receptacle ... By challenging "consumption" as it is conceived and (of course) confirmed by these "authorial" enterprises, we may be able to discover creative activity where it has been denied that any exists.' de Certeau, *The Practice of Everyday Life*, p. 167.

36 *Ibid.*, p. xxi.

37 *Ibid.*, p. 171.

38 J. Rose, *The Intellectual Life of the British Working Classes* (New Haven and London: Yale University Press, 2001), p. 371; P. Bourdieu, *Distinction: a Social Critique of the Judgement of Taste*, trans. R. Nice (London: Routledge and Kegan Paul, 1986), pp. 328–31. Bourdieu describes this as 'a collection of unstrung pearls, accumulated in the course of an uncharted exploration', pp. 328.

39 de Certeau, *The Practice of Everyday Life*, p. 174.

40 'And so the logic of double negation can lead the artist back, as if in defiance, to some of the preferences characteristic of popular taste ... The "artist" life-style which is defined by this distance from all other life-styles and their temporal attachments presupposes a particular type of asset structure in which time functions as an independent factor, partly interchangeable with economic capital. But spare time and the disposition to defend it, by renouncing what it could be used to earn, presupposes both the (inherited) capital needed to make renunciation materially possible and the – highly aristocratic – disposition to renounce.' Bourdieu, *Distinction*, pp. 294–5.

41 H. Bloom, *The Anxiety of Influence: A Theory of Poetry* (New York: Oxford University Press, 1973).

42 *Memoirs of Himself*, Tusitala XXIX, pp. 147–68, pp. 153–4.

43 *Ibid.*, p.157.

44 *Ibid.*, p. 154.

45 *Ibid.*, p. 154. Stevenson's engagement with adventure fiction and the idea of heroism is a prevailing theme in accounts of early reading. In *Memoirs of Himself* he describes affection for 'The first author whom it was my destiny to meet ... Mr Robert Michael Ballantyne. I dare say the reader is unacquainted with his works; they scare seem to me designed for immortality; but they were exceedingly popular in my day with the whole world of

children. Of these works I was myself a most earnest student' (*ibid.*, p. 161). In 'The Ideal House', his perfect library contains, among 'the three shelves of books that never weary', *Guy Mannering* and *Rob Roy, Monte Cristo* and the *Vicomte de Bragelonne*' (Tusitala XXV, pp. 190–5), while 'Popular Authors' devotes its attention to such a range of popular writers including W. Stephens Hayward, Bracebridge Hemming, Pierce Egan, Charles Reade, Viles, M. J. Errym, Reynolds, Sylvanus Cobb, Mrs Southworth, and J. F. Smith (Tusitala XXVIII, pp. 20–32). *The Pilgrim's Progress* is also part of the library; a volume inscribed 'Robert L. Stevenson. From Pappa and Mamma', is dated 1 January 1858 (R. G. Swearingen, *The Early Literary Career of Robert Louis Stevenson 1850–1881: A Bibliographical Study*, Vol. 2, PhD Dissertation, Yale University, 1970, p. 560).

46 'Bagster's Pilgrim's Progress', Tusitala XXVIII, pp. 153–63, p. 155.

47 *Ibid.*, p. 154. Swearingen, *The Early Literary Career*, contains an illuminating discussion of the relationship between religious and adventure narratives, as brought together in *The Pilgrim's Progress*: see pp. 502–8.

48 2/1/86 to Gosse, *Letters*, vol. 5, p. 171.

49 J. Frow, *Cultural Studies and Cultural Value* (Oxford: Clarendon Press, 1995), p. 60.

50 *Ibid.*, pp. 71–5; S. Hall, 'Notes on Deconstructing "the Popular"', in R. Samuel (ed.), *People's History and Socialist Theory* (London: Routledge, 1991), pp. 227–40, p. 235.

51 Frow, *Cultural Studies*, p. 87.

52 Barthes, *The Pleasure of the Text*, p. 36.

53 *The Anderson Auction Company Catalogue, Autograph Letters, Original Manuscripts, Books, and South Sea Curios from the Library of the Late Robert Louis Stevenson* Part I (New York: 1914); Part II (New York: 1915) lists much of the material sold by Belle upon Fanny's death. Alexander D. Wainwright, *Robert Louis Stevenson: A Catalogue of the Henry E. Gerstly Collection, the Stevenson Section of the Morris L. Parrish Collection of Victorian Novelists and Items from other Collections* (The Department of Rare Books and Special Collections of the Princeton University Library: Princeton: Princeton University Library, 1971) lists 'Books from Stevenson's Library'. See also George L. McKay, *A Stevenson Library: Catalogue of a Collection of Writings By and About Robert Louis Stevenson Formed by Edwin J. Beinecke*, 6 vols (New Haven: Yale University Library, 1951–64).

54 Swearingen, *Early Literary Career*, 1970).

55 N. M Brown, 'Ex Libris RLS: Much Travelled Books', *Scottish Book Collector*, 4:7 (1994), 5–8; 'Le Ona's Library', *Scottish Book Collector*, 4:8 (1994), 5–8; 'A Wreck of Books', *Scottish Book Collector*, 4:10 (1995), 7–9; 'Picking over the Bohns: Stevenson's Vailima Library', *Scottish Book Collector*, 5:1 (1995) 19–21; 'Stevenson's Scottish books', *Scottish Book Collector*, 5:3 (1996), 15–18; 'RLS Bibliopest', *Scottish Book Collector*, 5:6 (1996), 27–30; 'RLS, Frail Warrior', *Scottish Book Collector*, 5:7 (1996), 25–9; 'The French Collection: RLS's Vailima Library', *Scottish Book Collector*, 5:9 (1997), 22–5.

56 I am particularly indebted to Roger Swearingen and Neil Macara Brown for their generosity in sharing their research.

57 *Memoirs of Himself*, Tusitala XXIX, p. 156.

58 RLS 'Notes of Childhood', 1873 Beinecke Collection No. 6573, p. 10. Swearingen, *Early Literary Career*, p. 443.

59 Swearingen, *Early Literary Career*, p. 447.

60 *Ibid.*, pp. 502–3

61 *Ibid.*, p. 508.

62 'The Lantern-Bearers', *Scribner's Magazine*, 3 (February, 1888), 251–6, Tusitala XXX; 'Popular Authors', *Scribner's Magazine*, 4 (July, 1888), 122–8, Tusitala XXVIII; 'A Note on Realism', *The Magazine of Art*, 7 (November, 1883).

63 S. Colvin, Introduction to *The Letters of Robert Louis Stevenson*, vol. 1, Tusitala XXXI, p. xv. See also discussion by Ernest Mehew, *Letters*, vol. 1, p. 14.

64 [7]/8/94 to Mrs Humphry Ward, *Letters*, vol. 8, p. 342; 17/7/94 to Colvin, *Letters*, vol. 8, p. 339.

65 See H. J. Moors, *With Stevenson in Samoa* (London and Leipsic: T. Fisher Unwin, 1911), pp. 50–1. See Brown, 'A Wreck of Books', for a particularly detailed discussion of distribution and whereabouts of books that had been in his library.

66 'I remember that there were many bound volumes of *Longman's*, *Blackwood's*, and other magazines there, many of them no doubt containing contributions from his pen. It must not be forgotten, however, that he never brought his entire library to Samoa. A good many of his books dealt with Scottish history and folk-lore and those he had studied from cover to cover.' Moors, *With Stevenson*, p. 51.

67 Arthur Mahaffy, 'A Visit to the Library of R. L. Stevenson at Vailima, Samoa', *Spectator*, 30 November 1895, 762–3.

68 Brown, 'Picking over the Bohns', p. 20.

69 For further analysis of Stevenson's engagement with the military see Ralph Parfect, *Hell's Dexterities: The Violent Art of Robert Louis Stevenson*, PhD thesis, University of London, 2003.

70 30/2/85 [?/3/85] to J. A. Symonds, *Letters*, vol. 5, p.80. The Peninsular War was also to be the background for *Henry Shovel*, planned in 1891, but the project was again abandoned.

71 15/5/1891 to J. W. Balfour, *Letters*, vol. 7, p. 121.

72 'He is a Beast; but not human, and to be frank, not very interesting … O, this game gets very tedious.' 19/8/80 to H. James, *Letters*, vol. 6, p. 402.

73 Flora Masson, 'Louis Stevenson in Edinburgh', in R. Masson, *I Can Remember Robert Louis Stevenson* (Edinburgh and London: W. and R. Chambers, 1922), p. 127.

74 Barry Menikoff vividly describes experiences very similar to my own of attempting to trace Stevenson's borrowings from the records of the Advocates Library that remain in the National Library of Scotland. Menikoff goes on to recreate, in convincing scholarly detail, Stevenson's specific engagement with

texts dealing with Highland history, deployed in *Kidnapped* and *Catriona*. B. Menikoff, *Narrating Scotland: The Imagination of Robert Louis Stevenson* (Columbia: University of South Carolina Press, 2005), pp. 18–19.
75 See 'Some College Memories', Tusitala XXIX, pp. 12–18; Swearingen, *Early Literary Career*, p. 539.

2

The Calvinist configuration

> Do I not know, how, nightly on my bed,
> The palpable close darkness shutting round me,
> How my small heart went forth to evil things.[1]

In understanding Stevenson's theorisation of reading and its delights the particular dynamics of Scottish Calvinism provide a key context. Although in personal terms Stevenson spoke against Calvinist assumptions and appeared to seek both a lifestyle and a literary oeuvre which emphasised his distance from this world view, the aesthetic and philosophic implications of the Calvinist engagement with the Word – in which fiction is simultaneously negated as falling short of the word of God, but also creatively liberated from the constraints of realism because mimetic reproduction of God's word is impossible – underpin his theoretical writing and his fiction. Stevenson's identification of questions around processes of linguistic signification, the structuring of narrative pleasure, the development of the reader through reading and rereading, can be understood as emerging from the simultaneous rejection of and replication of Calvinist modes of thought, as can his position within nineteenth-century literary debates over realism, pleasure and the relationship between the reading public and literary hierarchies. Reinforcing his distance from the English literary establishment, contributing to his detachment from positions of critical authority, Stevenson's Calvinist consciousness created a structure of feeling which determined his acute and continued explorations of the reading process.

As historians of literary culture have noted, the Protestant Reformation stressed a model of reading which was 'for the individual an opportunity to inspect and constantly re-inspect his or self in search of the mysterious "signs" of salvation'.[2] Emphasis on the Bible as a self-interpreting text – not one which needed external authority – and as a text in which 'the ultimate interpretive responsibility devolved on the ordinary individual reader' was a powerful element within Scotland's own version of Protestantism, Calvinism.[3] Concurrent with this emphasis on private reading, that engaged relationship between reader and text, however, was the awareness that God alone is the final source of truth in the Word. While pushing the individual reader increasingly towards the search for textual meaning, a search for truth, this theology also produced a destabilising of literature's representational powers in its suspicion of the veracity of any other 'author'. Moreover, in its emphasis on the unknowability of the private self, however much one's election may be manifest in public deeds, Calvinism created a radical psychic uncertainty at the same time as it stressed the importance of individual negotiation between the sinner and God, the sinner and the Word. Calvin warned that confidence in the interpretation of signs could be a danger: of those inquiring into predestination he suggested 'let them remember ... they are penetrating the scared precincts of divine wisdom. If anyone with carefree assurance breaks into this place, he will not succeed in satisfying his curiosity and he will enter a labyrinth from which he can find no exit. For it is not right for man unrestrainedly to search out things that the Lord has willed to be hid in himself.'[4] While the individual is encouraged to 'read' and assess his or her self, there is no guarantee that such an assessment will match that of the divine Author. As François Wendel concludes in his influential study of Calvinist thinking, 'the separation of the elect from the reprobate is effected by God, but ... as far as we are concerned we cannot clearly distinguish the elect from the reprobate in spite of some "sure signs" to that effect given in the scripture'.[5] Gordon Marshall, writing of Scottish Calvinist teaching on hypocrisy, likewise notes that 'Calvinist pastors ... continually exhorted their flocks, on the one hand, to seek assurance, to prove themselves in the faith by their work ... but on the other, warned them repeatedly against the dangers of arrogant self-confidence and dead faith'.[6] As recently as 1999 the Professor of Systematic Theology at Scotland's Free Church College, arguing that as the 'first art critic was God himself ... Serious criticism must still ask, consciously or unconsciously, "What would God think?"', explored the conundrum that while 'it may be insurmountably difficult to ascertain what God does think and unwarrantably arrogant on our part to claim to know. The attempt must be made nevertheless.'[7] The Calvinist context which remained in particularly potent and 'pure' form in Scotland therefore configured a particular model of textual relations which foregrounded the role of the reader and the importance of interpretation while simultaneously problematising the veracity of any 'human' reading and questioning representational authority as inherent to and guaranteed within any text.

Stevenson's interest in and ambivalence about textuality emerged from this conflicting pressure which was expressed to a particular degree of abstraction in a Scottish context.[8] Yet while Stevenson's Calvinist inheritance is frequently viewed as limiting and possibly 'damaging' from a literary perspective (and indeed was perceived so to an extent by Stevenson himself), it also pushed him into exploration of fundamental questions about the relationship between the word and the world, allowing him to develop an understanding of the dynamics of fiction very different from the models of representation applied to the realist novel of the time. Above all, this Calvinist context shaped his recognition of reading as a process which cannot be taken for granted, or assumed to be straightforward: from this emerged a highly self-conscious scrutiny of his own engagement with books and that of others.

Stevenson's relationship to the pleasures offered by the text, his particular interest in the processes whereby the reader becomes 'lost in a book', his fascination with the relationship between language and the imagination, are shaped as much by the religious context of his upbringing and the national traditions of literature as by the context of debate within the literary establishment of his time. While his emphasis on literary pleasure and his delight in textual transgressions may in one respect have been a reaction against his upbringing, that highly developed interest in the phenomenology of the text, that 'suspicious' examination of how it operates, may also be understood as emerging from the philosophical context of Calvinism and may help explain why in his own critical writing and fiction he pushed that interest further and further. It is this nexus of influences which, as subsequent chapters show, gave him a distinctive position as critic, theorist and writer within the changing literary world of his time. Offering an alternative emphasis on the relationship between truth and the creator, Stevenson's complicated internalisation of the Calvinism of his childhood and of his literary inheritance also determined the ways in which his ideas on fiction extend beyond, although apparently deploying, the oppositional vocabulary of 'realism versus romance' in which late nineteenth-century aesthetic conflicts were played out, allowing him to move towards more specific and more sophisticated examinations of textual pleasure.

Personal context

Much has been written about the particular religious climate in which Stevenson grew up and which he later, painfully, rejected. Most influential on the young child was his nurse 'Cummy' (Alison Cunningham), who shared with him her enthusiasm for bloody tales of the Covenanters, read stories from the Bible, from Bunyan and from tales of religious martyrdom. As J. C. Furnas notes, 'the only grim thing about Cummy was her faith, learned under the elaborate expoundings of Calvinist divines in cold seaside churches … Cummy … mistrusted cards and dinner parties and took ardent sides in theological quarrels among Presbyterian sects, infecting Louis with hairsplitting partisanship'.[9] She also, however, introduced him to the lighter pleasures of *Cassell's Family Paper*. He knew his maternal grandfather, the Rev. Lewis Balfour, Church of Scotland Minister at Colinton, only as an old man, but the Balfour family history of an ancestor who had fought at Bothwell Brig in the Covenanting conflict of 1679 also had a powerful grip on young Louis's imagination.[10] His own father Thomas Stevenson's adherence to a strong and strict religious belief became an increasing source of familial tension although, as Jenni Calder points out, Thomas's own attempts at writing fiction had earlier been suppressed by his father.[11] As most biographers acknowledge, this religious influence offered an imaginative as well as moral framework for the child. Ian Bell suggests that 'Religion became his entertainment and he became a miniature fanatic, lecturing the adults on their failings'.[12] In his recollections of childhood Stevenson vividly depicts the impact of this climate of guilt, fear and glory upon his youthful imagination, producing recurring nightmares and terrors before sleep, described in poetry in 'Stormy Nights':

> Then, would my heart stand still,
> My hair creep fearfully upon my head
> And, with my tear-wet face
> Buried among the bed-clothes,
> Long and bitterly would I pray and wrestle[13]

and in prose in various essays: 'I remember repeatedly … waking from a dream of Hell, clinging to the horizontal bar of the bed, with my knees and chin together, my soul shaken, my body convulsed with agony.'[14]

One early twentieth-century commentator with an eye for the complexities of this influence was Alexander Webster, Minister of the Aberdeen Unitarian Church. Although drawing on John Kelman's 1907 study of *The Faith of Robert Louis Stevenson*, which seeks to make a claim for the Christianity of Stevenson's philosophy of life by linking the 'rejoicing man with the Eternal God', Webster offers a vivid, and rather more subtle assessment of his religious development:[15]

> Bred in it, and pressed to conform, he easily rebelled and went his own way. He could not take to the ultra-Calvinism of his father … Stevenson's nurse was a Calvinist also, and through her his mind was filled with the materials of orthodoxy. As has been said, 'Scotch Calvinism, its metaphysic and questionings of Fate, free will, foreknowledge absolute', what it invariably awakens, was much with him, in the sense of reprobation and the gloom born of it, as well as the abounding joy in the sense of the elect; the Covenanters in their wild resolution, the moss troopers and their dare

devilrie, Pentland risings and fight of Rullion Green: he not only never forgot them, but they mixed themselves in his very breath of life and made him a great questioner …

But much of the Calvinistic influence passed into his soul and qualified it. His sense of the terrible, the grim, and the ruthless was born of it.[16]

Stevenson himself, of course, acknowledged the power of this religious force: Calvinism, he wrote, 'is the religion of the strong; like the shrewd, hard climates of our northern coasts, it is fatal to the weakly but makes more manly and vigorous the selected few who can survive'.[17] He rejected, at much cost, the religion of his father and moved away from the restrictive Scottish morality in which he was brought up, but his analysis of its influence is subtle: Calvinism, he noted, prepares the Scots 'for the grim reality that must be faced at last, of a thwarted and painful existence, haunted by vain aspiration after impossible good'; both critics and biographers have seen the impact of his black and white morality in Stevenson's fiction.[18] Although critical of being fed as a child with the starkness of religious writing, through such encounters Stevenson developed a sensitivity to the multiplicity of reading matter and reading positions. Linking his religious upbringing to his own early guilt about literary pleasure, in *Memoirs of Himself* he assessed its impact on the workings of the imagination through a self-mocking anecdote which describes taking revenge on his nurse's strictures about reading through 'turning the tables' on her:

> She was reading aloud to me from *Cassell's Family Paper* a story called 'The Soldier of Fortune'. It was about the Crimean War, then lately ended; and from some superfluity of love affairs, Cummy … had expressed some fear lest it should turn out 'a regular novel'. That night I had a pain in my side which frightened me: I began to see Hell pretty clear, and cast about for any sin of which this might be punishment, and *The Solider of Fortune* occurred to me as my leading 'worldliness' of the moment. I foreswore [*sic*] it then and there; and next morning announced and uprightly held to my vow. So instead of something healthy about battles, I continued to have my minds defiled with Brainerd, McCheyne, and Mrs Winslow, and a whole crowd of dismal and morbid devotees.[19]

While ruefully acknowledging the 'defilement' of his mind with gloomy tales of Brainerd and McCheyne, Stevenson indicated that his nurse was far from happy in having to deny herself the pleasurable but worrying delights of *Cassell's Family Paper*.[20] He thus recognised the irony in this play of readerly guilt and gratification: for the child it is the light fiction (and guilt at enjoying it) which produces the fearful dreams while the fanaticism of religious martyrdom offers a temporary sense of safety; for the nurse, her own sense of religious responsibility both denies her alternative reading matter and returns her to texts most likely to upset the imagination of a sensitive boy. Characteristic of all Stevenson's essays on reading and its pleasures is this consciousness of the duality with which pleasure might be understood; so too is the technique of recontextualising moments of reading pleasure in a specific temporal perspective. In essay-length meditations on literature such as *'Rosa Quo Locorum'* and *Memoirs of Himself* this movement between the child reader and the evaluating adult led to nuanced analyses of the ambiguous pleasures of reading romance. Such retrospective accounts allowed him to recreate the influence of a powerful moral system while also suggesting his distance from it: 'The idea of sin, attached to particular actions absolutely, far from repelling, soon exerts an attraction on young minds … I can never again take so much interest in anything as I took in childhood, in doing for its own sake what I believed to be sinful.'[21] Here, as in other writing, the determining influence of Calvinism on Stevenson's mind is viewed through the mockery of distances in both time and sophistication. Its shaping of his identity as a man and a reader was, however, rather more complicated than simplistic notions of 'sinfulness', and less easily left behind in childhood.

Critical perceptions of the vivid and powerful influence of Calvinism upon Stevenson's childhood abound: early studies such as Kelman's emphasised that 'it would be difficult to find a record of nursery days more wholly saturated with religious thoughts than his'.[22] James Pope Hennessy warns that Cummy's influence should not be underestimated: 'there is no question that with her murky Calvinist and Covenanting convictions, her vivid awareness of the flicker of Hell-fire and of eternal damnation as well as in her choice of morbidly religious literature for reading aloud, she did implant in the little boy's mind many of the terrors that haunted him in the watches of the night'.[23] The implication of such comments is generally that this influence was, if not damaging, at least inhibiting: Calder, for example, while acknowledging that a reaction to Calvinist gloom was potentially creative, also notes that Stevenson 'never lost his preoccupation with evil, particularly with the duality of human nature, sin and respectability existing side by side'.[24] K. G. Simpson extends this interpretation into issues of literary form: 'the rigidity and joylessness of Scottish Presbyterianism accounts for much' of what he sees as conflict and disjunction in Stevenson's writing.[25] Roger Swearingen is unusual in offering a more positive account of Stevenson's religious background by arguing that the metaphysical intensity it offered was for him closely aligned to the moral polarities of romance and, as with Bunyan, provided powerful dramatic polarities that structure his fiction.[26]

Stevenson himself gave fuel to negative readings of Calvinism's effects by his descriptions of paternal austerity, nursery constraints and the hell-driven night terrors of a sickly child, but in the early years of the twentieth century his personal narrative found reflection in a wider critique of cultural damage to Scotland's creative output by its dominant religion. The poet and critic Edwin Muir, as part of his sustained attack on what he saw as the culturally and aesthetically detrimental effects of Scotland's own version of Calvinist doctrine, offered a strongly argued interpretation of Stevenson's emphasis on pleasure as a product of religion's damaging effects: 'So one of the earliest ideas which must have been implanted in Stevenson's mind by universal suggestion was that story-telling was an idle occupation, and could be tolerated only so long as it remained so.'[27] Stevenson, argued Muir, struggled against this emphasis on literature as lightest of recreational activities and sought to become a serious novelist but also suffered in self-presentation because of his upbringing:

> A society which makes a writer a mere entertainer tacitly deprives him of any civic status, puts him among the superior mountebanks, and, if he is a man of independence, drives him into a showy Bohemianism. The defiantly picturesque pose which Stevenson assumed was in part at least the cloak under which he hoped to conceal his humiliating function, that of having to please everybody.[28]

Muir's conviction that Stevenson 'insisted almost importunately in pleasing, and convinced himself that one this was one of the main duties of the writer' led him to conclude that 'The literary fop and the romantic story-teller were very largely make-believe'.[29] Such a perspective, emerging from a modernist aesthetic with an emphasis on high seriousness, and with an agenda to locate Stevenson (and other Scottish writers) through a detracting comparison with the nineteenth-century novel in England, presented Stevenson's critical writing as a default response, the defence of a recognised failure. To see the essays in his light, and to present his literary career, as Muir did, as a struggle towards the unfinished glory of *Weir of Hermiston* is, however, to underestimate the complexity of Stevenson's recognition of his own background, and the sophistication of his ideas on reading pleasures. While Muir's identification of an imposed ambivalence in Stevenson's self-representation is perceptive, his understanding of such contradictions as necessarily debilitating was part of a larger agenda which had a powerful influence on twentieth-century Scottish cultural criticism. Writers such as Fionn MacColla and William Power echoed Muir's view of Calvinism as a force which operated wholly to the diminution of Scottish culture.[30] Stevenson's own highly acute recognition of the impact of Calvinism on his imagination offers an alternative starting point for a broader cultural understanding of the Calvinist metaphysic and its various aesthetic effects.

What the biographical context of Stevenson's early years undoubtedly reveals is the development of Stevenson's view of himself as a 'transgressive' reader, an image which permeated his accounts of reading pleasures. The nightmare of guilt created by his early pleasure in *The Soldier of Fortune* is repeated again in 'Popular Authors', in his descriptions of first coming across penny romances that have been abandoned in a ruined castle, and following the taste for such reading until he encountered the *Mysteries of London* and 'fell back revolted'.[31] Even his excursions with his nurse, Cummy, who herself was the strongest exponent of religious faith, to purchase *Cassell's Family Paper* remains vivid in his mind as evidence of an intensely ambivalent cultural experience.[32] That sense of guilt at his pleasures as a reader is also, as Muir recognised, later transferred to a guilt at his ability to please.

Much of this sense of transgression is pinpointed as emanating from the figure of his father, who functions as representative of cultural constraint, symbolised by that 'spot of some austerity', his library:

> the proceedings of learned societies, some Latin divinity, cyclopaedias, physical science, and, above all, optics, held the chief place upon the shelves, and it was only in holes and corners that anything really legible existed as by accident. The *Parent's Assistant*, *Rob Roy*, *Waverley* and *Guy Mannering*, the *Voyages of Captain Woods Rogers*, Fuller's and Bunyan's *Holy Wars*, *The Reflections of Robinson Crusoe*, *The Female Bluebeard*, G. Sand's *Mare au Diable* – (how came it in that grave assembly!), Ainsworth's *Tower of London*, and four old volumes of *Punch* – these were the chief exceptions.[33]

Although he clearly enjoyed Scott's fiction, took delight in making up romances, and participated in the creation of *Treasure Island*, Stevenson senior nevertheless believed that the darker side of life should be confronted and that 'escapist' fiction contained certain dangers.[34] Indeed it was with some recognition of a shared ambivalence that Stevenson wrote to his father in 1883, raising the question of whether reading Scott was better for the soul than being morally instructed by Lockhart's *Life of Scott*:

> I have just finished reading a book which I counsel you above all things *not* to read; as it has made me very ill and would make you worse: Lockhart's *Scott*. It is worth reading, as all things are from time to time, that keep us nose to nose with fact, though I think such reading may be abused, and that a great deal of life is better spent in reading of a light yet chivalrous strain. Thus no Waverley novel approaches in power, blackness, bitterness and moral elevation to the diary and Lockhart's narrative of the end; and

yet the Waverley novels are better reading for every day than the life. You may take a tonic daily, but not phlebotomy.[35]

His father's reply echoed some of Stevenson's sentiments but fell back firmly on religion as the answer to his son's doubts about the balance between 'taking life too easily, and taking it too lightly'. In his reply he noted of Lockhart's work: 'I have read the latter and have rather a pleasant recollection of it. But I admit *the end* is not a pleasant recollection – the fact is Sir W. did not cultivate religion. He did not pay much attention to it and did not consequently get much comfort from it in this world.'[36] The relationship between aesthetics and hedonism is again brought to the fore in this discussion as the desirable 'benefits' of reading are differently defined.

Stevenson's positioning of himself as a reader seeking transgressive pleasures can be read as emerging from a specific context of literary activity in which he grew up, determining the ways in which he viewed the benefits gained from reading. Yet rather than assuming Stevenson's relationship with reading pleasures as damagingly defined by his Calvinist background, a recognition of its force and an acknowledged resistance to its strictures can be understood as also offering him a determinedly self-conscious position from which to analyse textual delight. In this sense he can be viewed as a 'ludic' reader, not only because a sense of play and interest in performance is a dominant feature of Stevenson's critical writing but also in terms of his insistence on the pleasure of consumption in reading. In his study of the psychology of reading, *Lost in a Book*, Victor Nell suggests that the view of popular culture as a noxious influence, which can be traced back to the Reformation, operates with a clear link between the doctrine of work and the growth in literacy. 'Mass reading' has for centuries, therefore, 'attracted the wrath of the Protestant conscience'.[37] Reading for pleasure, 'ludic reading' presents an alternative to the structures of literary value emerging from this influence but must nevertheless be understood in its context. The 'ludic reader', 'addicted' to reading, is someone who is skilled at reading, who can rapidly assimilate information, who has the skill to choose books that promise a good read across a range of literary categories, who expects that reading will be pleasurable – and was probably exposed to the delights of storytelling in early childhood.[38] Social and personal determinants, Nell argues, will affect even the ludic reader's perception of their choice of material – an argument which resonates with Stevenson's description of an early awareness of the transgressive nature of his reading:

> If ludic readers see themselves as depraved … they will be compelled to deal with the resulting discomfort by a variety of strategies. And the nature and

quality of the resolution readers find for the dissonance they experience will necessarily affect the rewards they derive from their reading, since the reinforcements to be derived from such socially sanctioned activities as painting in oils and attending the opera are likely to have a very different subjective quality than those gained from voyeurism or overeating.[39]

The very fact that Stevenson so often drew attention to and mused upon the nature of literary pleasure suggests an ability to articulate, justify and rationalise the rewards he himself gained from the activity of reading, but this in itself can be seen as strategic, a negotiation of that work/literacy link established by Protestantism as a means of determining the correct use of time and the dangers of worldly pleasure which underpins much of his writing.

The manoeuvres he engaged in to define his own position inevitably produced a focused analysis of the relationship between reading and the reader. In response to Cummy, who bred in him the fear of hellfire but also introduced him to light fiction through *Cassell's Family Paper*, and through the relationship with his father, who, although advocating that 'dark' material should be encountered in reading, was also clearly entranced by fiction, Stevenson developed an acute sensitivity to ways in which different reading pleasures could be understood. Thus the lens of self-examination in turn led to a focus on other reading positions as well as own, to the relationship between readers' hopes, desires, fears and the written word. It is this preoccupation, this alertness to the differing dynamics between the word and the world, which defined his position with the critical climate of his time. Such a framework of self-questioning also led him to explore the question of textuality in terms much closer to phenomenologists and reading theorists of the twentieth century such as Ricoeur and Barthes than to those of his own contemporaries, although his concerns might also be placed within a 'golden era' between 1890 and 1910 in which consciousness studies focused on reading research.[40]

Cultural context

While the personal religious context of Stevenson's childhood experiences had a clear influence on his subsequent development as a reader, writer and theorist of literature, so too did the broader cultural inheritance of Scotland's own particular version of Calvinism. Historians have long argued that the impact of Calvinism upon Scotland was particularly powerful and highly specific. The system of theology promulgated by the French reformer Jean Calvin in his *Institutes of the Christian Religion* became operational in Scotland from the 1560s, replacing the earlier influence of Lutheran traditions. The 'Reformed Confession of Faith' approved by the 'Reformation Parliament' in 1560 stressed good works as the fruit of election; salvation through faith alone; and the importance of the true preaching of the Word. The Scottish Reformation also turned its back on a range of religious iconography – crosses, crucifixes, rituals, vestments and surplices, organs and chorister. The focus was on 'preaching, Bible study, prayers, and metrical psalms sung to popular tunes'.[41] The role of John Knox in developing Scotland's own brand of reformation theology strengthened its distinctive focus: 'more adamantly opposed even than Calvin to any concession to Roman ceremonialism, he viewed with uncommon abhorrence the restitution of idolatry in any locality in which had been established'.[42] Scottish Calvinism was also 'distinctive among Reformed confessionalism in the extent to which it depicts, with apocalyptic undertones, the church of Christ locked in an ongoing struggle with Satan'.[43]

The effect of this system in Scotland was particularly powerful because of the discrepancy between an ideology and its material condition: the seeds of a metaphysic were planted long before the economic and behavioural codes aligned with it could be realised. Discussing the relevance of Weber's thesis *The Protestant Ethic and the Spirit of Capitalism* to Scotland, Gordon Marshall makes a strong case for Calvinism's influence on the spirit of modern capitalism but is forced to admit that the economic support for this abstract spirit was somewhat lacking in Scotland at the time of the Reformation.[44] Scotland's economic underdevelopment made it extremely difficult for the individual to 'prove' salvation in either commercial or social terms. Therefore, although Scotland's economy did pick up during the eighteenth century, providing a more practical basis for expressing religious precepts, Calvinism could only operate usefully, at least initially, in conceptual terms. Christopher Harvie paints a powerful picture of this process:

> A backward, semi-feudal, northern society adopted a religious ideology
> – Calvinism-associated with advanced urban commercial communities …
> The Calvinist theology, with its stress on an autonomous and capricious
> God … both liberated and imprisoned. On the whole it led to a practical
> stoicism. Predestination recognised the same sort of lottery in life as in death.
> Over this pit, Calvinism constructed rules to keep civil society together.[45]

Tom Nairn likewise suggests that, 'because it could not be the veiled ideology of a class, the Scottish reformation was bound to be an abstract millennial dream'.[46]

It is unsurprising then that the original metaphysical implications of Calvinism, which preceded and dominated its social patterns, lingered on as a pervasive force in Scottish thought, even after Reformation theology

had become moderated within nineteenth-century religious developments. Clearly for Stevenson its effects were still powerful on a personal
level, but the aesthetic implications of its broader influence were also
significant. Although interrelated, the three dominant characteristics
associated with Calvinism in relation to literature might be defined
as: its anti-art bias; its problematic relationship to 'the Word'; and its
questioning of literature's capacity to represent the world, of which God
is the author.

Aesthetic context

The most common perception of Calvinism's aesthetic impact is related
to its disapproval of idolatrous images, emerging in opposition to human
creativity and in censorship. Calvin's own plea for art, that in it 'we
depart not from his intention, when it is referred to that end, unto which
the author created and appointed them for us' points to the problem
that we cannot of course judge God's intentions: the artist, in adopting
the role of a knowing and omniscient creator, is dangerously close to
usurping God's role.[47] Another product of a strongly Protestant belief
system, Nathaniel Hawthorne, drew attention to this in the prologue
to *The Scarlet Letter*: '"What is he", murmurs one grey shadow of my
forefathers to the other. "A writer of storybooks! What kind of a business
in life – what mode of glorifying God, or being serviceable to mankind in
his day and generation – may that be. Why, the degenerate fellow might
as well have been a fiddler."'[48] As Austin Warren notes, Hawthorne was
embarrassed to tell a story, to construct a downright fiction and, in clear
parallel with Stevenson, was happier to call his work 'romance': 'When
a writer calls his work a romance, it need hardly be observed that he
wished to claim a certain lassitude both as to its fashion and material,
which he would have felt himself entitled to assume had he professed
to write a novel.'[49] Assessing the broad impact of Calvinist thought on
Scottish literature, Cairns Craig also focuses on a general unease with
artistic production: 'the created word has been caught in an inevitable
conflict with the Word of creation, and this profound awareness of the
necessary evil of the work of art is one of the determining elements of the
tradition of the Scottish novel'.[50]

While the anti-art perception of Calvinism has become a common-
place of criticism, the troubled issue of 'the Word' is more complex.
Calvinism is a belief system which in itself struggles with – and produces
struggles with – the written word. In social terms its emphasis on
preaching and Bible reading produces a veneration of the word of God
but also tensions around the text. Underpinned by changing relationships

between preaching and writing, Reformation structures revolved around the contradiction that 'on the one hand, there was the conviction that Christ's teaching was simple and had been addressed to all; on the other, fear of heresy led to a desire for control of interpretation through preaching'.[51] Moreover, while writing appeared to act as a guarantee of authenticity, 'a lie is as easy to print as the truth'.[52] Both epistemological and ontological questions were thus raised by new access to print media and changes in religious hierarchies. Because the verbal as well as visual image was often thought to be as dangerous in its potential, 'Words, like pictures or statues, were suspect for the very reason that they were powerful, capable of shaping and thus of waylaying the human imagination'.[53] As Crawford Gribben, writing of Protestant responses in the period between 1550 and 1682, suggests, 'Puritans refused to close the infinite God within a finite text'. As a result, their texts 'subvert their status as verbal icons, foregrounding their transitory nature only to point the reader past themselves towards a "transcendental signifier"'.[54] The force of this attention to the word was particularly strong in Scotland. The Reformed Church generally 'laboured to make lay Bible reading a central component of family worship' and 'consequently advocated the regular reading of the Bible and devotional books at home'.[55] The historian Philip Benedict notes that this emphasis on allowing believers direct access to the text of scripture produced 'an unusually high percentage of people who learned to read but not to write' to the extent that 'An investigation made in the middle of the seventeenth century by one Scottish Kirk session claimed to find no families in the parish lacking Bibles, and several English authors of the early eighteenth century claimed that Bible ownership was virtually universal in Scotland'.[56]

Familiarity with, and access to, the Word does not, however, necessarily make for an easy relationship with it, even if the harsh and doctrinaire Calvinism of earlier times was less evident in the period when Stevenson engaged with his own religious struggles.[57] That 'the Word' was a subject of heated debate in Scotland during Stevenson's lifetime is forcefully demonstrated by the 'Robertson Smith' controversy of the 1870s.[58] An almost exact contemporary of Stevenson, William Robertson Smith (1846–94), who was later to become a highly influential figure in the development of anthropology and sociology, emerged as a precocious talent within the Free Church of Scotland: by the age of twenty-three he had not only trained for the ministry but had been elected to the Chair of Hebrew in the church's college in Aberdeen. Having come under the influence of German Biblical criticism, his submission of a series of articles to the *Encyclopaedia Britannica*, and in particular the entry 'Bible' in volume three in 1875, began a debate which lasted for five years and resulted in him being dismissed from his post in 1881. In particular Smith's theories about the source and agenda of Deuteronomy were perceived as a threat to traditional understanding of the authorship of the Bible, strongly expressed by William Cunningham, Principal of New College, who wrote in his *Theological Lectures* (published in 1878) that 'the whole Bible was composed, even as to the words of which it consists, through the immediate agency of the Holy Spirit'.[59] Stevenson was well aware of the controversy and enthusiastic about the spectacle it provided: 'Robertson Smith is great fun' he wrote to his mother in July 1879.[60] The issue, however, had significant reverberations beyond the Church and offered more than entertainment: 'The long debates were fully reported and carefully read by the laity and so the reading public, for the time being, was given an understanding of the nature of Biblical Criticism superior to that of today. Not merely was the authorship of Deuteronomy the charge in the church courts; it was also foremost in the public mind.'[61] While Robertson Smith went on to become an internationally recognised scholar, Professor of Arabic at Cambridge and a influence on the anthropologist J. G. Frazer, the impact of the debate he sparked in Scotland testifies to the powerful feelings aroused by questions of textual authority and divine inspiration.

If the force of Calvinism upon textual engagement was evident in the relationship to 'the Word', its shaping effects upon aesthetic categories were also powerful. As a theology Calvinism relocated the sphere of human operations away from earthly reality, emphasising the importance of the individual relationship with God as of primary importance in shaping consciousness. Humanity must be continually aware of its flawed existence in a world governed by God; no one could be completely confident of their inclusion in the Elect, no matter how assiduous they might appear to be in good works: as Calvin stated in the *Institutes*: 'none excel by their own effort or diligence'.[62] Calvinism offers a system of absolutist perceptions, a universe defined through polarities, by a God who demands near impossible moral absolutes; salvation is, as we have seen, always a matter of uncertainty. From that Calvinist perception that only God has the power of the Word (and the means of interpreting it) comes that deep resistance to 'the ideology of the artist as the ultimate revealer of truths'.[63] In 'Lay Morals' Stevenson expressed his concern that 'Life may be compared, not to a single tree, but to a great and complicated forest; circumstance is more swiftly changing than shadow, language much more inexact than the tools of a surveyor'.[64] In the same essay he noted: 'No man was ever so poor that he could express all he has in him by words, looks or actions; his true knowledge is eternally incommunicable, for it is a knowledge of himself.'[65] Even that knowledge, however, is unstable: 'In the best of times, it is but by flashes, when our whole nature is clear, strong and conscious … that we enjoy communion with our soul.'[66] For a novelist 'working with inexact tools to define a shadowy, undefinable entity', the possibility and value of a realist imaging of the world by an earthly author is thrown into question.

While critics such as Craig have argued for the influence of this Calvinist perception on the production of fiction – evident in the modern novel as a doubting of the imagination and narrative and typographical experiments – the same unsettled relationship to the pleasures of the word, the same questioning of its efficacy in revealing the world, also holds good for Stevenson, and has implications for his relationship to literary realism and to romance. Fiction is not seen as offering representational insights into how to live in this world, so much as an 'unreal' dimension which provides moments of involvement, even of 'transformation', which are pleasurable and 'significant' in themselves. Fiction cannot represent the world, but recreates for the reader the desires and confusions that compel us. Stevenson's position within contemporary debates over realism and romance was thus very much determined by the religious and social context from which he emerged, pushing him towards theoretical abstractions unusual at the time: his resistance to and internalisation of Calvinist ideas thus defined his relationship to trends within the Victorian literary marketplace. This Calvinist inheritance shaped Stevenson's engagement with and understanding of literature on a deeper level than that of personal anxiety; rather the impact of this cast of mind drove him towards a phenomenological analysis of textual relations which anticipates later developments in reading theory and is distinct from the combination of morality and aesthetics which dominated debate around fiction in his time.

Reconfiguring Calvinism

Recognising a specific aesthetics of fiction as emerging from this historical and religious configuration counters the wider cultural critique of Calvinism developed by Edwin Muir and his contemporaries and, to an extent, aligns a reading of Stevenson with more recent and positive interpretations of the cultural and intellectual impact of Calvinism in Scotland. Beveridge and Turnbull, for example, have argued that the reflections of Presbyterian intellectuals on historical causality led to the discovery of unresolved tensions about human freedom and the efficacy of human agency which share similarities with Enlightenment thinkers.[67] From a literary perspective, Craig suggests that 'it is not a matter of whether the writer belongs or does not belong to a Calvinist tradition, but to the fact that the Calvinist distrust of the imagination, building on a powerful interpretive tradition in Judeo-Christian theology, has become part of the very fabric of the traditions of Scottish writing and Scottish thought'.[68] In a nuanced reading of Calvinism in relation to creativity, Robert Crawford also attacks Muir's view of the Reformation as 'oversimplified and damaging', but accepts that 'There can be few Scottish poets who have never ... wondered enviously what it might be like to come from a culture filled with hallowed images of Catholicism'.[69] Crawford advocates moving beyond the idea of Scottish Presbyterianism as anti-art and suggests replacing it with an idea that is 'both more generous and truer to the grain of Scottish cultural history, more attentive to the resonances of Scottish art'. He also warns, however, that such a move should seek to go beyond the binaries of a Catholic versus Protestant opposition.[70] Such potentially positive readings contribute to what has been described as a revisionist phase of 'secular Calvinism': 'For some of the post-1979 intellectuals at least, the Kirk and its Calvinist imprint of Scottish history offered a neglected and misrepresented cultural inheritance, a tradition ripe for critical renewal if secular Scots were to understand their own modern history and identity.'[71]

Such large claims, however, must be made with caution: as Christopher Whyte warns:

> To attribute to Calvinism ... a privileged status as a means of interpreting cultural and social realities in Scotland is also potentially to empower those capable of telling us what Calvinism 'means' and how it is to be understood. Fascinating as the undertaking promises to be, it has rarely been approached with the necessary degree of methodological complexity. In the case of Scottish literature, one would want to start by setting up a theoretical model of how religious belief and practice can interact with the creation of fictional and imaginative texts, a model, moreover, which is capable of more general application.[72]

This chapter has therefore attempted to trace, in general terms, the intellectual and psychological dynamics of the context in which Stevenson grew up, examining that particular nexus of influences and inheritances without presenting it as either entirely damaging or wholly liberating, nor seeing it as unproblematically representative of a more general Scottish psyche. The following two chapters focus upon specific areas – developments in nineteenth-century literary culture including the realism–romance debate, and the theorisation of pleasure – in an attempt to trace further the interactions of religious belief (in terms of both assimilation and rejection) with the creation of fictional texts.

The context of Calvinism inflected Stevenson's position as writer and theorist in various ways which distinguished his contribution to nineteenth-century reading debates. Firstly it produced a reluctance to establish himself in the godlike role of authoritative interpreter of our response to the world, an anxiety with implications for both his fiction and his critical writing. (And, as we shall see in the subsequent chapter, this contributed to his distance from critics who were his contemporaries.) Secondly, the problematising of fiction itself allowed for the development of a pointed interest in the ways in which reading engagement operates: what it means to experience pleasure in reading, what are the wider implications of being lost in a book, what relationship obtains between the written word and the world? Combined with his distance from the nineteenth-century critical establishment this produced a distinctive emphasis on: his own role as general reader; the plurality of reading positions, experiences and pleasures; questions about the structuring of meaning which preoccupied him in both his fiction and his literary essays.

While Stevenson may have viewed himself as moving away from the influences of Calvinism, rejecting the religion of his father and repeatedly stressing pleasure as the highest value that can be found in books, he was at the same time replicating in his literary theory an understanding of the relationship between the word and the world, between art and life, that was deeply underpinned by Calvinist theology. When William Robertson Smith became Professor of Arabic at Cambridge 'Colleagues in anthropology noted with some surprise that neither Biblical criticism nor his treatment by the Free Church diverted him from his family's doctrinal outlook. He was more of an orthodox Calvinist than many now within the Free Church.'[73] Stevenson clearly rejected the Church and its beliefs, but the rest of his life remained, in his attitudes to writing and reading, a negotiation of its precepts. Alexander Webster presents this in bleak terms:

> And yet the obnoxious thing haunted him, permeated his thought and shaped and coloured all his work. Japp says, 'When he reached out his hand with the desire of pleasure conferring, lo and behold, as he wrote, a hand from his forefathers stretched out, and he was pulled backwards so that, as he confessed, his writings were apt to shame, perhaps to degrade the beginnings'.[74]

It was, however, this 'obnoxious thing' that, with all its unresolved tensions, shaped Stevenson's interventions in critical debate, distinguishing his position from his contemporaries and directing him towards engagement with issues which have become of increasing interest in the analysis of reading. While Henry James may have identified an 'old superstition about fiction being wicked' in English fiction, that concern with dangerous immoralities in literature was gradually losing force.[75] In Scotland, however, the intellectual and metaphysical implications of the reading process remained a matter of controversy. For Stevenson anxieties around 'the Word' produced less a defensive reaction than a productive impulse. The chapters which follow explore one writer's relationship with a lingering belief system that dominated his culture and his imagination.

Notes

1 'Stormy Nights', *The Collected Poems of Robert Louis Stevenson*, ed. R. C. Lewis (Edinburgh: Edinburgh University Press, 2003), p. 257.

2 M. Calinescu, *Rereading* (New Haven and London: Yale University Press, 1993), p. 86.

3 *Ibid.*

4 John Calvin (born Jean Chauvin), 1509–64, published *The Institutes of the Christian Religion* in its first version 1536, final edition 1559. Its ideas were taken up and disseminated in Scotland by the reformer John Knox, and it was this version of Protestantism which came to dominate, expressed in the Scottish Confession of the Faith (1560). J. Calvin, *Institutes* Book III, xxi, 1, trans. F. L. Battles, 2 vols (London: SCM Press, 1961), pp. 922–3.

5 F. Wendel, *Calvin: The Origins and Development of his Religious Thought*, trans. P. Mairet (London: Collins, 1963), p. 266.

6 G. Marshall, *Presbyteries and Profits: Calvinism and the Development of Capitalism in Scotland 1560–1707* (Oxford: Clarendon Press, 1980), p. 64.

7 D. MacLeod, 'Calvinism and the New Millennium', R. D. Kernohan (ed.), *The Realm of Reform: Presbyterianism and Calvinism in a Changing Scotland* (Edinburgh: The Handsel Press, 1999), pp. 41–56, pp. 54–5.

8 'Spirit and world came to be divided absolutely. Given that in reality a life at one with the spiritual ideal is impossible, one such result of this was that tradition of contradiction to which such characters as Holy Willie, Robert Wringhim, and Dr Jekyll bear witness.' W. J. Donnelly, *Religion and the Poetic Imagination*, PhD thesis, University of Edinburgh, 1981, p. 148.

9 Furnas, *Voyage to Windward*, p. 13.

10 J. Calder, *RLS: A Life Study* (London: Hamish Hamilton, 1980), pp. 26–7.

11 *Ibid.*, p. 26.

12 I. Bell, *Robert Louis Stevenson: Dreams of Exile* (London: Headline, 1993), pp. 49–50.

13 'Stormy Nights', *The Collected Poems of Robert Louis Stevenson*, p. 258.

14 *Memoirs of Himself*, Tusitala, XXIX, p. 154. See also: 'I had an extreme terror of Hell implanted in me, I suppose, by my good nurse, which used to haunt me terribly on stormy nights, when the wind had broken loose and was going about the town like a bedlamite.' G. Balfour, *Life of Robert Louis Stevenson*, 2 vols, vol. 1 (London: Methuen, 1901), p. 32. Reference to

'[Notes of childhood], unpublished MS. Dated 18th May 1873' (MS Yale). Later drawn upon in *Memoirs of Himself* (1880) and 'Rosa Quo Locorum' (1893). R. G. Swearingen, *The Prose Writings of Robert Louis Stevenson* (London: Macmillan, 1980), p. 11.

15 J. Kelman, *The Faith of Robert Louis Stevenson* (Edinburgh and London: Oliphant, Anderson and Ferrier, 1907) p. 267.

16 A. Webster, *R. L. Stevenson and Henry Drummond* (London: The Lindsey Press, 1912) pp. 3–5.

17 'Selections from his Note Book', Tusitala XXIX, p. 192.

18 *Ibid.*, p. 192. See Swearingen on the young Stevenson: 'Heaven and Hell were to him abundantly real – not because he was callously disciplined by means of the doctrine of rewards and punishments but because only such places, the one as infinitely pleasing to contemplate as the other was horrible, seemed consonant with the presence, power, and mercy of the God in whom he so devoutly believed.' *Early Literary Career*, p. 468.

19 *Memoirs of Himself*, Tusitala XXIX, p. 154. For further details of the author of J. F. Smith, *The Soldier of Fortune*, serialised April to December, 1855, see Swearingen, *Early Literary Career*, p. 523 and p. 553, and references to Montague Summers, *A Gothic Bibliography* (London: The Fortune Press, 1941) for further details of *Cassell's Family Paper*.

20 David Brainerd (1718–47) and Robert Murray McCheyne (1813–43): both evangelical preachers who martyred their lives through dedication and missionary zeal.

21 *Memoirs of Himself*, Tusitala XXIX, p. 157.

22 Kelman, *The Faith of Robert Louis Stevenson*, p. 15.

23 J. Pope Hennessy, *Robert Louis Stevenson* (London: Cape, 1974), p. 30. See also Furnas, *Voyage to Windward*, pp. 29–32, Calder, *Robert Louis Stevenson*, p. 33, Bell, *Robert Louis Stevenson*, pp. 45–52, F. McLynn, *Robert Louis Stevenson* (London: Hutchinson 1993), pp. 13–26.

24 Calder, *Robert Louis Stevenson*, p. 33. She also writes: 'His father's gloom, Edinburgh's biting wind, the rough, dark, texture of the city and its life; with this behind him the pining for colour and vitality is not only understandable, but creative.' p. 215.

25 K. G. Simpson, 'Realism and Romance: Stevenson's Scottish Values', *Studies in Scottish Literature*, 20 (1985), 231–47, p. 233.

26 Swearingen, *Early Literary Career*.

27 E. Muir, 'Robert Louis Stevenson', *The Modern Scot* II: 3 (1931), p. 197.

28 *Ibid.*, p. 198.

29 *Ibid.*, p. 199; p. 203.

30 Power writes: 'Literature was to mean less and less for a people who had lost the sense of national continuity, who were immersed in perpetual squabbles over an open Bible every phrase of which was to have held equal and absolute authority as a rule of faith, life and politics, and who were under the domination of a largely lay Kirk that usurped the powers of parliament and extended its mosaic interference to every detail of private conduct.' *Literature and Oatmeal: What Literature Has Meant to Scotland* (London: George

Routledge, 1935), p. 20. See also F. MacColla, *At the Sign of the Clenched Fist* (Edinburgh: MacDonald, 1967).

31 'Popular Authors', Tusitala XXVIII, pp. 20–32, p. 28.

32 Prior to writing 'Popular Authors', he quizzed her in 1886 as to whether the expedition and the stories left as vivid an impression on her: 'The story I wrote you about was one you read to me in *Cassell's Family Paper* long ago, when it came out. It was astonishing how clearly I remembered it all, pictures, characters and incidents, though the last were a little mixed and I had not in the least the hang of the story.' Late August/86, *Letters*, vol. 5, p. 307.

33 '*Rosa Quo Locorum*', Tusitala XXX, pp. 6–7.

34 'Escapism', described by Victor Nell as 'the most richly pejorative of the descriptors applied to ludic reading' is, as he points out, a 'new coinage that appeared in the 1956 *Addenda* to the *Shorter Oxford English Dictionary* (1933b)', *Lost in a Book: The Psychology of Reading for Pleasure* (New Haven and London: Yale University Press, 1988) p. 32.

35 20/12/83, *Letters*, vol. 4, p. 221.

36 *Ibid.*, p. 221 n. 1.

37 Nell, *Lost in a Book*, p. 27.

38 *Ibid.*, p. 8. While ludic reading is not equated with the reading of fiction, Nell suggests that fiction occupies a uniquely important place in ludic reading. *Ibid.*, pp. 18–19.

39 *Ibid.*, p. 27.

40 *Ibid.*, pp. 73ff. Nell argues that this interest then lapsed until the 1950s.

41 *The Dictionary of Scottish Church History and Theology* ed. N. M. de S. Cameron (Edinburgh: T. and T. Clark, 1993), p. 120.

42 P. Benedict, *Christ's Church Purely Reformed: A Social History of Calvinism* (New Haven and London: Yale University Press, 2002), p. 158.

43 *Ibid.*, p. 162.

44 M. Weber, *The Protestant Ethic and the Spirit of Capitalism*, trans. T. Parsons (London: Allen and Unwin, 1930); G. Marshall, *Presbyteries and Profits*.

45 C. Harvie, *Scotland and Nationalism: Scottish Society and Politics 1707–1977* (London: Allen and Unwin, 1977), pp. 125–6.

46 T. Nairn, 'The three dreams of Scottish Nationalism', in K. Miller (ed.), *Memoirs of a Modern Scotland* (London: Faber and Faber, 1970), pp. 34–54, pp. 36–7.

47 M. P. Ramsay, *Calvin and Art: Considered in Relation to Scotland* (Edinburgh: Moray Press, 1938), p. 29.

48 N. Hawthorne, *The Scarlet Letter* (1850), ed. R. Butterfield (London: Dent, 1971), p. 16.

49 A. Warren, *The New England Conscience* (Ann Arbor: University of Michigan Press, 1966), p. 134.

50 C. Craig, *The Modern Scottish Novel: Narrative and the National Imagination* (Edinburgh: Edinburgh University Press, 1999) p. 201.

51 Jean François Gilmont, 'Protestant Reformations and Reading', in G. Cavallo and R. Chartier (eds), *A History of Reading in the West*, trans. L. G. Cochrane (Oxford: Polity Press, 1999), p. 223.

52 *Ibid.*, p.233, quoting a citizen of Zug in 1556, from J. O. Newman, 'The Word made Print: Luther's 1522 *New Testament* in an Age of Mechanical Reproduction', *Representations*, 11 (1985), 95–133, p. 97.

53 L. Gregerson, *The Reformation of the Subject: Spenser, Milton and the English Protestant Epic* (Cambridge; New York: Cambridge University Press, 1995), p. 3.

54 C. Gribben, *The Puritan Millennium: Literature and Theology, 1550–1682* (Dublin: Four Courts Press, 2000), p. 22.

55 The Reformed Church generally assumed that 'households should be a second place of worship ... They consequently advocated the regular reading of the Bible and devotional books at home.' P. Benedict, *Christ's Church Purely Reformed*, p. 509 'A number of Scottish churches passed out books of "Family exercises" to members in the 1630s and 1640s', *ibid.*, p. 511.

56 *Ibid.*, p. 515; p. 516.

57 Swearingen, for example, notes that 'The Presbyterianism which Stevenson was taught was orthodox. But it was an orthodoxy much liberalised by the great religious revival in Scotland during the 1830's and 1840's.' *Early Literary Career*, p. 457.

58 For further details of the Robertson Smith controversy and debates which surrounded Smith's contribution to the *Encyclopaedia Britannica* in 1875 see A. L. Drummond and J. Bulloch, *The Church in Late Victorian Scotland 1874–1900* (Edinburgh: The Saint Andrew Press, 1978); W. Johnstone (ed.), *William Robert Smith: Essays in Reassessment* (Sheffield: Sheffield Academic Press, 1995).

59 Alec C. Cheyne, 'Bible and Confession in Scotland: The Background to the Robertson Smith Case', Johnstone, *William Robert Smith: Essays in Reassessment*, pp. 24–40, p. 34, quoting W. Cunningham, *Theological Lectures on subjects connected with natural theology and evidences of Christianity, the canon and inspiration of scripture* (London: James Nisbet and Co., 1878), p. 409.

60 ?/7/79, *Letters*, vol. 2, p. 327.

61 Drummond and Bulloch, *The Church in Late Victorian Scotland*, p. 60.

62 Calvin, *Institutes*, Book III, 7, p. 941.

63 Craig, *The Modern Scottish Novel*, p. 218.

64 'Lay Morals', Tusitala XXVI, pp. 5–49, p. 11.

65 *Ibid.*, p. 5.

66 *Ibid.*, p. 28.

67 C. Beveridge and R. Turnbull, *Scotland After Enlightenment* (Edinburgh: Polygon (Determinations Series), 1997), chapter 5.

68 Craig, *The Modern Scottish Novel*, p. 201. See too G. Norquay, *Challenges to Realism: Moral Absolutism in the Novels of Robert Louis Stevenson, Robin Jenkins and Muriel Spark*, PhD thesis, University of Edinburgh, 1985.

69 R. Crawford, 'Presbyterianism and the Imagination in Modern Scotland', in T. Devine (ed.), *Scotland's Shame?: Bigotry and Sectarianism in Modern Scotland* (Edinburgh and London: Mainstream, 2000), pp. 187–96, p. 190. Beth Dickson, in an essay which examines a number of Scottish novels (but

none of Stevenson's) in relation to Calvinism, concludes: 'We are used to hearing Calvinists being condemned for their gloomy outlook on life, their insistence on hell, predestination and sin. What we are not so used to noticing is that the themes of hell, destiny, guilt, judgement and the overwhelming seriousness of life are the province of our contemporary and fashionable novelists, such as Gray, Kelman and McIlvanney. That a society which has foresworn [*sic*] its Calvinistic past because of its detrimental effects on human life should, when left to its own devices, come up with a secular version of it shorn of any conception of redemption or an after life seems perverse. It seems almost possible to argue the opposite of Edwin Muir's thesis, not that Calvinism produced gloom and pessimism but that it was because Scots found much to discuss about the darker side of nature that Calvinism appeared to them.' 'The Gospel and Scottish Fiction', *Scottish Bulletin of Evangelical Theology*, 14:1 (1996), 51–64, p. 64. For an argument against the perception of Calvinism as a repressive, damaging and anti-art force see MacLeod, who argues that Scottish literature has also been free and eager to attack Calvinism: D. MacLeod, 'Scottish Calvinism: a Dark, Repressive Force?', *Scottish Bulletin of Evangelical Theology*, 19:2 (2001), 195–225.

70 Crawford, 'Presbyterianism and the Imagination in Modern Scotland', p. 193.

71 W. Storrar, 'Three Portraits of Scottish Calvinism', in R. D. Kernohan (ed.), *The Realm of Reform: Presbyterianism and Calvinism in a Changing Scotland* (Edinburgh: The Handsel Press, 1999), pp. 17–30, p. 22.

72 C. Whyte, *Modern Scottish Poetry* (Edinburgh: Edinburgh University Press, 2004), p. 15. He continues: 'One would also have to steer clear of any reification of Calvinism, any suggestion that those phenomena to which the term has been applied across a period of more than four centuries can be assumed, without discussion, to be identical with one another ... The search for national character traits or a definable national tradition is repeatedly associated with an urge to denote one form of religious belief as also being specifically national. It is advisable to scrutinise line-ups of this kind closely and with a due measure of distrust.' (Dickson's comments (n. 69) might be read as approaching such national essentialism.) Gribben, making a more positive claim for the relationship between Hogg and Calvinism, likewise argues that discrimination is needed and generalisations all too easy: C. Gribben, 'James Hogg, Scottish Calvinism and Literary Theory', *Scottish Studies Review*, 5:2 (2004), 9–26, see pp. 12ff.

73 Drummond and Bulloch, *The Church in Late Victorian Scotland*, p. 74.

74 Webster, *R. L. Stevenson and Henry Drummond*, p. 9.

75 H. James, 'The Art of Fiction', *Longman's Magazine*, 4 (1884), 502–21.

3

A 'fictitious article': Stevenson and nineteenth-century literary culture

> But I am a fictitious article and have long known it. I am read by journalists, by my fellow novelists, and by boys: with these *incipit et explicit* my vogue. Beastly good thing anyway! For it seems to have sold the Edition … But I cannot take myself seriously as an artist; the limitations are so obvious. I did take myself seriously as a workman of old, but my practice has fallen off. I am now an idler and cumberer of the ground.[1]

Stevenson's self-deprecating representation, in this late letter to Colvin, drew upon an image of himself that he had deployed to good effect earlier in his literary career: if he was now only an 'idler' in his creative work, he had previously been but a 'gossip' in his critical endeavours.[2] By making his approach explicit through the very titles of 'A Gossip on Romance' and 'A Gossip on a Novel of Dumas's', Stevenson identified his voice with the pleasurable circulation of opinion without authority. In so doing he drew upon an image of narrator as gossip that had already enjoyed a certain literary currency, but also created an identity which allowed critical distance from his reading experiences: he was offering an explicit analysis of his subject, while acknowledging that he, like his audience, had succumbed to his reading material in casual and relaxed manner.[3] Such a formulation represents a degree of self-knowledge and a sophistication of literary strategy which goes beyond Edwin Muir's assessment of Stevenson as someone bound both by guilt at his reading pleasure and guilt at his desire to please readers, suggesting instead a determination to create a critical voice which nevertheless maintains the position of 'general reader' and establishes an unusually intimate relationship with the experiences of a wider reading public

Playing the part of 'general' reader', or of 'gossip', allowed Stevenson to explore reading pleasures through anecdotal engagement with his own literary history and detailed assessment of the time and place of reading activities. This performative aspect of his critical essays, in which he examined exchanges between his different selves and a range of texts, built on an aspect of Hazlitt's writing that he had found most appealing:

> If there is anything that delights me in Hazlitt ... it is the loving and tender
> way in which he returns again to the memory of the past ... The imagi-
> nary landscapes and visions of the most ecstatic dreamer can never rival
> such recollections, told simply perhaps, but still told ... with wit, prevision,
> delicacy, and evident delight. They are too much loved by the author not to
> be palated by the reader.[4]

Translating authorial recollection and past enthusiasm into present readerly enjoyment became a key element in shaping Stevenson's interventions in critical debate. As the second half of this book reveals, the performative exchanges of his critical essays were further extended in his fiction, in which he played out his relationship with key texts and literary forms. The focus of this chapter, however, is on this ways in which this self-representation as a gossiping member of the reading public can be understood as a response to the cultural formation of his Scottish background which in turn shaped and was shaped by his engagement with the late nineteenth-century literary marketplace.

If a Calvinist cast of mind poses problems for the writer of fiction, creating a reluctance to claim authorship of the word and authority over a representation of the world, it also, by implication, raises questions about critical positions which suggest a godlike mastery of the text's interpretation. Stevenson's desire to adopt the role of general reader when writing about literary consumption, presenting himself as someone whose relationship to the text possesses no particular authority and whose experience of its pleasures is characteristic of a wider public, operated on one level in defiance of an oppressive religious suspicion of reading pleasure. As general reader Stevenson flaunted his delight in the consumption of less than improving material and he did so in a context of increasing concern about the taste of a rapidly growing reading public. That democratising emphasis on the word and anti-hierarchical hermeneutic openness characteristic of Calvinist approaches to the Bible, epitomised in the preaching strategies of the Free Kirk, also, however, produced a reluctance to present himself as authoritative interpreter. The self-mockery directed towards his own role as critic, evidenced in a joking late letter to Henley – 'But you know I was always inclined to be a merciful and hopeful critic, except to poor George Eliot. Well, she died, and was none the worse for my opinion, nor aware of it' – suggests a highly individualised configuration of a reading position distinctive from more general developments within literary criticism at the time.[5]

Stevenson's highly self-conscious scrutiny of the activity of reading intersected with a range of contemporary cultural concerns. Firstly, it meshed with a general literary anxiety about the relationship between writer and reader. Historians of reading have suggested that some kind of 'reading revolution' took place at the end of the eighteenth century in which a move from 'intensive reading', that is, repeated readings of certain key texts, with the Bible as obvious example, to 'extensive reading' (less frequent readings of a much wider range of material) was accompanied by a movement from reading aloud to silent reading.[6] The role of the reader and the nature of reading thus changed considerably and this general movement brought with it a new kind of reading community, one no longer linked by shared experiences and with a far less organic relationship between reader and producer. The new, increasingly isolated reader, who searched for some kind of connection and familiarity in a relationship with the author, was also by the nineteenth century part of a rapidly expanding readership, the developing literary culture of the mass, described by Wilkie Collins in 1858 as the 'Unknown Public, now waiting to be taught the difference between a good book and a bad'.[7] The range of reading material available also increased enormously. As a result, 'nervousness regarding the role of the reader registers everywhere in the "dear reader" regularly invoked in fiction well through the nineteenth century'.[8] Patrick Brantlinger, in his study of the ways in which reading was figured in nineteenth-century fiction, demonstrates the uncertainty shared by novelists about how the reading public would interpret their work, while Garrett Stewart has argued that this anxiety around reading is consistently 'encrypted but persistent, made immanent in its own pantomimes of itself'.[9] Stevenson's ambivalences about reading, although inflected with his own psychic and cultural anxieties, nevertheless echo some of this wider uncertainty about the reading public.

Secondly, Stevenson's own need to take a stance on fiction has to be understood in the context of a more general and fiercely argued debate over its form and function. The period between 1880 and 1900 saw a huge growth in writing about this, more than had appeared in the whole of the previous half-century.[10] Manifested in 'the hundreds of articles on the subject of readers and reading' published in monthlies and quarterlies and in the 'more directly confrontational' exchanges of the weeklies, the material factors contributing to this change in literary dynamics were many.[11] They included: the growth of literacy; the demise of the three-decker novel and the expansion in mass publication of cheap books; the growth of the popular press and popular journalism; the introduction of syndication; the new professionalisation of authorship, evidenced by the establishment of the Society of Authors in 1884; and the growth of the role of the literary agent.[12] The institution of international copyright also led to new codes of usage in the international market.[13] Wilkie Collins's anxieties about the growth of the reading public, emerging as a call for new literary material suitable for a hitherto illiterate mass, represented a larger worry in the mid nineteenth century with the moral dangers of fiction which, by the end of the century, were more frequently expressed in terms of aesthetic concerns over form and generic hierarchies. While shaped by his own particular cultural inheritance, Stevenson's interventions in debates over the value of reading and of fiction quickly found an audience, as his famous dialogue with Henry James over the 'art of fiction' demonstrates. But the nature of his interventions gave him a different voice from many of his contemporaries and distinguished his role within another development at the time: the professionalisation of the literary critic.

The role of the critic was in a state of transition over the period of Stevenson's writing career, marked in particular by the movement towards an increased professionalism of approach. In the 1870s literary debate was conducted through the vast numbers of reviews and articles in widely read periodicals and newspapers, in collections of essays and in histories of literature, generally produced with some assumption of a homogeneous readership. By the beginnings of the twentieth century, increased consciousness of a new mass readership, divisive debates over the form and function of fiction, and an emphasis on scholarship which would endow this area with the intellectual weight suitable for a field of academic study, had combined to change the nature of literary criticism considerably.[14] Although, as Orel suggests, the values attributed to this transition – an undisciplined and impressionistic approach giving way to a more serious study of literature – can be too glibly applied, a sea change clearly does take place between the 1880s and the early twentieth century. The increasing self-consciousness evident in periodicals about the task of producing readers can be understood 'as registering a discomfort that accompanied important changes in the social role of periodicals, in the relation between individual publications and their contributors, and in the format of the periodical text'.[15] A shift away from the practice of anonymity to articles 'given authority' by the presence of a signature led to a growing distinction between the contributor and the general reader: 'In this way, the periodicals began to operate less as sociocultural authorities in their own right than as forums for the exercise of a sociocultural authority derived elsewhere – chiefly from the universities – that was vested in the university-trained individuals who exercised it as periodical editors and contributors'.[16] Eventually this process grew into an increasing systematisation of literary structures through university education and the publication of literary histories and anthologies. As Mays demonstrates, the increasing emphasis on expertise and the periodical policy of signature created university specialists rather than generalists – and ultimately undermined the authority of periodicals themselves.

Stevenson's representation of his critical voice as that of 'gossip' suggests that the role of the critic was another area in which his own background contributed to an individualised position within wider cultural developments.

The wider cultural climate can nevertheless be understood as contributing to the very pattern of Stevenson's literary career: changes in the material process of publication and the concomitant redefinition of 'literary value' had a considerable impact upon the choices of form open to writers – and were widely explored by Stevenson, as part of that 'relentless fragmentation and categorisation of fiction' which led to a proliferation of genres and changing literary hierarchies in the last two decades of the nineteenth century.[17] In this respect, the growth of the reading public, and its taste for increasingly diverse forms of fiction, to some extent benefited Stevenson, or at least mirrored his willingness to try out different fictional genres. Commenting on this symbiotic relationship between changing patterns of fiction-writing and Stevenson's own career, Keating notes that 'One of the remarkable features of Stevenson's career is the way that he moved over so many different kinds of fiction, proving a commercial success in most of them, functioning as a powerful influence on their subsequent development, and ignoring the advice of friendly admirers that he should sit still and concentrate on being an Artist'.[18] In both his fictional and his critical experiments Stevenson addressed wider concerns about the relationship between mass consumption and literary form; his intervention in these debates was at its most forceful (both from his own perspective and through the claims of others) in the 'battle' that was fought under the banner of realism versus romance. This therefore forms another significant area in which the dynamic between a personal cast of mind and more general cultural concerns was played out.

As both writer and reader Stevenson engaged with cultural debates, characteristic of his time, around the implications of commercial success and the relationship between popular consumption and aesthetic value in fiction. For that reason Stevenson's writing, and in particular *Dr Jekyll and Mr Hyde* has been evoked by nineteenth-century reading historians as highly representative of the tense relationship that had developed between writers and readers.[19] As this chapter demonstrates, however, while Stevenson's position may appear representative, both the particular perspective he brings to such debates and the strategies used to represent and define his contribution are in fact highly specific and are informed by a rather different set of concerns. Elements of his own personal biography and that wider structure of feeling produced by the context of Scottish Calvinism produced areas of difference as well as communal concern. In three sites of debate central to cultural developments at the time – anxieties about the reading public and increasingly commercialised contexts of publication; the growth in status and influence of the literary critic; and the oppositional aesthetics of realism and romance – Stevenson adopted a distinctive perspective. In the broader concern with the nature and function of literary pleasure which underpinned much of this discussion, his position is even more clearly divergent. His stance in relation to the growth of the reading public, the role of the literary critic and the realism/romance opposition are considered in this chapter, and the implications of his position on the pleasures of the text form the subject of the next.

The reading public

The impact of a rapidly growing reading public became a matter of concern for both writers and critics towards the end of the century.[20] Peter D. McDonald's study of British publishing identifies increasing anxieties within the commercial and cultural contexts of the fin de siècle over the role of its readership. Characteristic of such concerns, he suggests, is Edmund Gosse's response to the crowds attending Tennyson's funeral in Westminster Abbey: Clark Lecturer in English Literature at Trinity College, Cambridge, in possession of a huge library of first editions, many inscribed with signatures of his author friends, and at the heart of the 'literary' world, Gosse appeared threatened by the 'vast black crowd' outside the Abbey. His anxiety, as McDonald reads it, was based on the theory 'that any feeling's authenticity was inversely proportional to the number of people who shared in it' so 'the excitement about Tennyson's death has been too universal to be sincere'.[21] Similar worries were expressed by Henley's *Scots Observer*, which, in its later incarnation as the *National Observer*, linked the expansion of university education and the effects of the new Journalism with 'The Cheapening of Poetry'.[22] Gosse's concern was not only with the threat to what he described as 'sequestered scholarship' by the pressures of an ever-increasing marketplace but also with the new kind of readers who lacked the subtlety to appreciate good work. (Henley, as we shall see in Chapter 7, articulated specific anxieties about popular responses to *Treasure Island* for just such a reason.) In his 1891 essay Gosse reflected that 'The enlargement of the circle of readers merely means an increase of persons who, without an ear, are admitted to the concert of literature'.[23]

Stevenson's own anxieties about audience were also expressed in relation to the public's admiration. In 1885, prior to the death of his father and the relative independence that would bring, he commented to his cousin Bob that, having read a number of contemporary three-decker novels, he was struck by how 'wonderfully steep in the way of tedium and weakness' they were, and continued: 'I thought they could scarcely be worse. It's odd how, in all arts, downright badness is what the public hankers after.'[24] He was similarly dismissive of the reading public in a letter to the receptive ear of Gosse:

> What the public likes is work (of any kind) a little loosely executed; so long as it is a little wordy, a little slack, a little dim and knotless, the dear public likes it: it should (if possible) be a little dull into the bargain. I know that good work sometimes hits; but with my hand on my heart, I declare I think it by an accident. And I know also that good work must succeed at last; but that is not the doing of the public; they are only shamed into silence or affectation. I do not write for the public; I do write for money, a nobler deity; and most of all for myself, not perhaps any more noble, but more intelligent and nearer home.[25]

Yet while Stevenson condemned 'the bestiality of the beast whom we feed' and famously complained 'There must be something wrong in me, or I would not be popular', he did not share Gosse's nostalgia for 'sequestered scholarship'.[26] Instead he advanced a theory, later set out in more formal terms to some furore, that writers, while perhaps unappreciated, overplay their role as victims of the public:

> As for the art that we profess and try to practise, I have never been able to see why its professors should be respected. They chose the primrose path; when they found it was not all primroses, but some of it brambly, and much of it uphill, they began to think and to speak of themselves as holy martyrs. But a man is never martyred in any honest sense in the pursuit of his own pleasure; and *delirium tremens* has none of the honour of the cross. We were full of the pride of life, and chose, like prostitutes, to live by a pleasure. We should be paid, if we give the pleasure we pretend to give; but why should we be honoured?[27]

Writing, on this occasion, very much from the position of 'author', and apparently arguing from an aesthete's point of view, that the serious production of art should be sufficient reward in itself, Stevenson nevertheless distanced himself from those who depended upon moral approval. He did so through deployment of an image that in itself carried problematic commercial implications: the prostitute. This self-degrading image, paradoxically offered as a defence of his position, indicates Stevenson's difficulties, created by both personal and cultural pressures, in defending his role as artist while simultaneously acknowledging that such a role cannot be given too much 'authority' or moral weight.

Although 'writer as prostitute' may have shocked, it was an image that already had currency in relation to the role of the artist in the marketplace and, as Lisa Tickner notes in a discussion of Walter Sickert's deployment of the image, 'the modern artist could imagine an alliance with the prostitute in their mutual subversion of bourgeois value'.[28] It also represented an extension of Stevenson's earlier meditations on the relationship between literary production, income and the reading public. In his 1881 essay in the *Fortnightly Review*, 'The Morality of the Profession of Letters', he had taken issue with James Payn's contention that writers should, in order to make a living for themselves, investigate the kind of literature in demand and produce what was required.[29] Recognising the changing context of literary production, he noted that 'The total of a nation's reading, in these days of daily papers, greatly modifies the total of the nation's speech; and the speech and reading, taken together, form the efficient educational medium of youth', and acknowledged that in such times the writer had the power to do 'great harm or great good'.[30] But even in this essay which, of all his critical writing perhaps most accords with the discourses of moral concern then in circulation, he suggests that while the duty of the writer is 'truth to the fact', 'a good spirit in the treatment' is also important.[31] Moral purpose alone will not suffice. Implicitly in its title, explicitly in its dialogue with Payn, the essay attempted to define writing in motives other than purely financial but was attacked in *The Academy* by a reviewer who accused Stevenson of being mistaken in his sense of a greater freedom in the improved atmosphere of Grub Street, and ignorant of the pressures under which writers operate. Yet in the essay Stevenson had delineated a dynamic and complicated relationship between writer, public and text:

> We may seek merely to please; we may seek, having no higher gift, merely to gratify the idle nine day's curiosity of our contemporaries; or we may essay, however, feebly, to instruct. In each of these we shall have to deal with the remarkable art of words which, because it is the dialect of life, comes home so easily and powerfully to the minds of men; and since that is so, we contribute, in each of these branches, to build up the sum of sentiments and appreciations which goes by the name of Public Opinion or Public Feeling.[32]

Without advocating that every writer has to be propelled into art by a moral purpose, Stevenson recognised the wider context in which individual creativity operated. Responding to his critic by reiterating his refusal to accept the easy correlation of poor men producing the poorest writing, asserting that aesthetic ambition still had a place, he waspishly replied that the reviewer had offered clear evidence that 'the influence of literature lies chiefly in single and striking expressions, since not even a critic seems able to observe both the end and the beginning of an article so short as mine'.[33] His response not only condemned his critic but also reinforced the point that a writer has only limited control over the whims and understanding of the reading public.

Stevenson, as the reviewer suggested, may have been ignorant of the extreme pressures of Grub Street, but his protection from financial anxieties was nevertheless bought at the price of dependency on his father. After his father's death he brought into a more public forum his own controversial views on the writer's relationship to the public that he had earlier expressed privately to Gosse. 'Letter to a Young Gentleman Who Proposes to Embrace the Career of Art', published in *Scribner's Magazine* in 1888 but reprinted in *Across the Plains* (1892), again stressed the obligation of the writer to be true to himself or herself rather than giving in to commercial pressures, but with the qualification that, if they do so, they must also be realistic about the necessity under which they are working.[34] Clearly informed by his own early dilemma as a young gentleman, in a position of dependency, trying to produce work of quality in a commercial market, and by his experience of the power of public taste following the success of *Dr Jekyll and Mr Hyde* in 1886, Stevenson returned to that image with personal as well as cultural resonance: the artist, like the 'Daughter of Joy' who professes to be able to delight, 'chose his trade to please himself, gains his livelihood by pleasing others, and has parted with something of the sterner dignity of man'.[35] As he explained to his friend Low, his view of the artist as prostitute had been strengthened by his reception in America, where he felt approval might as suddenly be withdrawn as it had been bestowed. Such dependence upon the vagaries of the market did not however, he argued, diminish his pleasure in writing itself.[36] Again his views drew the attention of critics although the essay did not attract the public debate that he had hoped might equal the publication of 'A Humble Remonstrance', his dialogue with Henry James. Richard Le Gallienne, who admired the essay as a 'manly protest against the literary commercialism which has recently been somewhat blatant', recognised the prostitution image as the essay's most important element, suggesting that it contained 'the fascination of suicide'.[37] In *The Academy*, the critic astutely noted that Stevenson had conflated in the position of the prostitute the pleasures of a trade and the sale itself; if, as Stevenson suggested, the artist writes to please himself, then this is apart from the commercial transaction. Stevenson responded gratefully:

> I had to thank you … for a triumphant exposure of a paradox of my own: the literary prostitute disappeared from view at a phrase of yours – 'The essence is not in the pleasure but the sale.' True: you are right, I was wrong; the author is not the whore, but the libertine; and yet I shall let the passage stand. It is an error, but it illustrated the truth for which I was contending,

that literature – painting – all art, are no other than pleasures, which we turn into trades.[38]

Yet while he moved on from the dangerous image of writer as prostitute, Stevenson seemed unable to free himself from the connection between sexual debasement – the libertine – and the practice of fiction. The relationship between the pleasure of the writer, the pleasures of readers and the commercial recognition of a purchasing public remained troubling, and the concept of writer as prostitute offered a multi-layered representation of the contradictions he perceived.

If 'pleasure' remained a source of ambivalence (and of fruitful theoretical speculation), it did not prevent Stevenson pursuing his trade: 'he would engage himself in as many projects as he could, maximizing his profits as quickly as possible. He would arbitrarily raise his royalty rate, and when that was insufficient he would renounce royalty arrangements altogether and agree only to the outright sale of his copyrights.'[39] As Menikoff observes, Stevenson 'did not have an iconic view of the artist's work' but 'had no doubts about his capacity for fiction, or about his place among novelists … He also had an absolutely clear and convinced sense of his craft, as one of the few honest and honourable professions.' Nevertheless, Menikoff continues: 'paradoxically, Stevenson also wondered about the entire pursuit of art'.[40] It has been suggested by Richard Ambrosini that an overview of Stevenson's fiction and non-fiction writing career shows him developing 'an ethically motivated openness towards the challenges posed by the publishing market', that in his theorisation and embodiment of a psychology of reading based upon the mechanisms of pleasure, Stevenson was aiming to reach towards a wider public in ways which did not compromise his artistic and moral integrity.[41] Only by becoming a 'popular' author, Ambrosini argues, could Stevenson 'reach the universal source of every literary form, and develop the myth-making potentials of fiction'.[42] Persistence of the prostitution image may be read as part of a defiant celebration of such a stratagem, but it also suggests a keener sense of commercial pleasure than many of Stevenson's fellow 'artists' would be prepared to acknowledge. Readerly pleasures may be transformative but also operate in a context in which the consumer must be prepared to pay. The image of writer as prostitute, however much Stevenson may have justified it, still carries connotations of debasement; while he defended his right to write – as an artist – and stressed the commercial value of his work, he could do so only through a potentially degrading trope. Such ambivalence can therefore also be read as a defiant yet guilty response both to the concerns felt by his father over his son's failure to achieve professional success in the 'commercial' terms recognised by this family of engineers and to his own anxieties about the value and status of fiction-making. These anxieties may be under-pinned by more metaphysical negotiations than an ethically strategic adoption of the popular. In the context of Stevenson's Calvinist inheri-tance, the image also offers a means of evading condemnation of the writer for setting himself up in a position of godlike authority; the role of author, as various comments in his critical oeuvre suggested, is one not of control but of dependence, serving the needs of clients and open to a range of responses by interpreting readers. Stevenson may have been drawn, as Ambrosini suggests, towards the production of fiction which manifests the psychology of pleasure in reading, but both his writings on the subject and the fiction produced indicate a rather more troubled, suspicious and self-scrutinising engagement than the model of an ethical strategy allows.

Underpinning Ambrosini's analysis is the perceptive assertion that Stevenson's 'personal poetics of fiction ... led him to test the universality of his own reading experiences' by drawing on his childhood reading and his engagement with key texts such as the *Arabian Nights* and the fiction of Dumas.[43] What is undeniable in Stevenson's relationship to the reading public is his strong identification with its responses. By the end of his life Stevenson had produced a less moral and more clearly materialist definition of the reading public and its commercial impact:

> I fear with every book that it may have no merit; I never fear it will be so full of merit that the public can't see it. There are two publics; about 10,000 persons who like literature, *qua* literature if it's *good*; and about 100,000, who like ink upon paper; if it's interesting. You can't live on the first public; but the first public with its 10,000 voices is the great advertiser; they dance with the 100,000; they meet him (*it*, I should say) at dinner; and they sell it your book, whether it likes it or not.[44]

Containing his concerns about the trade/art dichotomy through this nuanced model, he divided his reading public into two. One, the smaller, carries into its judgements a sense of 'aesthetic value'; the other, the larger, works upon recommendation and will seek pleasure in 'ink upon paper'. Although this trope of envisaging two publics was a familiar one, exemplifying what Roslyn Jolly describes as the displacement of cultural anxieties on to groups at the margins of culture by establishing 'a distinc-tion between responsible and irresponsible readers (those who could determine their own consumption, and those whose consumption needed to be controlled from above) which tended to correlate with a distinction not only between the safe and the unsafe, but between the high-brow and lowbrow in fiction', and might be seen as allaying Stevenson's concerns about his role as writer, the interesting feature of his essays and letters is that he represented himself as both kinds of reader.[45] Whether this then formed the basis for an explicit and ethically informed engagement with 'the popular', or whether it represented a more troubled but intellectually productive interest in the phenomenology of reading, such a duality undoubtedly produced a particular and unrepresentative voice within wider concerns about the dangers of mass literacy. A Calvinist inheritance in this context both raised and lowered expectations of the writerly role, setting God as pattern of the ultimate authorial relationship with truth but also emphasising the impossibility of human art to come near this ideal. Imbued by a sense of the importance of work and a suspicion of art, Stevenson defiantly asserted the significance of pleasure. In that defiance he asserted the role of reader rather than claiming the troubled authority of the writer.

The role of the critic

Situating himself both inside and outside the 'reading public' also characterised and differentiated Stevenson's relationship with the developing role of the literary critic. The growing exposition of theories of the novel in this period clearly met with a response from Stevenson, whose discussions of the technicalities of writing can also be linked to the new concern with form evident in debates over the relative values of English, American and European fiction.[46] His position as a writer working within a wide range of literary genres, his increasing physical distance from the London literary world and the influence of Scottish literary tradition which he grew up with nevertheless combine to configure his interests in a pattern different from that of the emergent figure of the literary critic of the time.

It should be noted at this stage that, in tracing the development of literary criticism, a specifically Scottish dimension has to be taken into account. As historians and critics have argued, the teaching of English literature at university level was well established in the Scottish universities before it became part of the curriculum in English institutions. The establishment of courses in Rhetoric and Belles-Lettres at Scottish universities in the eighteenth century, as part of their central curricula, was then translated into the teaching of English Literature at universities such as University College London in the nineteenth century and eventually led to its admission as a subject into Oxford and Cambridge.[47] The new subject was installed at the very heart of mainstream university culture in Scotland as part of a project that may be understood as a kind of internal colonialism in which 'Scots schooled other Scots to conform to an Anglocentric norm in order to advance in Britain and the British Empire'.[48] While reinforcing the cultural antecedents of a

Scottish Presbyterian context for emphasising scrutiny of the word, this genealogy of criticism produces a different inflection from the concept of critical authority which came to predominate in the English literary establishment. And it was in the main this English critical domain that Stevenson looked to for points of comparison.

Those whom Stevenson viewed as 'critics', Edmund Gosse, George Saintsbury, Andrew Lang, were involved only in the early stages of this literary professionalisation.[49] Within the environment in which his own writing on fiction might be situated, there remained an emphasis on the critic as gentleman; while Gosse and Saintsbury held professional positions of a different kind,[50] there was still a distrust of an overly professionalised approach and Lang was in many respects 'more at home with writers of an earlier age', remaining 'a master of the familiar essay, an enthusiast of books and a patient analyser of one literary problem after another'.[51] Saintsbury, although doing more than any other critic of his century to proselytise for French literature, was disinclined to embrace the more experimental work of Zola and Daudet, and equally opposed to the schematic analysis of literature. There was, he argued, an immutable law that 'no perfect novel can ever be written in designed illustration of a theory, whether moral or immoral, and that art, like Atticus and the Turk, will bear no rival near the throne'.[52] His inclination as critic was, moreover, always towards the positive.

In the writing of Stevenson's friends and contemporaries credos of the emerging discipline of literary criticism can nevertheless be discerned. Saintsbury attempted to be as objective as he could manage – 'But let us try to be as little personal, both in this and other matters, as possible' – and suggested that this could be achieved through the possession of comprehensive knowledge of literature: the critic 'must read, and, as far as possible, read everything'.[53] This emphasis on an impersonal approach to the text was reiterated by Walter Besant in *The Pen and the Book* where he devoted a chapter to 'the critic and essayist'. Recommending this role to those in pursuit of a literary life, Besant too stressed the importance of wide-ranging knowledge: 'for critical work special knowledge is required: let the young critic therefore take up his own line and make it his own by study. He must therefore take care to acquire for himself standards and canons of criticism; he must read the critical works of those who can teach him – there are not many'. Citing John Morley, Leslie Stephen, Professor Dowden, Professor Saintsbury, Walter Pater, Sainte-Beauve and Austin Dobson as figures to follow, Besant warns: 'Let him be careful not to read inferior criticism which cannot help him and is likely to injure his taste.'[54] Like Gosse and Saintsbury, he was keen that the critic should avoid personal attacks on contemporaries: 'The substitution of courtesy and good manners in the critical columns in place of the old blackguard "slating" is only a thing of yesterday ... Let the young critic bear it in mind, and remember that it is due to himself as well as his author to treat him with the courtesy due from one gentleman to another.'[55] His strongest emphasis, however, was on the extent to which aesthetic objectivity should take precedence over emotional engagement: 'The born critic may be recognised by the way in which he approaches every subject. He preserves a somewhat cold manner: he is never carried away ... he keeps outside the story, by which he is seldom moved to laughter or to tears.'[56]

Echoing Saintsbury's views on criticism, Stevenson too expressed his dislike of overly biographical approaches to a writer's work, and wrote with some pain to Gosse in 1886, when he thought him involved in such an exercise with himself as subject.[57] In his inclination to be 'a merciful and hopeful critic', he also shared Saintsbury's desire to be positive in judgements wherever possible.[58] Stevenson, nevertheless perceived a distance between his own approach and that of the emergent professionals, repeating with some amusement to Henley, Saintsbury's judgement: 'As a mere literary critic Mr Stevenson does not take a very high place ... It is in fact, in the criticism of life, not of books, that Mr Stevenson is strong.'[59] And although he had engaged in theoretical debate over the novel with Henry James, he made similarly mocking differentiation between their style as critics: 'Have you, by any chance, seen his [James's] paper on Maupassant in a recent *Fortnightly*? If you have not, look it up, for it is exquisite. James's manner in these critical papers is my despair. I cannot conceive anything more essentially happy; and I do not like to think of my own big, red, Scotch knuckles, after I have seen him toss his lace and flash his diamonds.'[60]

The distinction was not, however, simply in elegance of style: if Stevenson agreed with assessments of him as better novelist than critic, it was on the grounds that his emotional engagement with novels precluded him from cool objectivity. Stevenson did 'get carried away', not only in the warm praise he heaped upon a variety of writers more latterly described as mediocre, but also because of the fervour a good book produced in him. The emotional nature of his response to literature is a recurring image in his letters: describing the encounter with Dickens's *Christmas Books* when in his twenties, he notes: 'I have only read two of them yet, and I have cried my eyes out and had a terrible fight not to sob. But, O, dear God, they are *good*.'[61] His response to Margaret Oliphant in 1879 is equally emotional in its enthusiasm for *The Beleaguered City*: 'I have thought often, how many arrows an author shoots into the air – I daresay so have you ... you have lodged some three or four in my heart. I have cried heartily. I feel the better for my tears; and now I want to thank you.'[62] In 1883 he confessed to Henley: 'Have you read Meredith's "Love in the Valley?" It got me, I wept.'[63] Fanny describes them sharing emotional reading experiences a year before that: 'I find upon looking up that Louis is in tears over *Back From the Dead*. Well, I cried, too, when I read it', although she continues more cynically: 'When I was younger I liked reading such things and dropped a pleasant tear over them, and thought myself a person of sentiment. I am too old for that now.'[64] To understand Stevenson's critical position therefore it is not only his overtly theoretical writing – 'A Humble Remonstrance' or 'Some Technical Elements of Style in Literature' – that needs to be considered but also those essays in which he simultaneously enacted and analysed the emotional intensity of literary engagement. This anecdotal mode allowed him to bring together the emotions of personal involvement with a theorisation of that involvement in a combination discouraged by the dominant critical discourse with its emphasis on distance, objectivity and specific literary contextualisation through 'knowledge'.

Essays such as a 'A Gossip on a Novel of Dumas's' or 'Popular Authors' open with highly personal accounts of reading experiences, allowing Stevenson to present himself as an authoritative commentator on cultural consumption but also as a consumer, thus representing within himself the increasingly divided readership of fiction. As questions were raised about who might best judge what people should read, definitions of the 'well-read man' were both shaping the practices of the reading public and articulating 'the difference between that public and those with the capacity and duty to oversee and guide it'.[65] This desire to safeguard 'good' reading by protecting and guiding the general reader led to 'the construction of a gulf between common and ideal readers, introducing a need for intervention in the former's readerly acts, specifying the particular modes that intervention should take, and defining the character of those best suited to take up this cultural work'.[66] It has also be seen as establishing a gendered divide whereby 'marginalised' groups such as women readers were increasingly the subject of concern.[67] While Stevenson participated in critical debate as 'writer' and, to an extent, 'critic', and while his fiction might be read – as it is by Brantlinger and Stewart – in terms of writerly anxieties about the psycho and social dynamics of reading, in his letters and essays he also projected himself as 'general reader', both in the sense imagined by De Certeau in the twentieth century and in the sense worried about by intellectuals in the nineteenth. Working within that gulf between the common and ideal reader, acknowledging – and enacting – a range of readerly roles, Stevenson was liberated into a less authoritative but paradoxically more flexibly theorised exploration of literary consumption. Given his fascination with the images of prostitution Stevenson might also be seen as embracing a more feminised role in this respect, passively consuming the delights that came his way – or at least refusing to take on the role of paternalistic censor of dangerously easy pleasures. Although capable of highly specific analysis of rhetoric, Stevenson was in the end neither a 'gentleman critic', nor the author of any 'arid' treatise on literature. The position he adopted in his critical and fictional manoeuvres, as the second half of this book demonstrates, functioned both as a rebellion against that Calvinist constraint embodied in his father (in that he is determined to emphasise the enjoyment, the play, the fantasy element in reading) but also as an internalisation of Calvinism's reluctance to claim any mastery or critical control over the unstable process of representation and knowing which is ultimately the province of God.

The critics' debate: realism and romance

In his relationship to contemporary cultural trends, manifested in debates over the reading public and the professionalisation of the literary critic, Stevenson's Calvinist inheritance emerges not only as something he fled from – because of its perceived constraints upon his imagination and lifestyle – but also something he reproduced in his thinking. His interventions in the theorisation of realism (or the relationship between art and life) provide further evidence of this pattern of rejection and replication. While his response to anxieties over the reading public and his understanding of critical authority are clearly shaped by the personal and cultural context of Calvinism situated with the changing literary climate of the period, it is in the debate over realism and romance that Calvinism's most powerful influence on an aesthetic position can be discerned. Hailed as their most successful practioner in the realism/romance debate, Stevenson may have appeared to be talking in the language of his contemporaries, yet in his critical writing he was addressing a much more interesting set of questions: 'romance', claimed by some as representing a revivification of masculine fiction, becomes for Stevenson the paradigmatic literary form through which to explore the dynamics of the reading experience.

In J. M. Barrie's 1890 parody of the contemporary literary world, 'Brought Back from Elysium', the figure representing 'The romanticist' scornfully informs the spirits of past novelists, Scott and Thackeray: 'Now that fiction is an art, the work of its followers consists less in writing mere stories (to repeat a word that you will understand more readily than we) than in classifying ourselves and (when we have time for it) classifying you.'[68] As the previous generation of novelists brought back from the Elysium Fields are confronted with the pressure to categorise and theorise, they express shock at this new world of the cheap press and a plethora of magazines, a world in which popularity is not only no longer regarded as a sign of merit but 'to be popular is to be damned'.[69] 'It is not our stories that we spend much time over' suggests the romanticist, 'but the essays, and discussions and interviews about our art. Why, there is not a living man in this room ... who has not written as many articles and essays about how novels should be written as would stock a library.'[70] Stevenson was a significant player within this new realm of increasing demarcation of literary modes and novelistic debate over the art of fiction. His complaint that 'it is thought clever to write a novel with no story or at least a very dull one' in 'A Gossip on Romance' (1882) prompted not only immediate agreement from the *Saturday Review* but also a demand that he should revive the genre himself because 'he has a vein of it ... he has at least had good training, for he has drunk largely of the genuine waters. He has steeped himself in the spirit of the 'King of the Romantics', in the spirit of Walter Scott.'[71] His response to Henry James's 'Art of Fiction' in 1885 likewise played a key part in the debate over the relationship of art to life and gave a more sophisticated dimension to the Anglo-American wrangling that had emerged in the previous polarisation of Howells and James with Besant.[72]

Unlike the poseurs satirised by Barrie, Stevenson was also prepared to consider his own fiction through the lens of this theoretical tension. In February 1886 he directly applied the terms of the realism/romance debate to his own writing and in particular the flaws he perceived in *Prince Otto*, suggesting to C. W. Stoddard, then teaching a class in literature at the Catholic University of Notre Dame, that the text might be used as illustration of contemporary literary conflicts:

> you may tell them ... that it is a strange example of the difficulty of being ideal in an age of realism; that the unpleasant giddy-mindedness, which spoils the book and often gives the air of wanton unreality and juggling with air-bells, comes from unsteadiness of key; from the too great realism of some chapters and passages (some of which I have now spotted, others I daresay I shall never spot) which disprepares the imagination for the cast of the remainder.

He then reinforced his own contribution to the debate by asking, 'Have you seen my "Note on Realism" in Cassell's *Magazine of Art*; "Elements of Style" in the *Contemporary* and "Romance" and "Humble Apology" in *Longman's*? They are all in your line of business; let me know what you have not seen, and I'll send 'em.'[73] Stevenson at this stage did appear to be moving in the direction of an 'arid treatise on literature'; he was also emphasising the writerly perspective of his own critical voice.[74] Powerful as these interventions, built upon and reinforced by the writings of friends such as Lang, Saintsbury and Gosse were, however, Stevenson's approach to the theorising of fiction began to move away from that of his fellow critics. Nor was his approach to realism and romance necessarily consistent with those such as Henley and Haggard who believed he would save the romance form. By the time Saintsbury was pronouncing on 'The Present State of the Novel' in the *Fortnightly* in 1887 and Rider Haggard was writing 'About Fiction' in the same year in the *Contemporary* and Lang was still engaged in defining 'Realism and Romance', Stevenson was using the opportunity of a series of essays commissioned for *Scribner's Magazine* to explore a very different set of aesthetic issues – popular fiction in 'Popular Authors', the imagination of boys in 'The Lantern-Bearers', the commercial context of creativity in 'Letter to a Young Gentleman Who Proposes to Embrace the Career of Art' – and, in a significant number of these, was doing so from the perspective of reader. By 1894, only a few weeks from Stevenson's death, while Andrew Lang was still exploring definitions of realism and romance in *The Saturday Review*, Stevenson had produced a body of fiction and criticism which played out the tensions between realism and romance but extended the terms of this debate into a performative analysis of reading dynamics.[75] By doubling the role of writer with the position of 'general reader' he not only moved away from 'critical mastery' found in his contemporaries but also used that readerly consciousness to take him into new questions about the workings of the imagination.

Realism

Although Stevenson's best-known contribution to the realism debate came in 1885, he was, from an early stage in his writing career (most often in his correspondence with his cousin Bob who as an art critic was engaged with similar questions) stressing the importance of patterns of literature rather than its referential qualities. In 1874 he wrote of the impact of seeing Japanese art for the first time: 'here was something at last that fetched me … this art is above all others in two points. First, in that it tells its story, not for the story's sake only, but so as to produce always a magnificent decorative design … Second. The colours are really fun. For themselves, you know; they are their own exceeding great reward; they're not a damned bit like nature, and don't pretend to be and they're twice as nice.'[76] Nearly a decade later, describing to Bob his 'breathless note on realism' written for Henley, he still prioritises 'pattern' in similar terms:

> [The Artist] goes to nature for facts, relations, values – material; as a
> man, before writing a historical novel, reads up memoirs. But it is not
> by reading memoirs that he has learned the selective criterion. He has
> learned that in the practice of his art; and he will never learn it well, but
> when disengaged from the ardent struggle of immediate representation, of
> realistic and *ex facto* art. He learns it in the crystallization of day dreams;
> in changing not in copying fact; in the pursuit of the ideal, not in the study
> of nature.[77]

The question of realism had therefore exercised Stevenson's imagination for some time before his famous exchange with James on the subject and to an extent he sought to escape from mystification of its dominance; as he wrote to Bob: 'I want you to help me get people to understand that realism is a method, and only methodic in its consequences.'[78] 'A Note on Realism' published in the *Magazine of Art* in 1883 again drew comparisons with the visual arts, returning to the idea, which appears in more developed form in 'A Humble Remonstrance', that literature – and the other arts – involves not just observation of detail but selection and construction into a valid form: 'These temples of art are, as you say, inaccessible to the realistic climber.'[79] Using Balzac, whom he had been reading at this time, as the central example in his argument, he began to set out his own position on realism which would find its fullest expression in 'A Humble Remonstrance' and the debate with James.

Less opposed to earlier forms of realism, which he saw in the historical novel and the work of Scott and Balzac, Stevenson argued in 'A Note on Realism' that their influence has become adulterated: 'a merely technical and decorative stage'. This 'suicide of the realists' was blamed on Zola: Stevenson accused him not only of too much attention to detail but of a cheap and sensationalist attraction to 'the rancid'. But in more measured terms, he also set himself apart from the continuing English debate over realism versus idealism, arguing: 'All representative art, which can be said to live, is both realistic and ideal; and the realism about which we quarrel is a matter purely of externals.'[80] Through a process of circularity and evasion, the essay returned to form as the ultimate element of importance; execution in the choice of idealism's lofty whole or the immediate and particular of realism will determine the shape of the resulting work. If too much attention to detail is given, the whole is lost; if the focus is only on the philosophical the work becomes 'null'. In its emphasis on form and principles of selection the essay might be read as anticipatory of fin de siècle aesthetics, but it is also underpinned by Stevenson's antipathy to 'representation of the world' as the main business of fiction, and his realisation that ambitions in this area could lead to inevitable disappointment, again conveyed to Bob:

> I suppose the real truth is that the objects themselves are far too complex for our comprehension, how much more for our description: five square feet of Scotch hillside would take a man a lifetime to describe, and even then, how lame, how empty: after he had chronicled heather, whins, bracken, juniper, grass, these little yellow flowers and the rest, it would only be to find that each of these objects taken separately are indescribable, and that their combination is as much above human powers as flying.[81]

His suspicion of a realist attempt to recreate the world, usurping the role of divine Author, thus brought together practical, aesthetic and philosophical concerns in a highly personal combination.

Responding to an article by Henry James on 'The Art of Fiction', 'A Humble Remonstrance' continued Stevenson's theorisation of his stance.[82] James's essay, published in *Longman's* in September 1884, was in itself a reply to pamphlet publication of a lecture on 'The Art of Fiction' given by the novelist Walter Besant on 25 April 1884.[83] Offering a justification for considering fiction as one of the 'Fine Arts', equal to music, painting and poetry, Besant had argued that, as an Art, fiction was governed by general laws which may be laid down and taught, although he also admitted that no laws can be successfully learned by those who do not possess the 'natural and necessary gifts'. The modern novel offered a means of converting abstract ideas into living models because in fiction the human interest comes before everything else. Recommending that the novelist develops powers of observation, selection and dramatic presentation – 'everything in Fiction which is invented and not the result of personal experience and observation is worthless' – he advised the novelist never to go beyond personal experience.[84]

In his reply James welcomed Besant's lecture for at least articulating a position, noting that until recently the English novel appeared to have no theory, no conviction, no consciousness of itself: 'there was a comfortable, good-humoured feeling abroad that a novel is a novel, as a pudding is a pudding, and that this was the end of it'.[85] While the old suspicion that fiction was 'wicked' did not dominate to the same extent, there was still a feeling that it should not be taken too seriously. At least, he suggested in a comment prescient in the light of Stevenson's response to his essay, that old Evangelical suspicion had some grounding in a valid idea: that the novel 'competes with life'.[86] As a central tenet of his argument James claimed that, just as the painting provides a picture that is 'reality', so the novel offers 'history'. Agreeing with Besant that the novelist should be understood as 'artistic', James condemned the belief that novels should be either instructive or amusing and that artistic preoccupations with form will somehow interfere with both these purposes.

James disagreed with Besant, however, in the idea that it is possible to say beforehand 'what sort of an affair the good novel will be' and suggested that 'the good health of an art which undertakes so immediately to reproduce life must demand that it be perfectly free'.[87] Working through the catalogue of 'rules' that Besant had laid down, he showed that, while one might not necessarily disagree, one need not assent to such a prescriptive set of guidelines. Although advocating realism of a kind, he suggested that those characters and situations that strike us as most real will be those that most interest us. While writing from 'experience' may be valuable, experience itself is never limited and never complete: 'it is an immense sensibility, a kind of huge spider-web of the finest silken threads, suspended in the chamber of consciousness and catching every air-borne particle in its tissue'.[88] His wider argument against Besant became therefore a defence of the 'organic' nature of the novel ('A novel is a living thing, all one and continuous') and an opposition to categorising novels as either those of incident or character, novel or romance: 'What is character but the determination of incident? What is incident but the illustration of character?' Such distinctions, noted by critics, have little use for producers of fiction. In his final brief, discussion of Besant's ideas on the conscious moral purpose of the novel, James stated his belief that English novelists have shown diffidence and timidity in this area, and reintroduced aesthetic questions of taste: 'There is one point at which the moral sense and the artistic sense lie very near together; that is, in the light of the very obvious truth that the deepest quality of a work of art will always be in the quality of the mind of the producer.'[89]

In his response to this essay, Stevenson questioned and redefined the terms used by both men: what, he suggests, they were in fact discussing was the 'art of narrative'. Although Besant may prefer the 'art of fictitious narratives in prose' as his subject, Stevenson argued the applicability of 'narrative' as a term to poetry, to drama, to biography and even to history in which, he suggested, can be found the same textual features and literary strategies that are apparent in fiction. What he was most uneasy with, however, was James's idea that a novel has the status of history: first questioning the 'propriety' of the word 'truth' in either context and then challenging James's central proposition, that art competes with life, Stevenson evolved a position that was neither an 'old Evangelical' nor a modernist one. Literature, he suggested, should be seen as a reorganisation and shaping of certain elements of life. His paradigm of art as geometry was in direct contrast to the organic images offered by James, as was his assertion that a novel exists by virtue of its immeasurable difference from life: an assertion that might be read as exemplifying a Calvinist suspicion of the idolatrous, and ultimately impossible, claim that art can 'represent' God's work. In concluding the essay, he returned to a strong reminder, again at odds with both Besant and James, that fiction cannot be a faithful account of life: 'And as the root of the whole matter, let him bear in mind that his novel is not a transcript of life, to be judged by its exactitude; but a simplification of some side or point of life, to stand or fall by its significant simplicity.'[90] Stevenson thus questioned the valorisation of realism at the time, going against a lingering anxiety from earlier in the century that the novel should not be read only for plot, but more importantly challenged James's assertion that the novel should 'compete with life'.[91]

In later years in the South Seas Stevenson found himself writing fiction that to an extent appeared closer to the 'realism' he had argued against, but in his letters the term 'realism' seems less 'a question of method' than a description of the material with which he engaged. *The Ebb-Tide* he described as 'a dreadful, grimy business in the third person; where the strain between a vilely realistic dialogue and an narrative style pitched about ... "four notes higher" than it should have been, has sown my head with grey hairs' and continued: 'I grind away with an odd, dogged, dour sensation – and an idea *in petto* that the game is about to be played out. I have got too realistic, and I must break these trammels – I mean I would, if I could; but the yoke is heavy.'[92] In terms of style and method, however, his interest was still in the significant pattern. Writing to Gosse in 1891, he advised: 'Wed yourself to a clean austerity'[93] and to James in 1893 he reiterated:

> My two aims may be described as
> *1st* War to the adjective
> *2nd* death to the optic nerve.[94]

His attention therefore was still not with the 'faithful' representation of the everyday world but with patterning out, through 'significant simplicity', some 'side' of life.

Romance

While Stevenson's exchanges with James and Besant were dominated by a terminological opposition of art and life, the other significant polarity structuring contemporary debate, that of realism and romance, was also evolving.[95] Peter Keating has identified Stevenson's influence in this debate as effacing any specific meanings to the term 'romance', until it became 'almost anything that wasn't realism'.[96] Such a reading has some truth but is not entirely fair: in the relatively early 'Victor Hugo's Romances' Stevenson clarified his thinking by beginning with Hugo's own assessment of *Quentin Durward*: 'Après le roman pittoresque mais prosaïque de Walter Scott il restera un autre roman à creér, plus beau et plus complet encore selon nous. C'est le roman, à la fois drame et épopée, pittoresque mais poetique, réel mais idéal, vrai mais grand, qui enchâssera Walter Scott dans Homère.'[97] After comparing Fielding with Scott, in terms of the latter's move away from character towards an understanding of 'personality ... resumed into its place in the constitution of things', Stevenson offered Hugo's own work as advance on this process by virtue of its self-consciousness. The best romances, he suggested, were those which make a powerful artistic impression and yet offer something as simple as nature. Romance thus became a means of embodying ideas that cannot be formulated in analytical words: 'It is not that there is anything blurred or indefinite in the impression left with us, it is just because the impression is so very definite after its own kind, that we find it hard to fit it exactly with the expressions of our philosophical speech.'[98] In Stevenson's construction 'romance', the source of early guilty pleasures, becomes shorthand for an alternative to the emphasis on all-encompassing representation implied by literary realism in which the author takes on the godlike role of both creator and interpreter. Much more to his taste was fiction in which the patterns offered by 'brute incidents' were allowed to stand for themselves: for Stevenson 'romance' appeared to offer the transformative patterning of significant simplicity he sought in fiction.

This transformation that can be brought about by the act of reading is described most explicitly in 'A Gossip on Romance', the essay which prompted the *Saturday Review* to call on Stevenson to revive the romance form.[99] Those who saw Stevenson as defender of romance gave their own definitions of its value: Haggard saw it as having potential, as an alternative to Naturalism, to meet the human need that was increasing among men and women who 'long to be brought face to face with Beauty, and stretch out their arms towards the vision of the Perfect'; Saintsbury welcomed both Stevenson and Haggard in their reversion to the 'simpler kind of novel' – 'they have 'pitched away minute manners-painting and refined character analysis. I hold that they have done rightly and wisely' – but also talked in utopian terms of the advances to be made once 'we have bathed once more and long in the romance of adventure and passion'.[100] And Lang echoed the emphasis in both Saintsbury and Haggard of the universal and timeless appeal of the form: 'It is now undeniable that the love of adventure, and of mystery, and of a good fight, lingers in the minds of men and women.'[101] Stevenson, however, was less interested in romance's envisioning of a brave new world or its timeless appeal than in the power it had upon the individual reader who succumbs to it.

In 'A Gossip on Romance' he differentiated between kinds of pleasure:

The pleasure that we take in life is of two sorts – the active and the passive. Now we are conscious of a great command over our destiny; anon we are lifted up by circumstance, as by a breaking wave, and dashed we know not how into the future. Now we are pleased by our conduct, anon merely pleased by our surroundings. It would be hard to say which of these modes of satisfaction is the more effective but the latter is surely the more constant. Conduct is three parts of life, they say but I think they put it high.[102]

Such a distinction can be extended into differentiation between fiction that addresses issues of conduct, moving the reader back into engagement with the world through its process of representation of 'real' issues, and fiction which allows a more 'effortless' relationship with the text in which there are less demands for agency upon the self. It was with this passive – yet transformed – reader that Stevenson's interest lay. As in other essays he sought to represent himself as part of that general audience, figured in terms characteristic of de Certeau's general reader, travelling the landscape in undirected ways. When he argued that '*Robinson* depends, for the most part and with the overwhelming majority of its readers, on the charm of circumstance' he is, by implication, part of that easily charmed majority, and included himself even more explicitly in the group that identified the *Arabian Nights* as a form of writing in which 'adventure, on the most naked terms, furnishes forth the entertainment and is found enough'.[103] Moreover, he set himself apart from the more elevated audience who prefer novels of manners and social detail to romantic fiction: 'English people of the present day are apt, I know not why, to look somewhat down on incident, and reserve their admiration for the clink of teaspoons, and the accents of the curate.'[104]

Yet such apparently passive reading, created by those moments when the reader is 'lost', is also presented as the most activating: 'when the reader consciously plays at being the hero, the scene is a good scene'. This is 'the triumph of romantic story-telling' – as opposed to 'character studies' in which 'the pleasure that we take is critical; we watch, we approve, we smile at incongruities, we are moved to sudden heats of sympathy with courage, suffering or virtue'.[105] Through the focus on romance Stevenson can be seen as moving towards addressing much wider questions about the psychology of reading process. As the following chapter shows, his speculations on activity and passivity as forms of pleasure anticipate reading theories interested in the relationship between reading and play, states of reading pleasure and states of hypnosis. Encounters with romance, moreover, led him into analysis of different stages of reading experience. Romance becomes associated not only with models of imaginative engagement in early childhood but also with the period of boyhood in which total immersion in a text is possible and 'Eloquence and thought, character and conversation, were but obstacles to brush aside as we dug blithely after a certain sort of incident, like a pig for truffles'.[106] In a late letter he expressed similar sentiments in relation to the readers of his fiction and his own habits;

> I am glad to have interested you; I will tell you in confidence – I only care to be read by young men; they alone can read. I read now, yes, and with pleasure; but some years ago I read with the greed and gusto of a pig, sucking up some of the very paper (you would think) into my brain. And that is the only kind of reading for which it is worth while to support the pains of writing.[107]

Again, his speculations anticipate those who have identified the adolescent reader as a particularly paradigmatic figure for the addictive dimension of reading. Stevenson's contribution to the realism and romance debate becomes therefore a means of articulating ideas connected with phenomenological analysis rather than with contemporary debates about the role and responsibility of art. The transformative experiences offered by the romance genre and the habits of different reading stages, powerful elements in his personal narratives of textual engagement, led him further into exploration of perhaps the most problematic literary issue of all for him: what constitutes and what is the value of reading pleasure.

Notes

1 6/10/94 to Sidney Colvin, *Letters*, vol. 8, p. 372.

2 H. J. Moors remarks that 'He was an indefatigable worker. Somewhere he writes in defense of the idler, yet he was no idler.' *With Stevenson in Samoa*, p. 100.

3 The image of 'gossip' already carried discursive significance: Thackeray structured *Vanity Fair* through the narrative inconsistency of gossip: 'In one early summary of the plot ... the narrator gives much information about a rumoured note of proposal to the young Rebecca Sharp, but no clear picture of events and their cause-and-effect relationship.' M. Lund, *Reading Thackeray* (Detroit: Wayne State University Press, 1988), p. 23. Meredith also foregrounded the voice of Dame Gossip in *The Amazing Marriage* (1895) as the powerful but unreliable image of public discourse. (Judith Wilt sees the 'treaty' between Dame and Novelist as representing Meredith's view that 'the impulses of romance and novel, action and analysis, mystery and understanding that these subplot characters represent ought not to be at war'. J. Wilt, *The Readable People of George Meredith* (Princeton: Princeton University Press, 1975), p. 221.)

4 'A Retrospect (A Fragment: Written at Dunoon, 1870)', *Further Memories*, Tusitala XXX, pp. 180–8, p. 180.

5 15/7/94, *Letters*, vol. 8, p. 330.

6 There are differences in the dating of this 'revolution', and also questioning of the 'linearity' of development it implies. The movement into a greater 'variety' of reading is also regarded as equally significant. See: R. D. Altick, *The English Common Reader: A Social History of the Mass Reading Public, 1800–1900* (London; Chicago: Chicago University Press, 1957); R. Wittmann, 'Was there a Reading Revolution at the End of the Eighteenth Century?', in G. Cavallo and R. Chartier (eds), *A History of Reading in the West*, trans. L. C. Cochrane (Oxford: Polity Press, 1999); R. Chartier, *Forms and Meanings: Texts, Performances, and Audiences from Codex to Computer* (Philadelphia: University of Pennsylvania Press, 1995); Darnton, *The Kiss of Lamourette*; R. Engelsing, 'Die Perioden der Lesergeschichte in der Neuzeit: Das statistische Ausmass und die soziokulturelle Bedeutung der Lektüre', *Archiv für Geschichte des Buchwesens*, 10 (1970), 944–1002; A. Manguel, *A History of Reading* (London: HarperCollins, 1996).

7 W. Collins, 'The Unknown Public', *Household Words*, 439 (21 August 1858), 217–22, p. 222.

8 W. Ong, 'The Writer's Audience Is Always a Fiction', *PMLA*, 90 (1975), 9–21, p. 17.

9 P. Brantlinger, *The Reading Lesson: The Threat of Mass Literacy in Nineteenth-century British Fiction* (Bloomington and Indianapolis: Indiana University Press, 1998), p. 19; Stewart, *Dear Reader*, p. 19.

10 J. C. Olmsted, *A Victorian Art of Fiction: Essays on the Novel in British Periodicals 1870–1900* (New York and London: Garland, 1979). See also Mays, who notes that the years between 1860 and 1900 saw 'an explosive expansion of the arena of "knowledge" that was signified by an overwhelming abundance of printed matter and an equally dramatic increase both in the number of readers and in the amount of time such readers devoted to reading.' K. J. Mays, 'The Disease of Reading and Victorian Periodicals', in J. O. Jordan and R. L. Patten (eds), *Literature in the Marketplace: Nineteenth-century British Publishing and Reading Practices* (Cambridge: Cambridge University Press, 1995), pp. 165–94, p. 165.

11 Mays, 'The Disease of Reading', p. 165.

12 See: Altick, *The English Common Reader*; Rose, *The Intellectual Life of the British Working Classes*.

13 See N. Cross, *The Common Writer: Life in Nineteenth-century Grub Street* (Cambridge: Cambridge University Press, 1985); N. N. Feltes, *Literary Capital and the Late Victorian Novel* (Madison: University of Wisconsin Press, 1993); K. Graham, *English Criticism of the Novel 1865–1900* (Oxford: Clarendon Press, 1965); J. Gross, *The Rise and Fall of the Man of Letters: English Literary Life Since 1800* (Harmondsworth: Penguin, 1969); P. Keating, *The Haunted Study: A Social History of the English Novel 1875–1914* (London: Secker and Warburg, 1989; Fontana, 1991).

14 See: D. Amigoni, *The English Novel and Prose Narrative* (Edinburgh: Edinburgh University Press, 2000); C. Baldick, *The Social Mission of English Criticism* (Oxford: Clarendon Press 1983); F. E. Court, *Institutionalizing*

English Literature: The Culture and Politics of Literary Study 1750–1900 (Stanford: Stanford University Press, 1992); D. J. Palmer, *The Rise of English Studies* (London, New York, Toronto: Oxford University Press (for University of Hull), 1965); J. Treglown and B. Bennett, *Grub Street and the Ivory Tower: Literary Journalism and Literary Scholarship from Fielding to the Internet* (Oxford: Clarendon Press, 1998).

15 Mays, 'The Disease of Reading', p. 168.

16 *Ibid.*, p. 169.

17 Keating, *The Haunted Study*, p. 340.

18 *Ibid.*, p. 343.

19 Brantlinger, for example, sees the tale as mirroring 'the story of an exemplary struggling author, torn between the desire to produce "masterpieces" and the knowledge that popular success lay in the contrary direction of both "shilling shocker" and "moral allegory"' (*The Reading Lesson*, p. 172). Stewart also offers provocative readings of the text in this context; see: 'The Gothic of Reading', *Dear Reader*, pp. 343–92.

20 Conrad, by contrast, proclaimed, 'I have some – literary – reputation but the future is anything but certain, for I am not a popular author and probably I never shall be. This does not sadden me at all, for I have never had the ambition to write for the all-powerful masses' (1887), *The Collected Letters of Joseph Conrad*, eds. F. R. Karl and L. Davies, I (4 vols) (Cambridge: Cambridge University Press, 1983–90), p. 390, quoted in P. McDonald, *British Literary Culture and Publishing Practice 1880–1914* (Cambridge: Cambridge University Press, 1997), p. 22.

21 P. McDonald, *British Literary Culture and Publishing Practice 1880–1914*, p. 6.

22 'The Cheapening of Poetry', *National Observer*, 5 (1892), 624; McDonald, *British Literary Culture*, p. 7.

23 E. Gosse, 'The Influence of Democracy on Literature', *Contemporary Review*, 59 (April 1891), 523–36, p. 530.

24 Mid-October/85 to Bob Stevenson, *Letters*, vol. 5, pp. 133–4.

25 12/1/86, *Letters*, vol. 5, p. 171.

26 *Ibid.*; Gosse, *Contemporary Review*, p. 532.

27 2/1/86, *Letters*, vol. 5, p. 171.

28 L. Tickner, *Modern Life and Modern Subjects: British Art in the Early Twentieth Century* (New Haven and London: Yale University Press, 2000), p. 44.

29 'The Morality of the Profession of Letters', *Fortnightly Review*, 157 (April 1881), 513–20; Tusitala XXVIII, pp. 51–61.

30 Tusitala XXVIII, p. 54.

31 *Ibid.*, p. 55.

32 *Ibid.*, p. 54.

33 27/4/81 to *The Academy*, published 7 May 1881, 339, in response to criticism of the essay which had appeared in 'Magazines and Reviews' in *The Academy*, 9 April 1888, 261.

34 'Letter to a Young Gentleman Who Proposes to Embrace the Career of Art', *Scribner's Magazine*, 4 (1888), 377–81, Tusitala XXVIII, 3–11.

35 *Ibid.*, p. 8.

36 W. H. Low, who describes Stevenson reading this essay aloud (*A Chronicle of Friendship* (1908), pp. 413–17), wrote a letter in response, also published in the September issue of *Scribner's Magazine*.

37 R. Le Gallienne, *The Academy*, XLI (14 May 1892), 462–4; further paragraphs were added to the review in 1896, in which he attempts to redefine pleasure (*Retrospective Reviews* (1896).

38 28/12/93, *Letters*, vol. 8, p. 211.

39 B. Menikoff, *Robert Louis Stevenson and 'The Beach of Falesá': A Study in Victorian Publishing* (Edinburgh: Edinburgh University Press, 1984), pp. 8–9.

40 *Ibid.*, p. 9.

41 Ambrosini, 'The Art of Writing and the Pleasure of Reading', p. 27.

42 *Ibid.*, p. 33.

43 *Ibid.*, p. 34.

44 c. 8/5/94 to S. R. Crockett, *Letters*, vol. 8, p. 286.

45 R. Jolly, *Henry James: History, Narrative, Fiction* (Oxford: Clarendon Press, 1993), p. 13.

46 See, for example, 'On Some Technical Elements of Style in Literature', first published in the *Contemporary Review* (April 1885); Tusitala XXVIII, pp. 33–50. As Ambrosini has suggested, Stevenson's interest in literary experimentation was also shaped by his view of the market as a testing ground for his fiction, 'The Art of Writing'.

47 The Scottish education system, of which Stevenson was a product, while increasingly drawn into English models, retained a tradition of supporting a broad general education. See Palmer in *The Rise of English Studies*, appendix 1. See also G. E. Davie, *The Democratic Intellect: Scotland and Her Universities in the Nineteenth Century* (Edinburgh: Edinburgh University Press, 1961); L. Ferreira-Buckley, 'Scottish Rhetoric and the Formation of Literary Studies in Nineteenth-century England', in R. Crawford (ed.), *The Scottish Invention of English Literature* (Cambridge: Cambridge University Press, 1998), pp. 180–206.

48 Crawford, 'Introduction', *The Scottish Invention of English Literature*, p. 8; F. E. Court likewise notes that, by the time David Masson retired from Edinburgh in 1895, the study of English literature 'had emerged as the printed "how to" guide to being English'. *The Institutionalizing of English Literature*, p. 132.

49 Gosse, like Saintsbury, but to a greater extent, was mocked by newer critics for his lack of disciplinary scholarship, most famously by John Churton Collins: 'English Literature at the Universities', *Quarterly Review*, 163 (1886), 289–329. Collins's attack was driven by his campaign for an English school at Oxford and a dislike of both the pedantries and the dilettantism of current literary criticism. (See Palmer, *The Rise of English Studies*, pp. 78–103; V. Cunningham, 'Darke Conceits: Churton Collins, Edmund Gosse, and the Professions of Criticism', in Treglown and Bennett (eds), *Grub Street and the Ivory Tower*, pp. 72–90.)

50 Gosse worked as a librarian at the British Museum from 1867 and in 1875 became a translator at the Board of Trade. From 1904 he worked as librarian at the House of Lords. Saintsbury was Professor of Rhetoric and Belles-Lettres at the University of Edinburgh 1895–1915.

51 H. Orel, *Victorian Literary Critics* (London: Macmillan, 1984), pp. 149–50.

52 Reviews of G. MacDonald, *Malcolm*, *The Academy*, 140 (9 January 1875), 34–5, p. 35. Court notes that Saintsbury 'in spite of his rigid Toryism, advocated the intrinsic merits of reading primarily for its own sake'. *The Institutionalizing of English Literature*, p. 156.

53 G. Saintsbury 'The Present State of the Novel I', *Fortnightly Review*, 42 (September 1887), 410–17, p. 411; 'The Present State of Criticism' in *A History of Criticism and Literary Taste in Europe*, 3 vols, vol. 3 (Edinburgh and London: William Blackwood and Sons, 1904), pp. 603–10, p. 609.

54 W. Besant, *The Pen and the Book* (London: Thomas Burleigh, 1899), pp. 64–5.

55 *Ibid.*, pp. 66–8.

56 *Ibid.*, p. 64.

57 'To begin with, this whole affair of the biographical treatment of people in their lifetime, goes sore against my heart. I admit it is a good form of advertisement; and I am no such self-deceiver as to suppose this does not weigh with me, for I earnestly wish my books to sell. In every other way it shocks me. I think the public should know nothing from behind the scenes, until the man himself is out of reach of hurt; and when I have been applied to for biographical details, I have always refused or (which I think best) sent a list of such facts as a diligent reader of the newspapers might have gathered for himself.' 17/3/86, *Letters*, vol. 5, p. 234. Low had told Stevenson that Gosse had been invited to write a piece on RLS for the *Century*.

58 In 1894 he complained to Henley of the latter's strictures against S. R. Crockett and compared this with his own, kinder perspective: 'What ails you at poor Crockett? He seems to me not without parts from what I have seen of him.' 15/7/94, *Letters*, vol. 8, p. 330.

59 A reference to Saintsbury's review of *Familiar Studies of Men and Books* in the *Pall Mall Gazette*, XXXV (18 March 1882), p. 5. 31/3/82, *Letters*, vol. 3, p. 309.

60 31/3/88 to Richard Watson Gilder, *Letters*, vol. 6, p. 143.

61 15/9/74 to Frances Sitwell *Letters*, vol. 2, p. 52.

62 January/79 to Margaret Oliphant, *Letters*, vol. 2, p. 301.

63 15/11/83, *Letters*, vol. 4, p. 203.

64 119/11/82 to J. A. Symonds, *Letters*, vol. 4, p. 28.

65 Mays, 'The Disease of Reading', p. 169. The wealth of reading material produced concerns about 'the vice of reading', but also led to anxieties that readers were reading incorrectly as well as excessively. As Mays notes, '"this hurried, careless, method of reading" represented "one of the chief dangers"' (Mays, 'The Disease of Reading', p. 171). Later in her essay she notes: 'The truly literate, well-read man was, quite simply, the man who read well, which is to say correctly in the normative terms established by these essayists. He

was distinguished neither by the sheer ability to read nor by what he read but by how he did so, for it was in the process of his reading (*qua* study) that his character was produced and demonstrated. In casting the dangers and promises of reading and literacy in these terms, the discursive construction of the reading problem thus functioned to establish and sanctify social boundaries in new terms' (p. 181).

66 *Ibid.*, p. 182.
67 R. Jolly, *Henry James: History, Narrative, Fiction*; A. T. Margolis, *Henry James and the Problem of Audience: An International Act* (Ann Arbor: UMI Research Press, 1985).
68 J. M. Barrie, 'Brought Back from Elysium', *Contemporary Review*, 57 (June 1890), 846–54, p. 848.
69 *Ibid.*, p. 849.
70 *Ibid.*, pp. 849–50.
71 'A Gossip on Romance', *Longman's Magazine*, 1 (1882), 69–79; Tusitala XXIX, 119–31; 'The Modern Novel', *Saturday Review*, 54:1411 (11 November 1882), 633–4, p. 634.
72 For various interpretations of this dialogue see: G. Dekker, 'James and Stevenson: The Mixed Current of Romance', in R. M. Polhemus and R. B. Henkle (eds), *Critical Reconstructions: The Relationship Between Fiction and Life* (Stanford: Stanford University Press, 1994), pp. 127–49; K. Graham, 'Stevenson and Henry James: A Crossing', in Noble (ed.), *Robert Louis Stevenson*; T. Hadley, *Henry James and the Imagination of Pleasure* (New York: Cambridge University Press, 2002); Jolly, *Henry James: History, Narrative, Fiction*; Norquay, *R. L. Stevenson on Fiction*; J. A. Smith, *Henry James and Robert Louis Stevenson: A Record of Friendship and Criticism* (London: Rupert Hart-Davis, 1948).
73 13/2/86 to C. W. Stoddard, *Letters*, vol. 5, p. 203. The class ran from February 1885 to June 1886.
74 *Ibid.*
75 A. Lang, 'Romanticism and Realism', *Saturday Review*, 78:2041 (8 December 1894), 615–16.
76 20/10/74 to Bob Stevenson, *Letters*, vol. 2, p. 64.
77 ?30/9/83 to Bob Stevenson, *Letters*, vol. 4, pp. 169–70; see also 9/10/83 to Bob, *Letters*, vol. 4, pp. 180–2.
78 *Ibid.*, vol. 4, p. 170.
79 *Ibid.*, p. 170. 'A Note on Realism' was published in *The Magazine of Art*, which at that time was edited by Henley (Tusitala XXVIII, pp. 69–75).
80 Tusitala XXVIII, p. 70.
81 17/11/68 to Bob Stevenson, *Letters*, vol. 1, p. 167.
82 H. James, 'The Art of Fiction', *Longman's Magazine*, 4 (September 1884), 502–21; R. L. Stevenson, 'A Humble Remonstrance', *Longman's Magazine*, 5 (December 1884), 139–47; Tusitala XXIX, pp. 132–43.
83 W. Besant, *The Art of Fiction: A Lecture Delivered at the Royal Institution on Friday Evening, April 25, 1884* (London: Chatto and Windus, 1884).
84 *Ibid.*, p. 15.

85 James, 'The Art of Fiction', p. 287.
86 *Ibid.*, p. 288.
87 *Ibid.*, p. 292.
88 *Ibid.*, p. 294.
89 *Ibid.*, p. 305.
90 'A Humble Remonstrance', Tusitala XXIX, p. 142.
91 John Tinnon Taylor notes that 'A particular stigma was attached to those who read only for the plot'. *Early Opposition to the English Novel: The Popular Reaction from 1760 to 1830* (New York: King's Crown Press, 1943), p. 9.
92 10/6/93 to Gosse, *Letters*, vol. 8, p. 103.
93 April/91 to Gosse, *Letters*, vol. 7, p. 105.
94 5/12/93 to James, *Letters*, vol. 8, p. 193.
95 Also implicit in Stevenson's apparent opposition to realism was his dislike of 'naturalism'. The debate has to be understood in the context of developments within the European novel and definitions of 'naturalism' as a literary school and method evolving in France; in particular the work of Emile Zola was to have a significant, if relatively short-lived, influence on theories of fiction. Stevenson, although he was often positive about Balzac, positioned himself against the naturalist attention to detail and the scientific observation of determining environments, arguing instead for a dynamic relationship between incident and character.
96 Keating, *The Haunted Study*, p. 348.
97 'In the wake of the romantic yet prosaic novel of Walter Scott there remained another novel yet to be created, and in our opinion a more beautiful and complete novel. This novel has at one and the same time elements of the epic and the theatrical, it is romantic yet poetic, realist yet idealist, true yet great, and will fuse together the worlds of Walter Scott and Homer.' 'Victor Hugo's Romances', *Familiar Studies of Men and Books*, Tusitala XXVII, pp. 1–23, p. 1.
98 *Ibid.*, p. 8.
99 'A Gossip on Romance', *Longman's Magazine*, 1 (November 1882), 69–79 (Tusitala XXIX, pp. 119–31); 'The Modern Novel', *The Saturday Review*, 54:1411 (11 November 1882), 633–4.
100 H. Rider Haggard, 'About Fiction', *Contemporary Review*, 51 (February 1887), 172–80, p. 173; Saintsbury, 'The Present State of the Novel I', *Fortnightly Review*, 42 (January 1887), 410–17, p. 415; p. 417.
101 A. Lang, 'Realism and Romance', *Contemporary Review*, 52 (November 1887), 683–93, p. 692.
102 Tusitala XXIX, p. 120.
103 *Ibid.*, p. 125; p. 126.
104 *Ibid.*, p. 124.
105 *Ibid.*, p. 128.
106 *Ibid.*, p. 119.
107 January/February/91 to W. Leslie Curnow, *Letters*, vol. 7, p. 82.

4

'Whores of the mind':
the analysis of pleasure

> We are whores, some of us pretty whores, some of us not, but all whores:
> whores of the mind, selling to the public the amusements of our fireside as
> the whore sells the pleasures of her bed.[1]

Suggestive of conflicts in Stevenson's own perception of pleasured reading
and writing, the figure of novelist as whore discussed in the previous
chapter also points to more general anxieties about literary production
and consumption.[2] The dangerously seductive power of fiction had been
a matter of concern from the 1860s onwards, usually with a specifically
gendered inflection: the woman reader is lured away from her moral duty,
her daily tasks and possibly her sanity through the arousal of passion
by unsuitable novels.[3] Stevenson's emphasis on commercial transaction
in this imagery of seduction was, however, particularly forceful and
specifically related to the writer as producer of pleasure, drawing the
public into a shared corruption but one in which the client, the reader,
possesses the economic power. Active as a 'whore of the mind', offering
textual seduction, the writer is nevertheless in a passively feminised
position, dependent upon convincing others of the value of their pleasures. Relationships between pleasure and artistic production, pleasure
and consumption, were, as we have seen, central concerns for writers
emerging from a Calvinist inheritance and a recurring subject of debate
between Louis and his father. The intersection of hedonism and aesthetics
was also a subject much worried about in the period generally. But even
in attempting to create an image which defined the commercial context
for writing, Stevenson was drawn towards terminology which brought
together the pleasure of the writer and the desires of the reader: to understand the psychology of readers, he had to turn to his own experiences
of reading delight. Deliberately provocative as the writer-as-whore image
might appear, unsatisfactory as Stevenson later acknowledged it to be, it
nevertheless recognised that the play of desires needs to be explored in
the purveyor as well as the consumer.

At the same time, however, his discussions of pleasure clearly deployed the dominant discourses of his time. If his understanding of writing as a trade in sexual desire was individualistic, he also drew upon shared representations of reading as a different kind of appetite. As his letter to Curnow in which he described reading 'with the greed and gusto of a pig' showed, he saw his needs as voracious.[4] In representing the act of reading through oral imagery he deployed a deeply familiar trope, but one in which the association with dangerous ingestion was particularly strong.[5] In the late nineteenth century literary consumption was variously understood as hunger, as greed, as intoxication.[6] Through such images wider anxieties about readers never being satisfied – hungering after a new book as soon as they finish an old one – were expressed. (Stevenson's own work was described in just such terms of a 'light diet' by John Jay Chapman, who wrote: 'I swear I am hungry for something every time I lay down Stevenson.'[7]) An extension of these concerns produced more admonitory images of reading as poison, or as a drug, while further translations led to reading being represented as a beneficial opiate, as medicine.[8] Again Stevenson's own reflections are discursively representative: he talked of turning to fiction when he needed a 'drug' to take his mind off illness and frequently stressed the value of reading cheerful books.[9] Yet while appearing to draw upon well-established motifs of reading pleasures already in circulation, the 'writer as whore' image provided a particularly personal angle from which to view his own experiences of such textual dynamics. The specific nature of his fascinated scrutiny of reading pleasures, developing as a response to the constraints of his Scottish background, fuelled by his increasing geographical distance from the literary establishment, and reinforced by his fusion of roles as popular novelist and man of letters, took him away from the terms of reference of his contemporaries and towards more abstract meditations on the imagination. This chapter examines the particular inflections of Stevenson's perspective on the satisfactions and seductions of reading within the context of contemporary literary debates, but also assesses the new directions in which his explorations led him, showing how he refined and redirected his own engagement with the poetics of pleasure.

The nineteenth-century context

One catalyst for argument on the contentious subject of literary pleasure in the last two decades of the nineteenth century was Sir John Lubbock's list of '100 best books' published in January 1886. In his study of literary capital, N. N. Feltes identifies this list and the subsequent correspondence about it as an important moment in the construction of late Victorian ideology, a point at which the change from Lubbock's original designation of 'good books' to 'best' and its concurrent numerical quantification suggests that 'the significance of the number was not arithmetical but ideological, signifying, as we shall see, attainable knowledge'.[10] Lubbock's list, and the article accompanying it, was based on a lecture given to F. D. Maurice's Working Men's College and reported in the *Morning Advertiser*, publicised by the *Pall Mall Gazette*, published in the *Contemporary Review* of February 1886 and reprinted in Lubbock's book *The Pleasures of Life*.[11] As Feltes notes, Lubbock's essay is, ironically in terms of its direction towards mass consumption, a materialisation of Matthew Arnold's 'literary touchstones' – the best that has been known and thought in the world. The prescription of a hundred 'best' books suggests to Feltes completion of the 'fetishization of "the classic": "the hundred best books" has an attainable completeness, a finality of its own existing precisely as a fetish which may be owned'.[12]

Lubbock's essay in the *Contemporary* is, however, significant in other ways. Given his original audience, and the fact that Sir John was author of the scheme of 'compulsory recreation' known as the Bank Holiday Act, it is not surprising that much of his essay should dwell on the recreational benefits of reading. Shifting rapidly, however, between an emphasis on the function of literature as a tool of study, improvement and moral guidance on the one hand and reading as the source of pleasant companionship and therapeutic relaxation on the other, the essay's voice carries a degree of uncertainty about the balance between these elements. In the familiar discourse of eating, the *Pall Mall Gazette* was highly critical of Lubbock's suggestions in terms of practicality: 'Altogether (apart from the question of time, science having not yet appreciably expanded the traditional threescore years and ten), it is certain that the digestion which could by any means assimilate such an incongruous mass (we had almost said mess) of intellectual provender is not given to one man in a thousand.'[13] The essay, however, was not entirely in favour of chewing through the worthily indigestible; agreeing with Lord Iddesleigh as to the 'charm of desultory reading', Lubbock pointed out the dangers of spending too long on any one book – 'Many readers ... miss much of the pleasure of reading by forcing themselves to dwell too long continuously on one subject' – and suggested that there are attractions in wide-ranging and rapid textual journeys.[14] In marked contrast to advice being given around the same time in a lecture to the London Society for the Extension of University Teaching in 1886, which warned of the dangerous multiplicity of reading material available, advised against trying to read everything too fast and concluded with the stern admonition against speedy ingestion 'Don't Bolt Your Books', Lubbock's interest was in facilitating the perusal of a number of books as an alternative to haphazard selection.[15] At some points then Lubbock's construction of reading came relatively close, in its emphasis on leisure, to a more playful, indeed 'ludic', model of reading than subsequent respondents to his list recognised. Lubbock even went so far as to suggest (rather tentatively) that the class represented by his audience might be more in need of such material:

> I am sometimes disposed to think that the great readers of the next generation will be, not our lawyers and doctors, shopkeepers and manufacturers, but the labourer and the mechanic. Does not this seem natural? The former work mainly with their head; when their daily duties are over the brain is exhausted, and of their leisure time much must be devoted to air and exercise. The labourer or mechanic, on the contrary, besides working for much shorter hours, have in their work-time taken sufficient bodily exercise, and could therefore give any leisure they might have to reading and study.[16]

In his emphasis on the extent to which reading might provide 'grateful recollections of peaceful home hours, after the labours and anxieties of the day', he was not suggesting merely an 'escapist' function for the 'general' reader, but was explicitly drawing upon a model of literary consumption set out by Frederic Harrison in his article on 'Choice of Books' in which he wrote: 'I put the poetic and emotional side of literature as the most needed for daily use.'[17]

The extended correspondence which arose in response to Lubbock's selection of books reinforced perceptions of his list as a significant contribution to the evaluation of literary texts in terms of their educative and moral potential. His emphasis on the poetic and emotional can also be contextualised in terms of debates in the late 1870s and beyond over the extent to which literature should engage the intellect or the emotions. Energetic as the response to his piece was, however, it shifted attention away from an important aspect of his discussion: Lubbock, in his advocacy of literature for the working classes, was working with a model of 'good' reading in which the pleasures of a text offer not simply escape from the daily grind but some kind of significant emotional fulfilment.[18] Although very few of the books he recommended to his audience would come under the designation of 'popular', the framework for his contentious selection hinted at the value of a kind of literary consumption which has stereotypically been associated only with the 'popular': eclectic perusal of material fuelled by readerly desires.

Lubbock had a very different agenda from Stevenson in his definition of literary pleasure, but they shared an interest in the effects of literature on the less sophisticated reader which was more sharply defined than that of most subsequent commentators on the subject; it was also manifested, in both writers, through cameos of the reading act. Some years before Lubbock's manifesto, in 'A Gossip on Romance', Stevenson had represented the impact upon a young Welsh blacksmith of hearing *Robinson Crusoe* read aloud: so entranced was he with the possibility of 'divine day-dreams, written and printed and bound' that he sat down and learned to read, first in Welsh, then in English.[19] In his 1888 essay 'Popular Authors' Stevenson presented with more ambivalence the emotional intensity and influence produced in a would-be adventurer by reading the sea-faring yarn *Tom Holt's Log*, which sends him to seek a career at sea and informs all his subsequent perceptions of the sea-faring life:

> He cannot realise, he cannot make a tale of his own life, which crumbles in discrete impressions even as he lives it, and slips between the fingers of his memory like sand. It is not this that he considers in his rare hours of rumination, but that other life, which was all lit up for him … that other life which, God knows, perhaps he still believes that he is leading – the life of Tom Holt.[20]

Lubbock also depicted the effects on the popular audience of a book 'not assuredly of the first order' (although clearly of a 'higher' order than *Tom Holt's Log*) through anecdote: a village blacksmith, sitting on his anvil in the summer evenings, reads *Pamela* to his audience of villagers who are so enthralled that, when the happy ending is reached, 'the congregation were so delighted as to raise a great shout, and procuring the church keys, actually set the parish bells ringing'.[21] In each small scene Lubbock and Stevenson were reaching towards an articulation of emotionally affective and pleasurable reading as somehow important. From different perspectives – one defined by a specific social agenda, the other emerging from a psychological interest in the transformative power of fiction – both Lubbock and Stevenson acknowledged the arousal of narrative pleasure as significant in itself. This model of engagement was not only different from that objectivity advocated for the critic by 'professionals' such as Besant and Saintsbury but also more nuanced than explanations for the attractions of popular reading offered by other novelists working in the field.

A more typical perception of the 'pleasures' of fiction was exemplified by Rider Haggard's assertion in 'About Fiction' (1887) that 'More and more, as what we call culture spreads, do men and women crave to be taken out of themselves'.[22] Echoing some of Lubbock's points but with a narrower emphasis, Haggard presented a model of reading as compensation for the trials of life and called for more reading material suited to the hard-working male reader. Such implicitly dismissive notions of fiction as a source of light pleasure to be consumed by the masses, transformative only in the sense of offering escape, became increasingly common in what H. G. Wells termed 'the Weary Giant theory of fiction'. Mocking the ideas expressed by those such as Haggard who talked of 'a weary public' which 'calls continually for books, new books to make them forget, to refresh them, to occupy minds jaded with the toil and emptiness and vexation of our competitive existence', Wells sneered at this 'man's theory of the novel':[23]

> The reader is presented as a man, burthened, toiling, worn. He has been in his office from ten to four, with perhaps only two hours interval at his club for lunch; or he has been playing golf ... or doing one of a thousand other of the grave important things which constitute the substance of a prosperous man's life. Now at last comes the little precious interval of leisure, and the Weary Giant takes up a book ... He wants to forget the troublesome realities of life. He wants to be taken out of himself, to be cheered, consoled, amused – above all, amused. He doesn't want ideas, he doesn't want facts; above all, he doesn't want – *Problems*. He wants to dream of the bright, thin gay excitements of a phantom world – in which he can be hero – of horses ridden and lace worn and princesses rescued and won.[24]

Stevenson's fiction might have offered just such pleasures to the 'weary giant', and he wrote enthusiastically about the value of 'cheerful' fiction, yet his deployment of the familiar imagery of reading as a drug to provide escape from pain suggests that he saw it as offering more than mere oblivion:

> When I suffer in mind, stories are my refuge; I take them like opium; and I consider one who writes them as a sort of doctor of the mind. And frankly, Meiklejohn, it is not Shakespeare we take to, when we are in a hot corner; nor, certainly, George Eliot – no, nor even Balzac. It is Charles Reade, or old Dumas, or the Arabian Nights; it is stories we want, not the high poetic function which represents the world ... We want incident, interest, action: to the devil with your philosophy. When we are well again, and have an easy mind, we shall peruse your important work; but what we want now is a drug.[25]

Romance operates in a transformative way, as a 'doctor of the mind', pleasure is specifically related to that absence of representation of the everyday characteristic of the romance form; stories offer a more significant resource than 'important' ideas. Although an element of release is implied in his vision, it goes beyond the amnesiac 'forgetting the troublesome realities of life' identified by Wells.

If Stevenson at times participated in a language of novel as opiate, consonant with the 'Weary Giant' theory of fiction, his own perspective might much more accurately be described as the 'child's theory of the novel'. In '*Rosa Quo Locorum*' he suggested that the working of the child's mind should be the object of greater inquiry than it was – 'From the mind of childhood there is more history and more philosophy to be fished up than from all the printed volumes in a library' – and in his discussions on pleasure it is the mind of the child that offers the most useful object of analysis.[26] The richness of this field is clearly illustrated by 'The Lantern-Bearers' (1888), an essay written in Saranac for *Scribner's Magazine,* at a time when his own childhood was very much in his mind as he reread old favourites and re-created the reading experiences of his early years. Revisiting his early memories of holidays in North Berwick, Stevenson explored his fascination with 'that small theatre of the brain which we kept lighted all night long'.[27] The fantasy world of the child, created for him and his boyhood friends by the possession of tin bull's-eyes lanterns which light their meetings at nightfall in secret places on the beach, becomes symbolic of the transformative power of the imagination. In the child's ability to transcend and rework the banalities of the everyday, a literary alternative emerges to realists who ignore fantasy and the imagination, concentrating instead on representing what they see as a way into the truthfulness of experience.[28] While the gang of boys may have appeared cold and wet to an outsider, and their talk nonsense, such an account would have been 'untrue' to the warmth of their experience: this is then another example of 'the truly haunting and truly spectral unreality of realistic books'.[29] Stevenson thus sets out his theory that the pleasure and power of fiction – 'that rainbow work of fancy that clothes what is naked and seems to ennoble what is base' – lies in its capacity to offer a transformative world which has a hold over the imagination, speaking to the reader, but does not claim to shape or dictate our relation to the everyday world. In this way Stevenson moves the debate over reading away from the oppositional perception of books as offering either escape or relevance and instead focuses on the exact nature of the imaginative experience with an attention similar in its intensity to a Calvinist scrutiny of 'the Word'.

Again and again in the series of essays written for *Scribner's* Stevenson drew on his childhood as the site of most illumination about such reading pleasures, building on earlier explorations of the child's imagination such as 'On the Movement of Young Children' (1874).[30] In 'A Penny Plain and Twopence Coloured' (1884), one of his most vivid essays on childhood imaginings, he had drawn upon the experience of buying cut-out paper toy theatres, produced by Skelt, which later becomes his own personal term for the land of fantastical imaginings. Here too the child's engagement with imaginative worlds was used to highlight the inadequacy of mimesis as a concept for understanding the working of literature:

it was 'a thing not one with cold reality, but how much dearer to the mind!'[31] Although the world of Skelt was crude, and the child's interest of a temporary kind, it shaped desires and expectations for both art and reality: 'I ... acquired a gallery of scenes and characters with which, in the silent theatre of the brain, I might enact all novels and romances; and took from these rude cuts an enduring and transforming pleasure.'[32] The scenery of this fantasy world, so lovingly detailed, becomes, as Stevenson described it, a prism through which all future experience is constructed: his first view of England is through the eyes of Skelt. The essay simultaneously explored and enacted desires which drive the imagination, re-creating the pleasures experienced by the child through the itemisation of lists of titles, names of characters and, most magically of all, the different coloured paints whereby Skelt is to be brought to life:

> With crimson lake (hark to the sound of it – crimson lake! – the horns of elf-land are not richer on the ear) – with crimson lake and Prussian blue a certain purple is to be compounded which, for cloaks especially, Titian could not equal. The latter colour with gamboges, a hated name although an exquisite pigment, supplied a green of such savoury greenness that today my heart regrets it.[33]

The final fantasy, in which Skelt himself is discovered, all his plays bought up, but when that treasure is attained they all turn to dust in his hands, served further as a metaphor for the role of the reader, endlessly desiring the ultimate fulfilment of the imagination, but inevitably to be disappointed if that gratification is no longer deferred.[34] The pleasure of reading, it would appear, lay in the experiencing moment and not in the message that could be taken from the text. It is therefore appropriate that the reader, directly interpellated towards the end of the essay, is explicitly asked to reflect upon his or her own experience of the relationship between resonant language and the imagination: 'Reader – and yourself?'[35]

This strategy has several implications: it shows Stevenson, in apparent opposition to the moral seriousness of reading that his father had emphasised, whereby it was of value to read depressing books, and defiantly asserting the importance of being 'lost in a book', of being a playful, 'ludic' reader. By constructing himself as child representative of the reading public, moreover, Stevenson not only laid claim for his role as figure of the 'general reader' but also allowed his readers to be drawn into experiencing the child's pleasure – particularly in the illustrated version of his essay which first appeared in *The Magazine of Art* thus creating a primary visual engagement with the drawings of Skelt's characters as well as the narrative. Situated as part of that general readership, looking back with nostalgia to earlier reading selves, the readers of Stevenson's essay could experience afresh the transformations of a fictional world. 'Reading about reading in childhood', as Calinescu notes in more general terms, 'helps us to remember, and perhaps even to recreate, the sense of enchantment produced in us by certain involved, quasi-hypnotic reading experiences we had long ago'.[36] Stevenson's focus on the pleasures of the child's imagination allowed him to perform (in every sense) an analysis of the ways in which reading works: the essay suggested that gratification is inevitably temporary; and that the power of language goes beyond the referential relationship of signifier and signified. His interest in the mechanics of pleasure can thus be expressed in terms which do not have to conform to debates about the morality of literature. Nevertheless, in articulating his understanding that pleasures lies less in seeing 'the real' represented than in encountering transformations of the everyday in which the psychic structures of desire can be played out, he can also be seen as responding to the Calvinist suspicion of 'unauthorised' representation of the world: the fictional experiences he advocates, imaged by the child's engagement with the text, make no such claims.

By moving away from claims for the authority of the word, stressing instead the element of story rather than any 'high poetic function', Stevenson followed a trajectory which resulted from Calvinism's implied mistrust of realist forms emulating representation of the world. (As K. G. Simpson has argued, Stevenson's lack of interest in the psychological dimension of character can be understood also as a product of religious influence: 'Given the Calvinist emphasis on the predetermination of human action there is little incentive to consider motivation of behaviour.'[37]) Stevenson's understanding of pleasure, epitomised by the child's experience of reading and dependent upon romance rather than realist forms of fiction, also produced manoeuvres in relation to low or popular fiction which again took him in different directions from his contemporaries, although their understanding of his approach to pleasure through deployment of the innocent reader created difficulties for his status as both writer and theorist.

In 'Popular Authors', another essay commissioned for *Scribner's* and one which allowed him to call upon his editors for a supply of books half-remembered from his childhood, Stevenson again reproduced the magical powers of names and adventures. Through his analysis of the work and literary careers of Stephens Hayward and Bracebridge Hemming, he gently interrogated established cultural hierarchies, questioning the desire for 'upper popularity' and suggesting that a writer such as himself might in some respects 'long for the penny number and the weekly woodcut!'[38] Again his analysis was brought to life by depiction of the setting for each of his own early reading experiences – the wet and windy day on which his mother first read him *Macbeth*; the books found on a boyhood expedition to Neidpath Castle. Although commenting on the relationship between commercial success and literary value, a concern dominant in debates on fiction at the time, Stevenson was much more interested in the power of popular texts to affect the 'general' (and child-like) reader. What relationship did the readers of such works perceive between the book and their lives? Had *Tom Holt's Log* inspired someone to go to sea? Did reading about a poor heroine's romantic and financial successes in *The Young Ladies' Journal* fill the young female reader with similar aspirations? Such encounters, the essay suggested, are not simply based upon a crude misapprehension of the 'reality' of such fictions: for the readers (like children) 'long, not to enter into the lives of others, but to behold themselves in changed situations, ardently but impotently preconceived.'[39] In other words, such tales offer a narrative reworking of their longings and aspirations. Stevenson thus sketched out a patterning of readerly desire which to some extent recognised the conditions of the readers' lives and offered a model for their pleasurable interactions with the text. The despised popular writers can 'supply to the shop-girl and the shoe-black vesture cut to the pattern of their naked fancies, and furnish them with welcome scenery and properties for autobiographical romancing'.[40] Again it was the 'transformative' power of language and narrative which fascinated Stevenson and once more it was the workings of the child's imagination which provided the most appropriate structure for understanding pleasure: 'Let us try to remember', he suggested, 'how fancy works in children; with what selective partiality it reads, leaving often the bulk of the book unrealised, but fixing on the rest and living it … It seems to be not much otherwise with uneducated readers.'[41] What the popular author does, he argued, is to supply 'some body of circum-stances to these phantom aspirations', although the reader, like the child at play, will follow only where they will. Those who achieve most success in this area are those who have the most sympathetic understanding of 'the popular mind' and can identify that will.

Stevenson's writings on pleasure are clearly informed by debates about the reading public and mass consumption; his intervention in 'Popular Authors' expresses familiar anxieties about the relationship between low and high art.[42] Yet, while engaging with questions about the relationship between mainstream literature and the reading public which preoccu-pied other critics, Stevenson did so through an unusual doubling of roles, self-identified as both a writer of commercial fiction – 'I was well thought of on my penny paper' – and as member of the reading public: 'SMITH … ERRYM … HAYWARD … these I read for pleasure'.[43] From both perspectives he might therefore claim a closer relationship for himself with the workings of 'the popular mind'. Through this dual performance – Stevenson, the writer who knows the complicated hierarchies surrounding this marketplace, mocking both the purveyors of popular fiction and those who look down at such men from the highroad of aesthetic principles combined with lack of commercial success, and Stevenson, as the reincarnation of earlier reading selves, who participated with relish in the consumption of the popular texts – he also found a position from which to negotiate his own mixed response to pleasure. He could focus on pleasurable stories which make little claim for the representative power of art but he could still assert their power in psychically activating the reader. As he had previously stated in 'A Gossip on Romance': 'the great creative writer shows us the realisation and the apotheosis of the day-dreams of common men. His stories may be nourished with the realities of life, but their true mark is to satisfy the nameless longings of the reader, and to obey the ideal laws of the day-dream.'[44] His centralising of the mechanics of pleasure thus becomes a defiant rejection of Calvinist opprobrium towards the seductions of art, but also an assertion of fiction's imaginative power in a way which does not usurp the authority of either God or Word.

Reader as child thus appears a more fruitful and less difficult image than the writer as prostitute in exploring the dynamics of the imagination. This device of deploying the child as paradigmatic reader did, however, create long-term problems in critical censure. Soon after Stevenson's death, H. G. Wells interpreted such textual performances as advocating the most simple form of escapism: entitling him 'The Lost Stevenson' in a review of *Weir of Hermiston*, Wells contributed to the emergent view of RLS as victim of critics, the public, and his 'own emotional patriotism', which drove him 'along the pathway of traditional romance'.[45] Too keen to let public acclaim determine his direction, confused by 'the huge reputation, the glamour of Scott and Dumas', he was unable to control the pull towards backward-looking romance and became 'not so much a romancer as a novelist entangled in the puerilities of romance'.[46] Finally, damningly, Wells links this stunted literary potential as a novelist with Stevenson's activities as an essayist: 'The toy theatre laid hold of his imagination in his boyhood and he never slipped its grip. He helped to hypnotise himself by his own ingenious criticisms.'[47]

This view of Stevenson as someone not only representative of his century's anxieties about readerly pleasure but also victim to the desire to please the reader is to be found in a number of critical perspectives both at the time and subsequently, and is frequently linked to his interest in the child's imagination. Echoing Wells's image of arrested development, Stevenson's fellow countryman J. M. Barrie (in an interestingly personal turn of phrase) described him as experimenting for too long: 'he is still a boy wondering what he is going to be'; when he embarks on his fictional journeys 'he always starts off whistling', but has not yet produced the awaited 'big' book.[48] An essay written after Stevenson's death by John Jay Chapman (the American writer who had visited the Stevensons in Bournemouth) also promulgated this powerful image: 'He became a remarkable, if not a unique phenomenon – for he never grew up. Whether or not there was some obscure connection between his bodily troubles and the arrest of his intellectual development, it is certain that Stevenson remained a boy till the day of his death.'[49] Henry James suggested that in England women novelists were more 'mature' in their concerns than their male counterparts, and (surely with Stevenson in mind) noted: 'The female mind has in fact throughout the competition carried off the prize in the familiar game, known to us all from childhood's hour, of playing at "grown-up" ... It is the ladies in a word who have lately done most to remind us of man's relations with himself, that is with woman. His relations with the pistol, the pirate, the police, the wild and the tame beast – are these not prevailingly what the gentlemen have given us?'[50] Fellow Scot Edwin Muir noted that Stevenson 'had spent his childhood and youth in a country where everything combined to prevent an imaginative writer from coming to maturity'.[51] More recently Leslie Fiedler's psychoanalytic critique of Stevenson as someone who could become a child or creative writer only through his relationship with older women, is reversed by Alan Sandison, who argues that the problem was not how to become a child again but how to grow up, endorsing 'Stevenson's distressed perception of himself as genuinely and irredeemably trapped in, if not childhood, at least late adolescence'.[52] Patrick Brantlinger also perceives weaknesses in Stevenson's advocacy of romance and his deployment of childhood imagination: 'But he associates romance or the fiction of "incident" and "adventure" with daydream, escapism, and childhood rather than any visionary romantic qualities that would both transcend and see more deeply into reality than the rational, realistic mind. At the end of 'A Humble Remonstrance', for example, he calls Sir Walter Scott both "a great romantic" and "an idle child", as if these phrases were synonymous.'[53] Stevenson's obsession with the child reader thus continues to attract critical disapproval. What Wells identified as characteristically 'ingenious criticisms' can, however, be understood as emerging both as a rebellion against and an internalisation of the Calvinist aesthetic which surrounded him in his early years: rebellious in its apparent valorisation of 'innocent' pleasure for its own sake, but also an expression of a deep unease with the claims made for the representative and educative power of fiction. More importantly, it was the very ingenuity produced by this doubleness that led Stevenson into exploration of questions that significantly engage later theorists of reading who provide more positive interpretations of both the child reader and the child as remembered reader.

From the perspective of subsequent reading theory, informed by psychoanalysis and linguistics, connections being made between the child and the reader produce more interesting possibilities than 'arrested development'. The assumption of Freud and his followers that, at its most basic, the thinking of the child is not seen simply as a stage towards the development of adult thought but 'as the matrix that permanently shapes adult experience and, in some versions of the theory, the model of the mind at its best' echoes Stevenson's emphasis on the child reader as a paradigmatic figure, while the philosophical writings of Gaston Bachelard also operate with an understanding that 'Within us, still within us, always within us, childhood is a state of mind'.[54] If Stevenson's writing on pleasure is linked with the thinking of such theorists then his approach to childhood and adolescent patterns of reading becomes less problematic. While his engagement with questions of literary pleasure might appear initially to share the same terms of reference as his contemporaries, Stevenson's considerations are characterised by an identification with the pleasured reader (general or child), a reluctance to adopt a consistently masterful interpretative role as critic and a nuanced appreciation of the commercial determinants of writerly and readerly roles. The influence of Calvinism shaped his participation in those debates; the terms of his argument were heavily inflected by the late nineteenth-century literary context and the world of letters in which he moved. When brought together, this Calvinist inheritance and the concerns of a rapidly changing literary culture fuse to produce a scrutiny of textual pleasure that anticipates, in a number of ways, subsequent and more explicitly theorised analyses of reading and that can be understood as a specific textual and intellectual project rather than the manifestation of a developmental crisis.

Reading pleasure

Fascinated by questions central to the study of reading – what does it mean to be 'lost in a book', what are the pleasures gained from this experience of immersion, why do particular words and phrases captivate? – Stevenson was also interested in more technical aspects of the ways in which specificity of time of reading, place of reading, form of fiction shape engagement and fulfilment. His relationship with pleasure, emerging as a response to his own personal literary history, can therefore also be located in the context of a less moralistic or aesthetic but increasingly scientific interest in the psychology of reading.

One product of the 'golden era of research into reading 1890-1910' which has relevance for the concerns of Stevenson is E. B. Huey's *The Psychology and Pedagogy of Reading*, published in 1908.[55] In this detailed explorations of the ways in which meaning is created, Edmund Burke Huey, Professor of Psychology and Education at the University of Western Pennsylvania, and founder of the laboratory of experimental psychology there, asked a number of questions about the ways in which meaning is created; distinguished between different stages of reading experience – child and adult – and presented his own strategy for teaching reading. Describing it as 'Problem enough, this, for a life's work, to learn how we read!', Huey examined the 'wonderful process, by which our thoughts and thought-wanderings to the finest shades of detail, the play of our inmost feelings and desires and will, the subtle image of the very innermost that we are are reflected from us to another soul who reads us through our book'.[56] Building on the work of William James on the psychology of the sentence and drawing on his view of consciousness as a continuous stream of processes, Huey had been publishing in this area since the late 1890s, developing a cognitive approach to the reading process through a range of experiments on visual perception in reading. Huey's influential questions about the relationship between language and meaning are chronologically paralleled by Freud's interest in the dynamic between daydreaming and literary production and Freud's research is the second area of development relevant to Stevenson. Although the main focus of Freud's concern in 'The Relation of the Poet to Daydreaming' (1908) is the psychology of literary creativity – examining the parallels between the child at play and the creative writer as both create a world of phantasy which is taken very seriously – the essay also addresses the relationship between the desire for the fulfilment of wishes and the structure of phantasy and daydreams. The imaginative world of the child is for Freud, as for Stevenson, central to understanding the literary process. While Stevenson's ideas on pleasure may be compared to those of novelists who were his contemporaries, it is also fruitful to read Stevenson's ideas on the child's imagination against those of both Huey and Freud.

Stevenson was, of course, aware of the work of William James, requesting that the *Principles of Psychology* be sent to him in Vailima.[57] He had also, as Farr argues, been deeply influenced by Herbert Spencer's biological inflection of Schiller's Romantic philosophy in his 1855 *Principles of Psychology* and, in 'Notes on the Movement of Young Children' (1874) and 'Child's Play' (1878), followed Schiller and Spencer in locating 'the distance between the enthusiastic immediacy of the child and his response to spectacles and the cooler mature detachment of the adult male as the incremental product of a sophisticated intellectual and moral education'.[58] He was, however, 'less interested in the ways by which, following Schiller and Spencer, the mature adult could exert increasing discrimination and refined tastes'.[59] Equally, while he engaged with issues preoccupying both the developing science of cognitive psychology and the emergence of psychoanalysis, and might be said to combine Huey's specificity of analysis of the reading process with Freud's interest in the deep structures of the imagination, his observations do not produce a theory of reading development similar to either. While a key feature of his phenomenological interest in aspects of imaginative response studied by Huey and by Freud is the centrality of the child, this figure remains for him the archetypal reader; romance (which some would argue is the favoured reading of the young) also becomes the most paradigmatic of fictional forms. This combination allowed Stevenson, like Huey and Freud, to explore important questions about what happens when we read, but also leads him towards a less developmental model than either.

When in his essays Stevenson explored the instant pleasures experienced when reading, his speculations were not dissimilar to Huey's in the area of linguistic signification: they shared, for example, an interest in the structures of what the latter called 'meaning-feelings', the associations produced by individual words and linguistic sequences.[60] Looking back on his own childhood, and that complex play of pleasure and guilt which characterised it, Stevenson commented on the power of resonant language, identifying this delight in words and phrases with early stages of the child's imagination, before 'fiction' is understood:

> 'The Lord is gone up with a shout, and God with the sound of a trumpet'
> – memorial version, I know not where to find the text – rings still in my ear
> from my first childhood, and perhaps with something of my nurse's accent.
> There was possibly some sort of image written in my mind by these loud
> words, but I believe the words themselves were what I cherished.[61]

In this characteristic act of reconstruction Stevenson found a means of illustrating the idea that it is not the representational power of the image but the language itself that signifies. He then cites as example of this phenomenon, the poetry of the Rev. Robert Murray McCheyne, but not before noting that the name itself possessed a kind of magic for himself and Cummy: 'My nurse and I admired his name exceedingly, so that I must have been taught the love of beautiful sounds before I was breeched.'[62] His suggestion that the child 'thinks much in images, words are very live to him, phrases that imply a picture eloquent beyond their value' not only explains his attachment to the resonant images which are such a key feature of his fiction but shows him moving into the territory of theorists such as Huey, who also sought to uncover the mechanics whereby meaning is constructed.[63] He was also building on the work of William James, who presented the activities of young children as paradigmatic in the construction of meaning: in his chapter on 'The Stream of Thought' in *Principles of Psychology* he notes that: 'We think it odd that young children should list with such rapt attention to the reading of stories in words half of which they do not understand, and of none of which they ask the meaning. But their thinking is in form just what ours is when it is rapid.'[64] Huey too suggested that 'the part played by imagery in reading ... is far larger in the reading of younger children'.[65] In *'Rosa Quo Locorum'* Stevenson went on to show how specific words acquire highly individualised association by the reader in terms of their own imaginative framework; for him the language of the psalms is imposed upon the landscape of Edinburgh: 'pastures green' become a 'certain suburban stubble-field' while 'Death's dark vale' is associated with a 'certain archway in the Warrington Cemetery'. The essay also dissects in fine detail the amalgam of images constituted by the phrase 'my table thou hast furnished'. (Questions about the attraction of particular words and phrases, beyond their representational quality, continue, of course, to preoccupy theorists of reading pleasure: Roland Barthes, in *The Pleasure of the Text*, ponders the attractions of an apparently mundane sentence – 'Cloths, sheets, napkins were hanging vertically, attached by wooden clothespins to taut lines' – which gives particular pleasure.[66])

This centrality of the child to Stevenson's explorations of creativity might also seem to bring him close to Freud in his thinking. Even in the early essay 'Child's Play' he worked with ideas now made familiar by Freud and others, and to which he would return in 'The Lantern-Bearers' and *'Rosa Quo Locorum'*, which identify the activity of play as a manifestation of creative energy emerging from simple and spontaneous responses related to dreaming and fantasising. Children, Stevenson suggested, 'walk in a vain show, and among mists and rainbows; they are passionate after dreams and unconcerned about realities'.[67] What he admired in particular was the child's unmediated relationship to the word, untainted by the 'theories and associations' which provide the coloured windows of the adult's perspective. In his 1908 essay on daydreaming Freud wrote: 'Should we not look for the first traces of imaginative activity as early as in childhood? The child's best-loved and most intense occupation is with his play or games. Might we not say that every child at play behaves like a creative writer, in that he creates a world of his own, or rather, re-arranges the things of his world in a new way which pleases him?'[68]

Stevenson likewise notes the particularly active engagement of the child's imagination: when the child enacts roles:

> He does not merely repeat them to himself; he leaps, he runs, and sets the blood agog over all his body. And so his play breathes him; and he no sooner assumes a passion that he gives it vent. Alas! When we betake ourselves to our intellectual form of play, sitting quietly by the fire or lying prone in bed, we rouse many hot feelings for which we can find no outlet.[69]

Such an image is a clear expression of the particular stage of reading involvement in which the child reader seeks to play the hero, a response identified by a much later reading analyst, J. A. Appleyard, as common in children between ages of seven and eleven, and described by Stevenson as characteristic of the 'bright troubled period of boyhood.'[70]

Stevenson, however, clearly regretted the loss of that capacity for involvement suffered by 'we grown-up people' who can 'tell ourselves a story, give and take strokes until the bucklers ring, ride far and fast, marry, fall, and die; all the while sitting quietly by the fire or lying prone in bed. This is exactly what a child cannot do.'[71] The child's energetic engagement becomes an alternative to the vitiated passivity of the adult reader, consuming a fictional world. From 'Child's Play' onwards Stevenson's writing was tinged with regret that the immediacy of such pleasures might be lost in the move towards maturity: what is gained by adulthood in specific terms of 'distance' also brings the loss of an imaginative dimension:

> To the grown person, cold mutton is cold mutton all the world over; not all the mythology ever invented by man will make it better or worse to him; the broad fact, the clamant reality, of the mutton carries away before it such seductive figments. But for the child it is still possible to weave an enchantment over eatables; and if he has but read of a dish in a story-book, it will be heavenly manna to him for a week.[72]

In this respect, as Farr notes, 'the gap between adult consciousness and the consciousness of the child functions as a crucial aporia, a sign of his fissured identity which is simultaneously constituted by, yet distinct from, his childhood self and the activity of play'.[73] Freud, in contrast to Stevenson, suggested: 'As people grow up, then, they cease to play, and they seem to give up the yield of pleasure which they gained from playing' yet continued, 'But whoever understands the human mind knows that hardly anything is harder for a man than to give up a pleasure which he has once experienced. Actually we can never give up anything; we only exchange one thing for another.'[74] Stevenson, moreover, did not share Freud's understanding of 'child's play' as 'determined by wishes; in point of fact by a single wish – one that helps in his upbringing – the wish to be big and grown up'.[75] For Stevenson the figure of the 'child reader' figures paradigmatically, represented not only as one stage in reading development but as the most desirable form of engagement with a text, an attachment which, as we have seen, posed problems for critics in his time and subsequently.[76]

Yet, if Stevenson's main aim is identified as the theorisation of the reading process, rather than an evasive strategy of defending dubious pleasures, this emphasis is less problematic. Indeed, it has parallels with the phenomenological approach of Gaston Bachelard, who in his explorations of the significance of childhood and its imagining also attempts to bring together philosophy and psychology through a personalised discourse. In *The Poetics of Reverie*, for example, Bachelard describes the state of 'reverie', a conscious but dreaming condition, as one which poeticises the dreamer and becomes an opening for creativity: the child is a central figure in the process:

> In the course of earlier work we often stated that one could scarcely develop a psychology of the creative imagination if he did not succeed in distinguishing clearly between imagination and memory. If there is any realm where distinction is especially difficult, it is in the realm of childhood memories, the realm of *beloved images* harboured since childhood. These memories which live by the image and in virtue of the image become, at certain times of our lives ... the origin and matter of a complex reverie: the memory dreams, and reverie remembers. When this reverie of remembering becomes the germ of a poetic work, the complex of memory and imagination becomes more tightly meshed; it has multiple and reciprocal actions which deceive the sincerity of the poet. More exactly, the happy childhood memories are told with a *poet's sincerity*. The imagination ceaselessly revives and illustrates the memory.[77]

Bachelard's point is of multiple significance in understanding Stevenson's thinking and textual strategies: firstly, it offers a certain similarity in the emphasis that is given to the childhood imagination, as carrying an archetypal significance:

> personal memories, clear and often retold, will never completely explain why reveries which carry us back towards our childhood have such an attraction, such a soul quality. The reason for this quality, which resists the experience of life is that childhood remains within us a principle of deep life, of life always in harmony with the possibilities of new beginnings.[78]

From Bachelard's perspective, as with Stevenson's account, childhood is less part of a process of development than a continuing source of imaginative energy. Moreover, access to memories of childhood, the reconstruction of the child's imagining, not only offers a positive release for the writer but also presents a point of shared communication with the reader: the imagining of childhood becomes in itself something which transcends the personal and psychological. In terms of his literary strategies Stevenson consistently sought to foreground this bond between writer and reader in the recreation of intense imaginative engagements. Finally, Bachelard's discursive style, meditative, personal, theorising without explicit reference to theory, again suggests illuminating parallels with Stevenson: for both this ruminative style is essential for holding the reader in shared understanding of the reading experience.

While Farr suggests that 'Stevenson's romance with the past locates true aesthetic pleasure in a residual stage of boyishness as a form of immature consolation, rather than a politically emancipatory project of mature self-governing individuals in a rational State', Stevenson's deployment of the child as a key figure in his explorations of both creativity and reading pleasure might be also understood as less a defence or retreat but rather an attempt to confront central processes within the imagination.[79] Just as childhood imaginings remain within us as a source of creative potential, which we do not 'grow out of', so the experience of childhood readings might also be seen to offer a purer reading experience which remains as an underpinning to later textual relations. Writing the child reader becomes therefore the most powerful way both of reminding adult readers of their childhood memories and of returning them to the intensity of these reading experiences: as Bachelard again notes, 'For that is the decisive phenomenological fact: childhood, in its archetypal quality, is *communicable*'.[80] As subsequent chapters on Covenanting histories and Dumas's fiction show, Stevenson's analytic concern with the plurality of reading experiences and his intense scrutiny of what pleasures and states of mind are permissible or desirable in the process of reading directed him not only towards time and place but also to a focus on 'rereading' as evidence of the multiplicity of both interpretation and pleasure. Stevenson's strategy of focusing on the persona of the child reader, of deploying anecdotes about his early engagement with books, offers both a specificity of encounter and an address to shared experience.[81]

The paradigm of romance

Through this process of reconstructing childhood reading experiences, Stevenson could best represent his understanding of literary pleasure and his continuing preoccupation with what it means to be 'lost in a book'. If the child reader offered the clearest example of such immersion, it was the romance form which presented the purest opportunity for losing oneself, the best example of the sway a text might hold over the reader.

A heightened awareness of the power of fiction over his imagination, first constructed in terms of pleasurable transgression, focused his critical attention on the psychic pull of the fictional experience in an unusually intense way. Such abandonment allowed that duality of role he appeared to find so attractive: emotionally activated, the reader of romance was also passively transported to another world. The process whereby the reading self, subsumed into identification with another self, enters a world that, for a brief period, operates to its own internal rules fascinated him. Immersion in a world with its own shape and reality which can, temporarily, be shattered as soon as the reader looks up from the page, the loss of a world outside the book, continues to interest theorists of reading. It is a sensation evocatively described by the phenomenologist George Poulet:

> A book is not shut in by its contours, is not walled-up as in a fortress. It asks nothing better than to exist outside itself, or to let you exist in it. In short, the extraordinary fact in the case of a book is the falling away of the barriers between you and it. You are inside it; it is inside you; there is no longer either outside or inside.
>
> Such is the initial phenomenon produced whenever I take up a book, and begin to read it ... For the book is no longer a material reality. It has become a series of words, of images, of ideas which in their turn begin to exist. And where is this new existence? Surely not in the paper object. Nor, surely, in external space. There is only one place left from this new existence: my innermost self.[82]

In 'A Gossip on Romance' Stevenson focused on just such a dynamic of textual interaction: 'In anything fit to be called by the name of reading', the essay began, 'the process itself should be absorbing and voluptuous; we should gloat over a book, be rapt clean out of ourselves, and rise from the perusal, our mind filled with the busiest kaleidoscopic dance of images, incapable of sleep or of continuous thought'.[83] In the course of this curious sentence the activity of reading moves from producing a somatic state, rapt and gloating, to a state in which sleep is impossible; its patterning thus embodies the dichotomy between losing the waking self in the book and being unable to lose that self in the relaxation of sleep. This state, with its combination of activity and passivity, is described as being not so much inevitable as ideal, a notion reiterated in 'A Chapter on Dreams', an essay read as indicative of the relationship between Stevenson's own thinking on the creative process and ideas on creativity emerging from the developing science of psychology.[84] It is also, however, revealing on the reading process; Stevenson interprets his dreams in the role of reader and those dreams offer a reading experience so intense that no subsequent book can equate with the encounter: 'About the same time he began to read in his dreams – tales for the most part, and for the most part after the manner of G. P. R. James, but so incredibly more vivid and more moving than any printed book, that he had ever since been malcontent with literature.'[85] Both active in consuming and interpreting but also passive or 'lost in a book', the configuration of the dream reader re-creates that sense of being simultaneously inside and outside a world and a self, of 'gloating over a book' and being 'rapt', which engaged Stevenson and later resurfaced in Poulet's description of 'the remarkable transformation wrought in me through the act of reading'.[86]

This aspect of reading dynamics has subsequently been given more academic analysis in empirical studies of reading which trace the relationship between trance states and literary engagement. Building upon Freud's assumption of a relationship between daydreaming and creativity, the work of Josephine Hilgard on personality and hypnosis is particularly relevant in its analysis of imaginative encounters. Hilgard identifies a particular kind of reading 'involvement,' in which 'the very "being" of the person is swept emotionally into the experience described by the author' and links this in terms of capacity for experience with those who are more likely to prove hypnotisable.[87] Hilgard's distinction between 'involvement' and other forms of absorbed reading, which can be either more intellectual or more passive forms of engagement, is refined (from a more clearly literary perspective) by Victor Nell, again developing a distinction between 'involvement' – as definite emotional commitment which leads to transportation to another world – and 'attentional absorption', a state of highly concentrated attention, not characterised by personal involvement: while the involved reader can identify with fictional characters, be there, participate, the absorbed reader – in a position more akin to the critic – 'does not identify with the character and never takes part in the action himself. He might feel sympathy for a character, but he is not deeply empathetic. Sometimes he theorises about a book.'[88] In his own literary essays Stevenson's self-identification with a general reader and his re-creation of intense literary engagement for the reader allowed him performatively to explore that process of involvement, offering analysis without claiming full critical detachment.

More significantly, both Hilgard and Nell also emphasise the fact that strong reading involvement of this kind is dependent upon a recognition of the 'unreality' of the fiction: 'the reader feels that he or she has been transported to another place which, though real, is known to be false, since there is still an observing ego, distinct from the participating ego'.[89] There is thus 'a strange duality' to the 'entranced reader's experience', so that internal reality of the imaginary world is sustained while at the same time – even when the reader is most involved – that world never lays claim to an external reality in the way that dream worlds appear to do.[90] In exploring different susceptibilities to 'involvement' and to hypnosis, Hilgard identifies a high correlation between what she terms adventurers in 'physical space' and a susceptibility to hypnosis. She suggests three points of similarity between adventure and hypnosis: 'reality-testing processes are altered' in terms of the reality-testing ego being present but only on a marginal basis; 'responsiveness to external cues, especially the power of words, is retained' – in both processes one is guided by the influence of the environment – that is, words; and 'processes compatible with childhood can be reexperienced' … 'a regressive movement towards magical wish fulfilment and impulse gratification'.[91] Those books in which the reader can move into an altered state of consciousness – lost as in hypnosis – and the structures of adventure therefore appear to share common ground.[92] It is perhaps unsurprising then that the process of involvement, being lost in a book to the extent that, like the child, we identify with the hero and play out his dramas, was central not only to Stevenson's reflections on reading but also to his valorisation of romance. In romance, as he argued in 'A Gossip on Romance', it is the quality of the brute incident which imprints itself upon the reader's mind, making romance 'the poetry of circumstance'. Romance, rather than realism, becomes a term for the most creative form of textual engagement, the most 'activating'. Realism, with its focus on character, is by contrast more deadening: 'the more clearly they [the characters] are depicted, the more widely do they stand away from us, the more imperiously do they thrust us back into our place as spectator'.[93] Adventure romance offers a form of fiction which permits the greatest involvement and that purity of experience which the child can enjoy. 'The desire for knowledge, I had almost added the desire for meat', he wrote, 'is not more deeply seated than this demand for fit and striking incident.'[94] Richard Ambrosini argues that Stevenson wrote 'adventurous romances, rather than realistic psychological novels, because he was convinced this was the most elevated path towards artistic expression in prose narrative', but in his endorsement of a particular form of textual involvement Stevenson also developed a model of reading pleasures which acknowledged textual power but positioned the experience in such a way that did not suggest the dangerous authority of realist representation perceived in Calvinist terms as a threat to the creative and interpretative powers of God.[95] In romance interest turns 'not upon what a man shall choose to do but on how he manages to do it'.[96] The fiction Stevenson wrote about most enthusiastically did not take the reader into 'a world' which imitates the concerns of the everyday, but rather moved the reader out into another dimension of fantasy in which his or her anxieties and desires might be played out through psychic transformations that avoid laying claim to any ultimate authority. Just as the child reader becomes the image of unfettered reading pleasure, of engagement without the pressure to differentiate between levels of 'reality' in experience, so romance appears as an alternative to a realism tied to faithful representation and demanding responsible interpretation

Stevenson's conjunction of romance as in some ways the 'truest' literary form and of childhood reading experiences as the most pure can also be found in subsequent studies of reading development, but configured rather differently. His remark in 'A Gossip on Romance' that 'the triumph of romantic story-telling' is 'when the reader consciously plays at being the hero' anticipates later analyses of enthusiastic romance-reading which locate that identification with character as characteristic of readers between six and twelve: a stage at which the child

> focuses on issues of identity, in the image of the powerful or clever hero or heroine who in one guise or another is the principal archetype of most stories school-age children read. The prominence of this archetype suggests that a main reward of reading fictional stories at this age is to satisfy the need to imagine oneself as the central figure who by competence and initiative can solve the problems of a disordered world.[97]

Stevenson's own view expressed in 'Child's Play', that early reading demands immediate involvement – children need to play out events, say with a sword, because of their lack of experience of the world through which they could imaginatively flesh out the tale – likewise establishes an opposition between the passivity of adult readers and the activity of the child. For Appleyard, however, the appeal of adventure fiction, which virtually all children in these years consume, lies in reassurance: 'Over and over, in constantly changing settings, the heroes and heroines face new versions of anger or evil or crime, but the structure of the situations, the behaviour of the characters, and above all the outcomes are reassuringly familiar.'[98] In presenting this view he draws upon Northrop Frye's influential genre theory which defines romance as the literary form that deals with 'the search of the libido or desiring self for a fulfilment that will deliver it from the anxieties of reality but will still contain that reality'.[99] The familiarity of such stories, the element of repetition, constitute part of the form's attraction, not least because of the element of control implied: 'The continually reenacted victory of the heroes and heroines of juvenile narratives assures the young reader that the adventure of travelling into the world and meeting its challenges can have a happy ending.'[100] His comments on the relationship between character and plot in romance again echo those of Stevenson: 'when the game so chimes with his fancy that he can join in it with all his heart, when it pleases him with every turn, when he loves to recall it and dwells upon its recollection with entire delight, fiction is called a romance'.[101] However, while Stevenson's engagement with fiction demonstrated an interest in the psychology of play, his advocacy of romance is less clearly linked to the reassuringly familiar, and contrasted with the pacifying qualities of realist conventions: 'It is not character but incident that woos us out of our reserve.'[102]

To an extent this idea anticipates the more empirical approach of reading psychologists who note that in romance and early reading there is an emphasis on plot rather than character in adventure, which can be understood in terms either of desire for maturity – 'fictional characters represent what children at this age *want to be*' – or acknowledgement of development: 'they represent what children *were* and are reluctantly giving up'.[103] In this analysis both suggestions are compatible with a developmental model that sees the child as growing into an engagement with other literary forms – particularly in terms of Frye's other categories of tragedy (wishes and dreams ending in catastrophe and death) and irony or satire (discrepancy between dreams and the ambiguous reality of actual experience) or comedy ('the transformation of this limited world into a new community freed from the power of death').[104] Such imagining is presented as being beyond the power of young children. While identifying characteristics of the romance genre and the youthful reader noted by Stevenson, such approaches produce a developmental model in which the intensity of the romance reading experience is a product of the childhood imagination but will ultimately be left behind as a more complex world view comes into play.

Stevenson, however, represented this process not as a movement into complexity and maturity but as one of loss: the power to experience is increasingly controlled by interpretative frameworks. As he had noted in 'Child's Play', our hermeneutic frame is increasingly less pure: 'all things are transformed and seen through theories and associations as through coloured windows. We make to ourselves day by day, out of history, and gossip, and economical speculations, and God knows what, a medium in which we walk and through which we look abroad.'[105] In that sense, Stevenson's advocacy of romance, while sophisticated in the analysis of the form, could easily be read as a manifestation of that critical common-place of his arrested development.[106] Such a model works, however, only if the move towards literary realism itself is understood as a develop-ment into maturity. As earlier discussion has suggested, this model is less tenable if viewed through a Calvinist-inflected perspective, not only suspicious of the aims of realism but also embodying a model of morality which is based upon striking oppositions rather than the reciprocal and relativist morality of nineteenth-century realism. Stevenson identified what he saw as 'problems' in the reading experience of such 'character-studies' or realist fiction. In those, he argues, the same process of total absorption cannot take place, but rather 'the pleasure that we take is critical: we watch, we approve, we smile at incongruities, we are moved to sudden heats of sympathy with courage, suffering or virtue'.[107] For Stevenson then, the most activating (the most 'writerly', in Barthesian terminology) texts are those in which we experience rather than view events.[108] Active pleasure, Stevenson appears to suggest, comes when we are immersed in the text to the extent of not knowing that we are there; the immediacy of such experience is the most satisfying aspect of reading, and this is what is open to the child reader and to the reader of romance. Not only does this offer the most energising form of pleasure, it is also that which most liberates us from being tied to the everyday. Driven by a resistance to Calvinist thinking suspicious of the idle pleasures of art, Stevenson defiantly embraced the experience of reading romance as both liberating for, and characteristic of, the imagination. Yet his movement in this direction was also, paradoxically, propelled by a Calvinist world view which recognised that even the most detailed realist texts are unstable and potentially misleading in terms of their representative and interpretative nature.

Overlapping with the interests of both cognitive psychology and psychoanalysis but more clearly paralleled by the phenomenological philosophy of Bachelard, Stevenson's particular form of reading analysis was prompted by a particular cast of mind emerging from a highly specific background and time. Both resisting and replicating a Calvinist inheritance through his difficult relationship to literary pleasure, the terms of his ambivalences are then further complicated by being situated within broader cultural debates over the nature and value of the reading experience. If his interest in, and celebration of, the child as epitome of reading pleasure might seem to some an evasion of adult responsibility, it can also be understood as strategy for dissecting the creative imagination. It is this combination of the internalisation and explicit rejection of a Calvinist-inflected world view which led Stevenson into his scrutiny of the relationship obtaining between word and world, into the examination of the mechanics of pleasure and into his negotiations around the role of the artist in the context of commercial production. The perspective created in his essays, that of the general reader, sharing and enacting responses with his readers, was itself a response to the network of influences he was negotiating. The three chapters which follow continue to explore these recurring preoccupations as they are mapped out in a series of textual interfaces in which questions about reading, raised in the essays and letters, are played out as he vagabonded his way through different forms of fiction.

Notes

1 2/1/86 to Gosse, *Letters*, vol. 5, p. 171.
2 'A key problem for critics of all persuasions ... was and remains pleasure, *le plaisir de texte*: what attitude should one adopt towards a form of reading that was and also is a main form of entertainment for the *literate* masses.' Brantlinger, *The Reading Lesson*, p. 21
3 See K. Flint, *The Woman Reader 1837–1914* (Oxford: Clarendon Press, 1993). The gendering of this debate was particularly powerful in the 1860s in relation to sensation fiction.
4 January/February/91 to W. Leslie Curnow, *Letters*, vol. 7, p. 82.
5 N. Holland, *The Dynamics of Literary Response* (New York: Oxford University Press, 1968), identifies the oral as most common fantasy of reading.
6 Readers might be viewed as dehumanised machines of consumption, but 'while reading habits resembled the automatic motions of the machine, they were also and more consistently described with reference to bodily ingestion – eating, drinking and drug-taking.' K. J. Mays, 'The Disease of Reading', p. 172.
7 Letter to Mrs C. Grant LaFarge, 11 August 1895, quoted in Maixner, *Robert Louis Stevenson: The Critical Heritage*, p. 488.
8 As Brantlinger has noted, the movement from authorial intimacy with the reader to a belief in the vulgarity of the reading public produced a concern about the toxic effects of literary consumption, figuring reading not as food but as poison. Co-existent with such images from an early stage in the novel's development, was an emergent counter discourse of 'reading as medicine'. *The Reading Lesson*, p. 9.
9 'As I live, I feel more and more that literature should be cheerful and brave-spirited, even if it cannot be made beautiful and pious and heroic. We wish it to be a green place. The Waverley novels are better to re-read than the ower-true life, fine as dear Sir Walter was. The Bible, in most parts, is a cheerful book.' 12/3/83 to James Dick, *Letters*, vol. 4, p. 251.
10 Feltes, *Literary Capital and the Late Victorian Novel*, p. 44.
11 'Sir John Lubbock on Reading', *Morning Advertiser*, 11 January 1886, p. 2; 'On the Pleasure of Reading', *Contemporary Review*, 49 (February 1886), 240–51; *The Pleasures of Life* (London: Macmillan, 1887); 'Sir John Lubbock's Liberal Education', *Pall Mall Gazette*, 42 (11 January 1886), 4.
12 Feltes, *Literary Capital and the Late Victorian Novel*, p. 46.
13 *Pall Mall Gazette*, 42 (11 January 1886), 4.
14 *The Contemporary Review*, 49 (February 1886), 244.
15 Mr Goschen, on 'How to Speak, How to Read and How to Think', reported in the *Pall Mall Gazette* (1 March 1886), 11.

16 *The Contemporary Review*, 49 (February 1886), 245.

17 *The Contemporary Review*, 49 (February 1886), 250; Lubbock quotes Frederic Harrison, 'On the Choice of Books', *Fortnightly Review*, n.s. 25 (April 1879), 497.

18 Freud problematised the definition of this term in somewhat similar terms in the early twentieth century: 'You ask me to name "ten good books" for you, and refrain from adding to this any word of explanation', 'Contribution to a Questionnaire on Reading' (1907), *Shorter Writings, Standard Edition of the Complete Psychological Works of Sigmund Freud vol. IX (1906–1908)*, trans. under the General Editorship of James Strachey in collaboration with Anna Freud, assisted by Alix Strachey and Alan Tyson (London: The Hogarth Press and the Institute of Psycho-analysis, 1959; London: Vintage Press, 2001), pp. 245–7.

19 'A Gossip on Romance', Tusitala XXIX, p. 125.

20 'Popular Authors', *Scribner's* Magazine, 4 (1888), 122–8; Tusitala XXVIII, pp. 20–32, p. 32.

21 Lubbock, *The Contemporary Review*, 49 (February 1886), 242.

22 H. Rider Haggard, 'About Fiction', p. 173.

23 *Ibid.*, p. 174.

24 H. G. Wells, 'The Contemporary Novel', *An Englishman Looks at the World* (1914), pp. 148–69; reprinted in P. Parrinder and R. M. Philmus, *H. G. Wells's Literary Criticism* (Brighton: Harvester Press, 1980), pp. 192–206, p. 192.

25 1/2/80 to J. Meiklejohn, *Letters*, vol. 3, pp. 61–2.

26 '*Rosa Quo Locorum*', was written in Sydney in 1893. Tusitala XXX, pp. 1–8, p. 1.

27 'The Lantern-Bearers', *Scribner's Magazine*, 3 (1888), 390–4, reprinted in *Across the Plains* (1892). Tusitala XXX, 29–40. For a detailed reading of this essay's imagery see L. Farr, 'Surpassing the Love of Women: Robert Louis Stevenson and the Pleasures of Boy-loving', *Journal of Stevenson Studies*, 2 (2005), 140–60.

28 'There, to be sure, we find a picture of life in so far as it consists of mud and of old iron, cheap desires and cheap fears, that which we are ashamed to remember and that which we are careless whether we forget', Tusitala XXX, p. 36. In attacking realism he opposed the idea that environment has a determining effect on the psyche and that the description of surfaces leads to an understanding of character.

29 Tusitala XXX, p. 39.

30 For discussion of this essay see Ambrosini, 'The Art of Writing and the Pleasure of Reading'.

31 'A Penny Plain and Twopence Coloured', *The Magazine of Art*, 7 (April 1884), 227–32; Tusitala XXIX, pp. 103–9, p. 107.

32 *Ibid.*, p. 109.

33 *Ibid.*, p. 106.

34 As in 'Child's Play' it is the process not the product that is important. A similar point is made in 'A Letter to a Young Gentleman', when Stevenson

described the artist with a true vocation being like the child at play 'at being a pirate on the dining-room sofa'; the question of 'Is it worth doing' simply does not occur. Tusitala XXVIII, p. 5.

35 'A Penny Plain', p. 109.
36 Calinescu, *Rereading*, p. 96.
37 Simpson, 'Realism and Romance: Stevenson's Scottish Values', p. 241.
38 'Popular Authors', *Scribner's Magazine*, 4 (1888), 122–8, Tusitala XXVIII, pp. 20–32, p. 25.
39 *Ibid.*, p. 30.
40 *Ibid.*, p. 31.
41 *Ibid.*, p. 30.
42 See Ambrosini, 'The Art of Writing' for a reading of this as an ethical strategy.
43 Tusitala XXVIII, p. 25.
44 Tusitala XXIX, p. 123.
45 *Saturday Review*, 81 (13 June 1896), 603–4; Parrinder and Philmus, *H. G. Wells's Literary Criticism*, pp. 99–103, p. 101.
46 *Ibid.*, p. 102.
47 *Ibid.*, p. 103.
48 J. M. Barrie, 'Robert Louis Stevenson', *Gavin Ogilvy; An Edinburgh Eleven: Pencil Portraits from College Life* (Edinburgh: Hodder and Stoughton, 1894); *An Edinburgh Eleven* (Edinburgh: Hodder and Stoughton, 1929), pp. 111–22, p. 113.
49 J. J. Chapman, 'Robert Louis Stevenson', *Emerson and Other Essays* (1898) pp. 217–47, reprinted in Maixner, *Critical Heritage*, pp. 489–94, pp. 490–1.
50 'Mathilde Serao' (1902), *Notes on Novelists* (London: J. M. Dent, 1914), p. 237. See discussion in Hadley, *Henry James and the Imagination of Pleasure*, pp. 11–12.
51 Muir, 'Robert Louis Stevenson', p. 196.
52 A. Sandison, *Robert Louis Stevenson and the Appearance of Modernism: A Future Feeling* (London: Macmillan, 1996), p. 20; L. Fiedler, 'R.L.S. revisited', *No! in Thunder, Collected Essays of Leslie Fiedler*, vol. 1 (New York: Stein and Day, 1971), pp. 299–300.
53 Brantlinger, *The Reading Lesson*, p. 169.
54 J. A. Appleyard, *Becoming a Reader* (Cambridge: Cambridge University Press, 1990), p. 38; G. Bachelard, *The Poetics of Reverie: Childhood, Language and the Cosmos*, trans. D. Russell (Boston: Beacon Press, 1969), p. 130.
55 Nell, *Lost in a Book*, p. 74; E. B. Huey, *The Psychology and Pedagogy of Reading: With a Review of the History of Reading and Writing and of Methods, Texts and Hygiene in Reading* (London: Macmillan, 1908; Cambridge, MA and London: The MIT Press, 1968).
56 *Ibid.*, pp. 5–6.
57 Early November/91 to Edward L. Burlinghame, *Letters*, vol. 7, p. 189.
58 Farr, 'Surpassing the Love of Women', p. 147. 'Notes on the Movement of Young Children', first published in *Portfolio*, 5 (August 1874), 115–17; Tusitala XXV, pp. 196–201.

59 Farr, 'Surpassing the Love of Women', p. 157.
60 'Feelings, and the motor-reactions or tendencies from which feelings cannot be disjoined, are far more fundamental and usual than images, and these constitute the consciousness of meaning', Huey, *The Psychology of Reading*, pp. 165–6. In this discussion Huey draws heavily on William James and Théodore Flournoy, 'Temps de lecture et omission', *L'Année Psychologique*, II (1896), 45–53.
61 '*Rosa Quo Locorum*', Tusitala XXX, p. 1.
62 *Ibid.*, pp. 1–2.
63 *Ibid.*, p. 2.
64 William James, *Principles of Psychology* (1890), 2 vols, vol. 1 (Cambridge, MA, and London: Harvard University Press, 1981), p. 255, n. 23.
65 *Psychology of Reading*, p. 163.
66 Barthes, *The Pleasure of the Text*, p. 26. Later Barthes suggests that the pleasure of reading a list of food could lie in the fact that 'the novelist, by citing, naming, *noticing* food (by treating it as notable), imposes on the reader the final state of matter, what cannot be transcended, withdrawn', p. 45.
67 'Child's Play', *Cornhill Magazine*, 38 (September 1878), 352–9; included in *Virginibus Puerisque*, Tusitala XXV, pp. 106–16, p. 115.
68 S. Freud, 'Creative Writers and Day-dreaming' ('The Relation of the Poet to Day-dreaming'), originally delivered as a lecture 6 December 1907, *Standard Edition of the Complete Psychological Works of Sigmund Freud vol. IX (1906–1908)*, pp. 143–53, pp. 143–4.
69 'Child's Play', p. 112.
70 Appleyard, *Becoming a Reader*; 'A Gossip on Romance', p. 118.
71 'Child's Play', p. 109.
72 *Ibid.*, p. 106.
73 Farr, 'Surpassing the Love of Women', p. 151.
74 Freud, 'Relation of the Poet to Day-dreaming', p. 145.
75 *Ibid.*, p. 146.
76 Even Farr, who offers a nuanced reading of his deployment of the boy reader in terms of models of masculinity, sees in this attachment evidence of 'arrested development', 'Surpassing the Love of Women'.
77 Bachelard, *The Poetics of Reverie*, p. 20.
78 *Ibid.*, p. 123.
79 Farr, 'Surpassing the Love of Women', p. 158.
80 *Poetics of Reverie*, p. 127.
81 Bachelard notes: 'To reach the memories of our solitudes, we idealise the worlds in which we were solitary children. So it is a problem in practical psychology to take into account the very real idealisation of childhood memories and the personal interest we take in all childhood memories. And for that reason there is communication between a poet of childhood and his reader through the intermediary of childhood which endures within us.' *Poetics of Reverie*, p. 101.
82 G. Poulet, 'Criticism and the Experience of Interiority', in R. A. Macksey and E. Donato (eds), *The Structuralist Controversy: The Language of Criti-*

cism and the Sciences of Man, trans. C. Macksey (Baltimore: Johns Hopkins University Press, 1972), pp. 56–72, reprinted in J. P. Tompkins (ed.), *Reader Response Criticism from Formalism to Post-structuralism* (Baltimore and London: Johns Hopkins University Press, 1980), pp. 41–9, pp. 42.

83 Tusitala XXIX, p. 119.
84 'A Chapter on Dreams', *Scribner's Magazine*, 3 (1888), 122–8; reprinted in *Across the Plains* (1892). Tusitala XXX, pp. 41–53. See Sandison, *Stevenson and the Appearance of Modernism*; for discussion of its connections with *Dr Jekyll and Mr Hyde* see R. R. Thomas, 'The Strange Voices in the Strange Case: Dr. Jekyll, Mr. Hyde, and the Voices of Modern Fiction', in W. Veeder and G. Hirsch (eds), *Dr Jekyll and Mr Hyde after One Hundred Years* (Chicago: University of Chicago Press,1988), pp. 73–93.
85 Tusitala XXX, p. 43.
86 Poulet continues: 'Not only does it cause the physical objects around me to disappear, including the very book I am reading, but it replaces those external objects with a congeries of mental objects in close *rapport* with my own consciousness.' 'Criticism and the Experience of Interiority', in Tompkins (ed.), *Reader Response Criticism*, p. 43. He also notes: 'Whatever sort of alienation I may endure, reading does not interrupt my activity as a subject … When I am absorbed in reading, a second self takes over, a self which thinks and feels for me.' *Ibid.*, p. 45.
87 J. R. Hilgard, *Personality and Hypnosis: A Study of Imaginative Involvement* (Chicago: University of Chicago Press 1970), p. 23.
88 *Ibid.*, pp. 40–1; Nell, *Lost in a Book*, pp. 213–15.
89 Nell, *Lost in a Book*, p. 215; the argument also draws on A. Tellegen and G. Atkinson, 'Openness to Absorbing Self-altering Experiences ("absorption")', a Trait Related to Hypnotic Susceptibility', *Journal of Abnormal Psychology*, 83 (1974), 268–77.
90 Nell, *Lost in a Book*, p. 212.
91 Hilgard, *Personality and Hypnosis*, pp. 136–7.
92 Adventuring as child-structured activity goes, of course, beyond the literary: see M. Brearley: 'I have often been asked whether cricket becomes "merely a job", and whether professional players play from love of the game. Have we lost all contact with the spontaneous play of children? … Logically, a game is complete without any spectators at all, unlike a play at the theatre, which name itself implies a spectacle. It is unduly puritanical, however, to feel that the only satisfactions of the game should come from within, and from earning the respect of one's peers, the other players, for there are many different kinds of satisfaction, just as there are many different kinds of game-playing.' M. Brearley and D. Doust, *The Ashes Retained* (London: Hodder and Stoughton, 1979), p. 124; see also 'Of the many inspired reflections on the "miracle of Istanbul", as it will come to be know, the most eloquent came not from a professional writer, but a player. "I'm enjoying this triumph like a child," said Xabi Alonsono, scorer of Liverpool's equaliser. If there is a secret to the magic it might lie there. In our innocent past.' K. Mitchell, 'Magic and Hypnotism of the Rolling Ball', *The Observer Sport*, 29 May 2005.

93 'A Gossip on Romance', p. 128.
94 *Ibid.*, p. 122
95 Ambrosini, 'The Art of Writing', p. 33.
96 'A Gossip on Romance', p. 118.
97 Appleyard, *Becoming a Reader*, pp. 59–60.
98 *Ibid.*, p. 62.
99 N. Frye, *Anatomy of Criticism: Four Essays* (Princeton: Princeton University Press, 1957).
100 Appleyard, *Becoming a Reader*, p. 63.
101 'A Gossip on Romance', p. 129.
102 *Ibid.*, p. 128.
103 Appleyard, for example, wonders why the characters in these books appear simple when children themselves at this age are undoubtedly complex, and asks: 'Is it fair to call the characters in these stories flat or stereotypes? Or to say that character is a negligible element in children's stories in comparison with action? Hardly. If children are limited in their capacity to imagine and identify with complex characters who develop and change as the story goes on and have elaborate inner lives, the converse is also true; they can readily imagine and identify with a character defined by the right traits and relationships and skilled at the right tasks, and they do not tire of seeing this kind of character repeatedly exercise these traits and skills in the kind of episodic tale that most adult readers would find tedious. Good children's stories illustrate as well as adult fiction the point behind the much-quoted questions of Henry James, "What is character but the determination of incident? What is incident but the illustration of character?"' *Becoming a Reader*, p. 75.
104 Frye, *Anatomy of Criticism*, pp. 63–4.
105 Tusitala XXV, pp. 108–9.
106 Again see Farr for a more sophisticated version of this.
107 'A Gossip on Romance', p. 128.
108 Again Stevenson's understanding of childhood in relation to creativity appears closer to the writings of Bachelard than the empirical analyses and developmental models of Appleyard and others. As Bachelard, who suggests in *The Poetics of Reverie* that this 'function of the unreal' may last throughout life, notes: 'In the child's reverie, the image takes precedence over everything else. Experience comes only later … The child sees everything big and beautiful. The reverie towards childhood returns us to the beauty of the first images.' *Poetics of Reverie*, p. 102; 'Childhood sees the World illustrated, the World with its original colours, its true colours … In our reveries we see our illustrated universe once more with its *childhood colours*.' *Ibid.*, p. 117.

5

'A landmark on the plains of history': Covenanting history and *The Master of Ballantrae*

The figure that always fixed my attention is that of Hackston of Rathillet, sitting in the saddle with his cloak about his mouth, and through all that long, bungling, vociferous hurly-burly, resolving privately a case of conscience ... It is an old temptation with me, to pluck away that cloak and see the face – to open that bosom and to read the heart. With incomplete romances about Hackston, the drawers of my youth were lumbered. I read him up in every printed book that I could lay my hands on ... All was in vain: that he had passed a riotous nonage, that he was a zealot, that he twice displayed ... some tincture of soldierly resolution and even of military common-sense, and that he figured memorably in the scene of Magus Muir, so much and no more could I make out. But whenever I cast my eyes backward, it is to see him like a landmark on the plains of history, sitting with his cloak about his mouth, inscrutable.[1]

In his published dialogue with Henry James, Stevenson placed history as central to understanding the relationship between art and life. 'It is in every history', he wrote, 'where events and men, rather than ideas, are presented – in Tacitus, in Carlyle, in Michelet, in Macaulay – that the novelist will find many of his own methods most conspicuously and adroitly handled.' In particular the writing of history raises key questions about the relationship between word and world: 'on a more careful examination truth will seem a word of very debatable propriety, not only for the labours of the novelist, but for those of the historian'.[2] His view emerged from considerable experience: the voracious consumption of history as a reader and a drive to produce history as an author were dominant elements in Stevenson's literary career. From his boyhood immersion in tales of Scotland's bloody religious past, through excursions into European military and social history, to his determination to acquaint himself with the background to his new environment in the South Seas, Stevenson read history prodigiously. Every publication he conceived led to numerous requests for reading material, ranging from large-scale background to fine detail, all motivated by the desire to be accurate in renditions of the past.[3] Making his way across the United

States from New York to California in 1879 on his first trip to America, Stevenson carried Bancroft's six-volume *History of the United States* – purchased in New York – in his knapsack, although it was in every sense 'essentially heavy fare'.[4] At times, his writing was also overburdened with the weight of historical reading matter: in 1873 he complained that he had read so much Scottish Covenanting history that he was unable to write because 'the whole subject turns round about me and so branches out to this side and that that I grow bewildered' although he added his belief that 'one cannot write discreetly about any one little corner of a historical period, until one has an organic view of the whole'.[5] His formulation of projects in which he himself would play the role of historian was equally energetic:[6] a history of his own family, 'a family of engineers' from the essay of that name, was mooted at several times in his life and research begun although never completed;[7] in letters he wrote almost feverishly of his plans for three histories of Scotland, including one on the Union; and he was equally fervent about Highland history in the 1880s – around the time he made an ambitious if ill-judged attempt to put himself forward for the chair of Constitutional Law and History at Edinburgh University.[8] Later, when in the South Seas, he adopted various strategies to produce 'historical' material from his new home in the face of opposition from both his wife and his friends in England who wished keep him on the steady, and rather more profitable, path of producing fiction.[9] At one stage, when teaching Austin Strong in Samoa, he even contemplated producing his own 'History for Children' based upon lessons to the boy.[10] As Barry Menikoff's recent study of his relationship to Highland history powerfully demonstrates, Stevenson's engagement with the past is central to any understanding of his fiction.[11]

Yet, as critics have noted, although he was driven by and towards 'history', and obsessed with historical detail, none of his novels has at its heart that engagement with historical change that can be found in the novels of Scott or Thackeray. Rather than a concern with historical causality, Stevenson displayed a fascination with the intensity of dramatic incident in a historical context and focused his intelligence on the processes involved in reading the difference of events and people in the past.[12] Just as there was a degree of failure in his aspirations to play the historian – while 'in a very real and important sense it could be said that throughout his career Stevenson's Literature fed off his History', none of the planned historical works ever appeared – his success as a writer of historical fiction has also been questioned.[13] Torn between a desire to produce 'plain facts' as a 'realist' writer, and an urge to escape into the world of romance, Stevenson, argues K. G. Simpson, was beset with 'a recognition of the moral responsibility of the writing coexisting, in understandable unease, with a longing to escape to an imaginative realm where the ethical dimension of the literary is minimised, if not removed entirely'.[14] Simpson's sense of an unease, a misdirection, in Stevenson's deployment of a historical imagination is echoed in Andrew Noble's analysis (of *Kidnapped* in particular) which concludes with the indictment that Stevenson 'surrendered to that commercially rewarding body of sentimental fantasy, a weird kind of literary "mythology", perpetrated both by Scottish intellectuals and a wider public, which has been the compensatory matter of Scottish history since at least the onset of the Industrial revolution'.[15] Perhaps because the relationship between his reading, his research and his writing was such a complicated one, history as text was central to his speculations on the dynamics of reading. It was his early encounters with Scotland's religious past, a powerful shaping element in his own Calvinist inheritance, which in particular provided him with material for his most interesting speculations on the relationship between the event itself, the writer's account and the reader's experience.

His general reflections on this interaction are set out with most sophistication in 'A Humble Remonstrance', where his ideas on the extent to which the same narrative structures operated in fiction and history came into conflict with Henry James's own attempts to reconfigure this relationship. James's definitions of history and fiction were reworked over the course of his career, but in his debate with Stevenson he insistently defended the analogy between fiction and history as a means whereby the novel's capacity to represent life might be taken seriously.[16] As Jolly argues, 'James sought to give the conventional analogy between history and the novel a new force by bringing it up to date with changes in historiographical practice over the century.'[17] The new scientific approach of nineteenth-century history imbued the historical model with an authority and status to which the novelist could gain access and, she argues, cultural anxieties about fiction drove James to embrace it.[18] Stevenson, in contrast, appeared to defend the precedence of the novelist – or of fictional strategies. With a familiar suspicion of claims for textual authority, Stevenson chose to emphasise the determining effects of narrative form in both fiction and historical writing, and appeared less concerned than James with constructing arguments that would validate the 'seriousness' of the novel.

In his response Stevenson's anxieties took him in a different direction from James: his concern was with the reader's experience, rather than with the status of the writer, and with the extent to which aesthetic responses might shape historical engagement with painful experience:

so that even when we read of the sack of a city or the fall of an empire, we are surprised, and justly commend the author's talent, if our pulse be quickened. And mark, for a last differentia, that this quickening of the pulse is, in almost every case, purely agreeable; that these phantom reproductions of experience, even at their most acute, convey decided pleasure; while experience itself, in the cockpit of life, can torture and slay.[19]

Negotiating the dichotomy between written words and lived deeds, Stevenson confronted what Ricoeur has called 'the upheaval which affects discourse itself when the movement of references towards the act of showing is interrupted by the text'.[20] Through acknowledgement of those processes of delight and excitement, emotions evident in accounts of his own reading of history, Stevenson was concerned with the peculiar nature of that moment at which 'Words cease to efface themselves in front of things; written words become words for themselves'.[21] Emerging from a Calvinist perception of the dangerously iconic nature of words, which demands both an alert acknowledgement of their power and a scrutinising recognition of their inadequacy, Stevenson's interest is less with the relationship of 'art' to 'life' than with the dynamic between the immediacy of lived experience and the experience of narrative. His much quoted reflection that 'Life is monstrous, infinite, illogical, abrupt and poignant; a work of art, in comparison, is neat, finite, self-contained, rational, flowing and emasculate' was followed by the much stronger assertion that 'Life imposes by brute energy, like inarticulate thunder'.[22] While recognising that narrative style inevitably shaped the truth of both fiction and history, in his reading of history Stevenson appeared to demand the closest possible correlation between words and deeds: the most significant historical accounts, he argued, emerge from the words of those involved in an event:

> It is only out of memoirs written by violent and sincere partisans, that we can ever learn how deeds appeared to the actors themselves, what moral obliquities led them open-eyed into mistakes and crimes and what sort of strength supplanted them through great, heroic undertakings; every self-deception, every dishonesty even, possess for the critic a sort of hidden sincerity.[23]

In a historiographical model very different from the scientific approach underpinning that of James on the novel, those who are least 'objective' become those who produce the most satisfyingly accurate version of the historical event: they are closest, it seems, to that 'inarticulate thunder'. As Stevenson wrote after reading Clarendon:

> It is a pet idea of mine that one gets more real truth out of one avowed partisan than out of a dozen of your sham impartialists – wolves in sheep's

clothing – simpering honesty as they suppress documents. After all, what one wants to know is not what people did, but why they did it – or rather, why they *thought* they did it; and to learn that, you should go to the men themselves. Their falsehood is often more than another man's truth.[24]

Stevenson's concern with the representation of historical experience was in some respects characteristic of his time; as Stephen Bann has argued, the nineteenth century saw the development of a 'new historical sensibility, striving to annihilate the gap between the model and the copy, and offering the Utopian possibility of a restoration of the past in the context of the present' – a desire to be fulfilled to some extent by the photograph.[25] In historical fiction, as exemplified by Thackeray, a favoured author of Stevenson, there was also a drive towards historical mimeticism. From his childhood, however, with the consumption of tales of Scotland's past, Stevenson's sense of the historical had been closely related to notions of allegiance, to systems of belief, whether in the religious affiliations of martyrs or the nationalist implications of Jacobitism, which resulted in this explicit admiration of the 'partisan'. Representation of 'the past' demanded therefore confrontations with 'truth' in different senses: a negotiation of his present world view with powerful belief systems from the past; a balance between attention to authentic detail and the pull towards captivatingly symbolic incident; and a broader ontological engagement with the relationship between language and authority. In order to explore Stevenson's response to these conflicting imperatives, this chapter examines questions of narrative form, language and truth which emerge out his relationship with one specific and, for him personally resonant, period of Scottish history.[26] Offering bloody cruelty, strong characters, passionate adventures, and familiar locations, the history of the Scottish Covenanters was the subject in which Stevenson, from boyhood to his last days in Samoa, appeared to find most 'quickening of the pulse'; it was also a field in which that tension between words and things, models and copies was played out in relation to sources and discourses rather different from those familiar to his contemporaries. Although it was less evident as subject matter in his fiction than might have been expected, its preoccupations and discourses had from boyhood shaped his sense of narrating the past.

Reading Covenanting history

Writing to J. M. Barrie, from Vailima, in 1893, Stevenson observed:

> When I was a child and indeed until I was nearly a man I consistently read Covenanting books. Now that I am a graybeard … I have returned and for weeks back have read little else but Wodrow, Walker, Shields, etc. Of course

this is with the idea of a novel; but in the course of it I made a very curious discovery. I have been accustomed to hear refined and intelligent critics – those who know so much better what we are than we do ourselves ... trace down my literary descent from all sorts of people, including Addison, of whom I could never read a word. Well, laigh i' your lug, sir – the clue was found. My style is from the Covenanting writers.[27]

By self-admission, it was the histories of the Scottish Covenanters, those who defended the National Covenant from its signed renewal in 1638 and who fought for their own particular versions of Presbyterianism until the 'Glorious Revolution' of 1688–89, which first grasped Stevenson's imagination. The National Covenant epitomised an extreme division between Church and State, embodied in the assertion of Presbyterian democracy against perceived Church corruption and state intervention in religious liberty, and played out in resistance to Charles's attempts to impose his authority in Scotland by a predominantly English army. The Solemn League and Covenant (1645) represented a combined pledge of English Puritans and Scottish Presbyterians to religious unity and autonomy. The subsequent persecution of the Covenanters following the restoration of Charles II, with the ejection of minister from churches, and field preaching in 'Conventicles', further reinforced this narrative of powerful religious conviction, resistance and martyrdom.[28] Stevenson read this material furiously – not only the accounts of battles, political shifts and divisions but also the many stories of individual figures, such as the preacher and prophesier Alexander Peden, and the martyr James Renwick. From 1868 to 1869 he planned a Covenanting Story-book, drawing up a list of seven stories set in seventeenth-century Scotland.[29] His first paper to the Speculative Society was on 'The Influence of the Covenanting Persecution on the Scottish Mind'.[30] By the age of twenty-three he was so immersed in the period that he was unable to draw upon the material to write.[31] In his forties his letters from Samoa were still full of requests for Shields and Wodrow, as he added to his 'library of these quaint, unwholesome authors'.[32]

Stevenson, of course, was well acquainted with the work of Scott, who was also drawn to Covenanting history and traditions, evident in the inclusion of five Covenanting ballads in *Minstrelsy of the Scottish Border* and in his use of this religious struggle as context for his fiction, most notably *Old Mortality* (1816).[33] James Hogg, too, was a writer whose voice Stevenson saw as emerging from familiarity with the Covenanting tales, and he commented upon their shared frame of reference:[34] 'I believe the common ground had been supplied by common devotion to Covenanting literature – of which I read more when I was young than you could dream.'[35]

John Galt, a novelist to whom Stevenson rarely alluded, also drew heavily upon the Covenanters for his subject material, most notably in *Ringan Gilhaize* (1823). In the early years of the nineteenth century such religious conflict clearly remained alive and of interest to both writers and readers.[36] Evangelical fervour in Scotland in the period was marked by the number of monuments erected to Covenanting martyrs and, by the early nineteenth century, 'one could abhor and reject the violent rhetorical annunciations and destructiveness derived from self-obsessed religious fervour, as the same time as one could admire the patient endurance and fortitude of ordinary Scots men and women in the severest of circumstances'.[37] Culminating in the Disruption of 1843, issues around religious patronage and state control, dominant in the Covenanting struggles, continued to be politically contentious; this period saw a proliferation of reprinted texts from Covenanting writers and eighteenth-century historians, who represented the past from a number of subtly different, and politically engaged perspectives.[38] Even those opposed to the violent expression of fanaticism saw some virtues to be learned from Covenanting heroics. Such partisan viewpoints formed the resources for Stevenson's reading, although by the time he contemplated writing about the period its political resonances were less contentious, and less associated with revolution than in Scott's time. The popularity of the subject at the end of Stevenson's life, when S. R. Crockett also gained commercial success by his ventures into the field, suggested that this was indeed by then a relatively safe area for fiction.

Given Stevenson's fascination with the Covenanters and his acknowledgement of their influence, surprisingly little of this material occupies a central place in his published writing. It formed the subject of his first publication, *The Pentland Rising*, gave context to the religious fanaticism in 'Thrawn Janet', was an evident influence on 'The Tale of Tod Lapraik' within *Catriona* (1892) and created a powerful historical backdrop to *Weir of Hermiston*; but apart from that early history, published when he was sixteen, it was not explicitly explored. A story from boyhood, 'The Plague-Cellar', takes the Pentland Rising as its backdrop, but otherwise only a short unfinished novel written late in his life – the three chapters completed of *Heathercat* – and some fragments of essays remain as direct 'fictional' evidence of his interest.[39] It may be, as he stated in 1873, that he had read too much to extrapolate the material for fiction, yet in 1894 he suggested the reverse to Samuel Crockett: that he had not yet understood enough of them and that Crockett, who was at the time preparing *Men of the Moss Hags*, his own Covenanting romance, should wait 'For three years, because by that time, I shall be really seeing my subject; and then I'll race you!'[40]

A second inhibitor for Stevenson lay in his own ambivalent relationship to the belief systems of the Covenanters: although he described himself as a 'child of the Covenanters', he was not drawn in any simple empathy to that complicated group of people: as he commented to Crockett, 'I fear you misunderstand my attitude about these ticklish gentry. I have but little use for them except in so far as they were sincere and are picturesque.'[41] While the mindset may have been recognisable to him, their power over his imagination was closely linked to grim tales of his childhood and those fears of hell that he fought to reject. Nevertheless, as Swearingen has suggested, the subject matter of Covenanting tales may have functioned as a bridge between secular romance and Christian literature, offering striking narratives of heroic convictions.[42] Stevenson's own explanation, that it is a fondness for rhyme in language that he gains from these 'covenanting buckies', hardly seems an adequate explanation for their hold on him or their influence on his fiction, but does point to a recognition that their influence relates to linguistic issues.[43] Stevenson's claim in the letter to Barrie that his style is attributable to the reading of Covenanting tales offers therefore a more convincing suggestion, but with this body of historical material that Stevenson returned to again and again, the shaping influence of its discourses and conventions needs to be understood on a level beyond subject matter, a fondness for rhyming language or vivid pictorialism. In order to unravel the impact of Covenanting literature, the 'Covenanting buckies' have to be identified and differentiated in terms of their specific textual strategies, their influence sought in less obvious places and their significance understood in terms of readerly experience as well as writerly guidelines.

Writing Covenanting history

For his first publication, *The Pentland Rising*, that 'slim green pamphlet' published, through his father's patronage, in 1866 on the two hundredth anniversary of the Battle of Rullion Green at which the ill-equipped Covenanting forces who had risen against their oppressors were decisively overcome, Stevenson read widely and eclectically.[44] The text itself included references to and lengthy quotations from Robert Wodrow's *The History of the Suffering of the Church of Scotland from the Restoration to the Revolution* (published in two volumes in 1721 and 1722); from Wodrow's source, James Kirkton's manuscript history, *The Secret and True History of the Church of Scotland from the Restoration to the Year 1678* (written in 1693, published in edited, retitled and recontextualised form by Charles Kirkpatrick Sharpe in 1817); and from the more moderate Episcopalian accounts found in Bishop Gilbert

Burnet's *History of My Own Times* (1724–34).[45] It also contains the more vehement voices to be found in the extreme Presbyterian collections of speeches and tales of atrocity published in *Naphtali* (1667), *A Hind Let Loose* (1678) and Defoe's *Memoirs of the Church of Scotland* (1717).[46]

The two main sources, however, were Wodrow and Kirkton, both writers involved in the events they chronicled. Robert Wodrow (1679–1734) was a victim of 'persecution' from a very early age: shortly after his mother gave birth at the age of fifty-one, his Covenanting father narrowly escaped imprisonment when he sneaked into her bedchamber to obtain what he thought would be his last interview with her, and had to flee in disguise moments before soldiers thrust swords into his wife's bed, whereupon she desired them to desist, 'for the bird is now flown'.[47] As a historian Wodrow receives a mixed response from modern practitioners: William Ferguson writes of this 'much maligned figure' that although his style was unattractive, 'his real significance lay in the techniques he employed'; that 'his awesome appetite for knowledge and zest in its pursuit made him an important historian and a significant figure in the culture of the Scotland of his day'; another less kindly describes him as like a squirrel hoarding nuts, in his indiscriminate amassing of material; and Angus Calder talks of 'this densely documented, uniquely tedious, deeply prejudiced book'.[48] Stevenson himself preferred the style of the nineteenth-century Aikman, in his *Annals of the Persecution* (read later in 1868) but only because 'it contains more detailed accounts than anything I ever saw, except Wodrow, without being so portentously tiresome and so desperately overborne with footnotes, proclamations, acts of Parliament and citations'.[49] Wodrow's desire to include as many different accounts and voices in his jumble of a text may nevertheless have had an effect upon Stevenson's understanding of different narrative models as well as meeting his criteria for 'lived' experience. James Kirkton (?1620–99), Wodrow's main source, was even more fully involved in events: deprived of his charge in Meretoun, Berwickshire, for refusing to conform, he was seized as a government spy, escaped to Holland and returned in 1687. At the Revolution of 1689 he was settled again in Meretoun, was attacked in the satiric *Scotch Presbyterian Eloquence* and ridiculed as Mr Covenant Plaindealer in Pitcairne's *Assembly*.[50]

That both historians could claim involvement with the Covenanting cause, if not with all its events, suggests that their words, as 'partisans', would carry particular resonance for Stevenson as in their own lives they had bridged that problematic distance between 'words' and 'events'. Their different accounts of the night preceding the Battle of Rullion Green (the key event of the Pentland Rising) and of an incident which followed it demonstrate the extent to which Stevenson worked with these partisan sources in his early writing. All three writers presented the Covenanters as having marched a considerable way in terrible conditions before the battle. Wodrow's account is (surprisingly) succinct although sympathetic: 'When they came that length in the morning, they looked rather like dying men than soldiers going to a battle. It would almost have made their very enemies themselves to relent, to have seen so many weary, faint, half-drowned, half-starved men, betwixt enemies behind and enemies before.'[51] Wodrow's main source, Kirkton, using what has been described as a 'dry, cool way of speaking', presents a more moving picture:[52]

> To Bathgate they came through pitifull broken moores in ane extraordinary dark and rainy night, and two hourses after day-light was gone. No accommodation can they find there to men both wett, weary and spent; and about twelve o'clock at night, upon ane alarme from the enemy, they are constrained to begin their march toward the New Bridge, wither when they were come in the morning, they looked rather like dyeing men than souldiers going to conquer. It would have pitied a heart to see so many faint, weary, half-drowned, half-starved creatures betwixt their enemies behind and before. That night it was believed they lossed more than the half of their poor army, who stuck in the clay, and fainted by the way.[53]

Stevenson, who could not supply 'hidden sincerity or partisanship', sought to compensate by an account which is longer and more dramatic than either:

> Chilled to the bone, worn out with long fatigue, sinking to the knees in mire, onward they marched to destruction. One by one the weary peasants fell off from their ranks to sleep, and die in the rain-soaked moor, or to seek some house by the wayside wherein to hide till daybreak. One by one at first, then in gradually increasing numbers, till at last, at every shelter that was seen, whole troops left the waning squadrons, and rushed to hide themselves from the ferocity of the tempest. To right and left nought could be descried but the broad expanse of the moor, and the figures of their fellow-rebels, seen dimly through the murky night, plodding onwards through the sinking moss. Those who kept together – a miserable few – often halted to rest themselves, and to allow their lagging comrades to overtake them. Then onward they went again, still hoping for assistance, reinforcement, and supplies; onward again, through the wind, and the rain, and the darkness – onward to their defeat at Pentland, and their scaffold at Edinburgh.[54]

With prolepsis used to give events greater dramatic significance, deeper emotional reverberations are created through identification of the participant's hopes and expectations, while the visual dimension to the scene is also powerfully expressed. This 'colouring' of incidents continued in the account of the battle itself, as if in anticipation of Stevenson's later exhortation that 'the story, if it be a story, repeat itself in a thousand coloured pictures to the eye':[55]

> The sun, going down behind the Pentlands, cast golden lights and blue shadows on their snow-clad summits, slanted obliquely into the rich plain before them, bathing with rosy splendour the leafless, snow-sprinkled trees, and fading gradually into shadow in the distance. To the south, too, they beheld a deep-shaded amphitheatre of heather and bracken; the course of the Esk, near Penicuik, winding about at the foot of its gorge; the broad, brown expanse of Maw Moss; and, fading into blue indistinctness in the south, the wild heath-clad Peeblesshire hills. In sooth, that scene was fair, and many a yearning glance was cast over that peaceful evening scene from the spot where the rebels awaited their defeat; and when the fight was over, many a noble fellow lifted his head from the blood-stained heather to strive with darkening eyeballs to behold that landscape, over which, as o'er his life and his cause, the shadows of night and of gloom were falling and thickening.[56]

Adapting the naturally theatrical aspects of the landscape, Stevenson presented it in painterly gradations of colour; again emotionally anticipating the conclusion by seeing the battle only in terms of imminent defeat. Such an account might be described as overtly 'novelistic': it attempts to render scenes visually but also through sentiments and characterisation, and by constantly reminding the reader of the part this event plays within the larger historical pattern it firmly establishes our sense of a plot trajectory through which this experience can be framed.[57] The passage is also strikingly 'poetic' in the symbolic density of the language. Embellishing his sources for the effect of intensity and immediacy, Stevenson drove the reader further toward confrontation with textuality, into words that 'cease to efface themselves'.

The tale of poor Mr Arthur Murray of Potterow offers an even more striking example of this technique. Although this character is not mentioned by Wodrow, Kirkton described how

> up and downe the countrey many grew sick of grief, and some died. Particularly Mr Arthure Murray, ane honest outted minister, dwelling in a suburb of Edinburgh, by which Dalyell's men entered the city after the victory. He hearing they were passing, opened his window to view them, where he saw them display their banners tainted in the blood of these innocent people, and heard them shout victory, upon which he took his bed and died within a few days.[58]

Although Stevenson did not give the event undue space in his account, the reader is again led to witness the scene in dramatic terms:

With colours flying, and with music sounding, Dalzell victorious entered Edinburgh. But his banners were dyed in blood, and a band of prisoners were marched within his ranks. The old man knew it all. That martial and triumphant strain was the death-knell of his friends and of their cause, the rust-hued spots upon the flags were the tokens of their courage and their death, and the prisoners were the miserable remnant spared from death in battle to die upon the scaffold.[59]

The reader views the scene from Murray's perspective, with an interiority not found in any of the other accounts, but again the visual element is also strong, the metonymic details of the flag become a powerful symbol of the bloody and tattered status of the rebels, playing on the double association of 'remnant' with torn fabric and God's few. While attempting a more 'novelistic' rendition of the scene, Stevenson's account is again notable for the way in which the language with its deliberate archaisms and symbolism draws attention to its own textuality. Writing which attempts to render the 'cockpit of life' more vividly achieves that quickening of the pulse through stylistic devices that draw attention to the quality of writing, to the text as text – exactly the problem Stevenson was later to identify as endemic to all histories. The young writer enhanced the accounts of the partisans, Wodrow and Kirkton, in order to render the experiences more vivid to his reader, yet it is those very literary qualities which stand between the reader and events.

Although he was later highly dismissive of the text, *The Pentland Rising* may be seen as a learning experience for Stevenson.[60] In attempting to render the immediacy of an event, he adopted certain strategies: interiority, a narrative movement inside the emotional responses of those involved in events, a device familiar to the conventions of literary realism; the elaboration of a recognisably 'literary' narrative voice; a temporal overview, suggestive of an omniscience again associated with realism; and significant detail as a means of embodying the wider dimensions of the experience – the flag or the landscape operate symbolically. Of those strategies, the first three – those most closely associated with nineteenth-century realism – are much less evident in his later writing while that deployment of weighted detail remains. James commented favourably on Stevenson's 'talent for seeing the familiar in the heroic, and reducing the extravagant to plausible detail' that made *Kidnapped* 'read like a series of inspired footnotes on some historic page'; it is the same technique that produces that 'delightful quickening of the pulse' that Stevenson saw as essential to the recreation of the historical event.[61]

Patrick Walker and John Howie

In his life-long perusal of Covenanting texts Stevenson not only read weighty authorities such as Wodrow and Kirkton; in letters from the summer of 1878 he requested the writings of Patrick Walker and John Howie, examples of a rather more popular Church history and very much part of his national culture.[62] Patrick Walker (?1666–?1745) was a favourite of Stevenson: a copy of *Biographia Presbyteriana* was given to him by his father in 1869, the book itself makes a brief but significant appearance in *Kidnapped*, and Stevenson often referred to Walker in letters.[63] The mysterious Walker appears to have been even more 'involved' in events than Wodrow or Kirkton: reputedly at the Battle of Bothwell Brig, the first incident in which he was concerned was the shooting of a dragoon in 1682. Sentenced to banishment, he was never transported but kept in confinement in Edinburgh until 1685. After imprisonment and torture, he joined friends in Calder Muir, and remained there until the Revolution 'when we find him again active in the removal of curates, and in destroying their canonical apparatus, a commission he executed with great good will, it being quite congenial to his taste'.[64] He was less prominent, however, once more moderate measures prevailed: 'From this period, there appears no further trace of him until his settlement in Edinburgh, where he kept a small shop for the sale of Religious Tracts &c. at Bristo Port, opposite the Society Gate.'[65] His *Life of Alexander Peden* was brought together with his other biographies in 1725, in a collection by James Duncan, which states in its introduction: 'The life of Mr A. Peden, from its greater popularity, has been many times reprinted in an abridged form, and on coarse paper, it being one of the most popular *chapman*-tracts of its time, and as such has ever continued a great favourite in the Scotch cottage library.'[66] Walker's writing then, even if the veracity of its authorship has been questioned by at least one scholar, was a significant part of the circulation of material which contributed to the different strata of discourses around Covenanting history.[67]

John Howie (1735–93), a collector of Covenanting material and author of number of religious texts, produced *Biographia Scoticana, or a Brief Historical Account of the Lives, Characters and Memorable Transactions of the most Eminent Scots Worthies* in 1775; it was reprinted in various versions through the late eighteenth and early nineteenth century and published as *Scots Worthies* in 1870.[68] Covering much of the same material as Walker in detailing the lives of prominent Covenanting campaigners and martyrs, it remained popular as a standard within the 'library of many a pious Scottish household'.[69] It was a work much used by Sir Walter Scott who, as one critic puts it, was oddly attracted to this 'coprophilous old bigot'.[70] Stevenson, although he demanded a copy be sent to him, disliked Howie almost as much, describing his work as 'a rotten book, and not worth a rush at best'.[71] Those features Stevenson disliked so much about Howie's narrative and found attractive in Patrick Walker's (in addition to the fact that the latter was 'closer', in sympathy and in time, to events) offer further insights into his deployment of 'historical' sources and narrative models.

The two sources clearly had different aims. Howie wrote with a moral purpose: there was an education in both individual and national morality to be had from the lives he represented: 'In these lives we have a short view of the actions, excellencies and failings of our ancestors, as examples both for caution and imitation ... Was there ever an age, since reformation commenced in Scotland, that stood in more need of useful, holy, and exemplary lives being set before it?'[72] Closer to the events themselves, Walker's task was less evidently one of narration than the collection of material. According to anecdote, 'mounted on a little white poney' when gathering stories, Walker offered no coherent or linear narrative, had a plain style and had a conviction of authenticity deriving from his own beliefs.[73] In national terms Walker's aims were rather less uplifting and certainly more apocalyptic than Howie's: 'And how long this melancholy Day may last, there is not a Prophet, nor any one that can tell us the Time how long, nor when the Deliverance will be, from under the Power of these Plagues spiritual and temporal, under which the Nation and Church of Scotland are brought very low.'[74] Walker would rather make the reader weep for shames, past and present, than educate through positive role models.

Their treatment of one well-known story, the life of Alexander Peden, a prominent field preacher and prophet, who had been minister at New Glenluce in Galloway until he was 'outted' from his post and who died in 1686, further illustrates the difference between the writers. Peden's career was, by all accounts extraordinary and, although the spiritual significance and supernatural import of his biography are debated, the same incidents appear in all versions of his life. The incident from Peden's biography that provides the most obvious contrast between Walker and Howe is the well-known martyrdom of John Brown of Priesthill.[75] When married by Peden, Brown's bride was given a warning that she should keep a winding-sheet nearby, for her husband would be taken from her when she least expected it. At this point Howie rather sourly remarks, in a commonsensical repression of fanaticism, that:

> From incidents and anticipations of this kind, some have weakly imagined, that this worthy minister was endowed with the gift of prophecy; whereas, no more appears, than that he possessed a natural, or, if you will, a spiritual sagacity, by which he could perceive that, in the temper of those times, a

man of John Brown's decision of character, and zeal for divine institutions, was not likely to escape the fury of the enemy.[76]

Accounts nevertheless agree that in May 1685 John Brown was sought out, at home, by Claverhouse and slaughtered in front of his wife and child. Howie's account of this event sought to justify the ways of God to man, offer an exegesis of the incident and provide consoling emotions for the reader both through the sentiments expressed and through the poetry of his language.[77] His narrative began with a consoling moral message and provided an emotional diegesis for the dialogue which follows:

> There is a light in the Christian's life that discovers the spots of the wicked and torments them before the time. When Claverhouse could bear his prayers no longer, and had succeeded after interrupting him twice, with the most blasphemous language, to raise him from his knees, John Brown said to his wife – 'Isabel this is the day I told you of before we were married,' and added with his usual kindness, 'You see me summoned to appear in a few minutes, before the court of heaven, as a witness in our redeemer's cause, against the Ruler of Scotland. Are you willing that I should part from you?' 'Heartily willing,' said she, in a voice that spoke her regard for her husband, and her submission to the Lord, even when he called her to bow before his terrible things. 'That is all I wait for: O death, where is thy sting! O grave, where will be thy victory!' said John Brown, while he tenderly laid his arms around her, kissed her and his little boy, and lastly Janet, saying to her, 'My sweet bairn, give your hand to God as your guide; and be your mother's comfort.'[78]

Howie proceeds to enter the perspectives of all participants in the scene, including the shamed troops who slunk from 'the awful scene' and finishes with another consolatory account of the poor wife left with the body, culminating in an burst of bejewelled colour:

> But think not, reader, that she was miserable; it is only when we have brought on ourselves our afflictions that we are miserable under them. Nor think that she was alone. Are not angels ministering spirits to believers in their troubles? ... Thy God saith, For a moment have I forsaken thee, but with great mercies will I gather thee. O thou afflicted, tossed with tempests, and not comforted, behold I will lay thy stones with fair colours, and thy foundations with sapphires. And I will make thy windows of agates, and thy gates of carbuncle, and all thy borders of pleasant stones.[79]

In this account the 'brutality' of the scene is diluted by the dispersal of emotions as the reader is led to see through the eyes of the daughter, the troops and, of course, the narrator. Such narrative diegesis, with its highly charged and Biblical language, extends to an interpretation of the meaning of events, offering guidance to the reader as to the moral message to be taken from the incident.

Patrick Walker's earlier account is much shorter, and yet in many ways more powerful. His version of Brown's death is contextualised by a prophesy from Peden – 'in the Morning, when he took his Farewell, he came out at the Door, saying to himself, *Poor Woman, a fearful Morning* twice over, *a dark misty Morning*' – but presents a far less elaborate dialogue between Claverhouse and his victim. There is no attempt to enter into the emotions of the participants, the shooting itself is described in brutal terms: 'the most part of the Bullets came upon his Head, which scattered his Brains upon the Ground' and there is little consolation in the picture of Brown's wife at the end:

> Claverhouse said to his Wife, What thinkest thou of thy Husband now; Woman? … left her with the Corps of her dead Husband lying there; she set the Bairn upon the Ground, and gathered his Brains, and tied up his Head, and straightened his Body; and covered him with her Plaid, and sat down and wept over him; it being a very desert Place, where never Victuals grew, and far from Neighbours.[80]

The tale is then concluded with another instance of 'supernatural' powers excluded by Howie: Peden, the same morning but staying in a distant place, announces he should go to John Brown's wife, who is weeping beside her husband's body. Rather than encouraging empathy, this coda pushes the reader towards a view of the event's significance in a wider and more metaphysical narrative.[81]

In Howie's narrative moral interpretation and consolation are always present; in its emphasis on character, its interest in delineating the full panoply of emotions involved and its aim of extracting a meaning from events, it is not only the more overtly 'novelistic' account but also the one which deploys some conventions of literary realism. By contrast that spare account of Patrick Walker's, manifestly less interested in character than the emblematic quality of incident and behaviour, offers a representation in which narrative mediation or consolation is reduced to a minimum and in which the 'cockpit of experience' is allowed, as it were, to speak for itself. It is in his narrative model that the 'quality of the brute incident' later espoused by Stevenson can be most clearly discerned, expressed in the voice of 'inarticulate thunder'.[82] Through his use of a range of Covenanting sources in *The Pentland Rising* and from his subsequent wide reading of popular histories of the period, Stevenson had the opportunity to view the relationship between words and things, narrative and event, played out in a variety of forms. From that period of history which related most directly to choices of partisanship, questions of allegiance which he had to decide in his own life, Stevenson also found a forum in which the central philosophical and aesthetic implications of a Calvinist world view could be confronted.

The Master of Ballantrae

While Stevenson may not have produced a Covenanting novel, the influence of this exposure to a range of different narrative models through reading Covenanting literature (and by his own early experiment into the form) can be found throughout his oeuvre, and not only in those texts which directly address the period or impact of the Covenanters. Indeed, Stevenson's engagement with the aesthetic issues raised by this combination of religion and history is most evident in a novel which adopts quite a different historical context: *The Master of Ballantrae*. Written in conditions of some austerity at Saranac Lake and serialised between 1888 and 1889, *The Master of Ballantrae* takes as its subject the aftermath of the Jacobite rebellion, played out in divisions between the two brothers, Henry and James, of the house of Durrisdeer.[83] This tale, complicated in the shifts of sympathy between the protagonists, oscillating between historical realism and supernatural melodrama, and narrated through a series of narrative fragments, was reviewed by his old friend W. E. Henley in the *Scots Observer* in terms which irritated Stevenson.[84] Although the author objected to the review designating his novel 'A Masterpiece in Grime', complaining that he couldn't see what was so grimy about it, Henley's remarks are illuminating:

> The book shows us how thorough a Scot Mr Stevenson is: beneath all that fascinating, many coloured web which he has woven of wild romance and capricious fancy and extravagant fun, the hard, gloomy, uncompromising side of the Scottish intellect asserts itself. In *The Master of Ballantrae* the spirit which animated the old Scottish theologians and preachers and soldiers – the severe, unflinching, pleasure-hating spirit to which the race owes so many of its defects and so much of its fibre – seems to have entered into the Kingdom of Romance and made part of that Kingdom its own.[85]

If the spirit inhabiting *The Master of Ballantrae* comes from the Covenanters, however, elements of its style, structure and concerns also bear their imprint.

Firstly, a case could be made for a direct influence in terms of content: most obviously, the novel forces the reader into a series of confrontations with polarities, not just in the 'political' divisions between the two brothers, one of whom took up the Jacobite cause and thus lost his place as 'the Master' of Ballantrae, while the other kept the family's political options open by staying at home and remaining loyal, but also in the extremes of outlook they represent: James as a wild and opportunistic adventurer, Henry cautious and dogged in his beliefs and behaviour. In the twists and turns of the plot the reader is also led into making a series of moral judgements, which often turn out to be both transient and unsure: both these aspects of the novel can be read as underpinned by the fierce division of feelings produced by the Covenanters – extreme (and severe) in their own behaviour but also the victims of cruel persecution. Furthermore, the ambiguous figure of the Master himself bears obvious resemblances in his duality to a key figure of the 'Killing Time', John Graham of Claverhouse, First Viscount Dundee, scourge of the Covenanters as 'Bluidy Clavers', but also 'Bonnie Dundee', hero of the Jacobites, after his death at the Battle of Killiecrankie in 1689.

The capacity for cold-blooded killing demonstrated by Claverhouse in the narrative of John Brown's death clearly fascinated Stevenson, who returns to such incidents of chilling violence again and again in his fiction.[86] In the behaviour of the Master on various occasions, there are echoes of Walker's representation of Claverhouse as a figure in whom an arrogant failure to acknowledge moral responsibility to either God or man is combined with a striking power. When Brown's wife asks him 'how will ye make Answer for this Morning's Work?' he replies: 'To Man I can be answerable; and for God, I will take him in my own Hand.'[87] Scott, of course, had done much to promulgate the image of 'Bonnie Dundee', as did later historians such as Robert Chambers whom Stevenson had also read. As Chambers notes in his 1829 history: 'To such a degree, indeed, did his actions excite public sentiment in that superstitious age, that he was generally believed to have entered into a league with the powers of darkness, by which, in consideration of the abandonment of his salvation, he was rendered invulnerable in this world.'[88] A similar belief comes to surround the Master. Often alluded to by Jessie Brown as 'my bonnie laddie', the Master, in his power to excite desire, resembles Chamber's description of Claverhouse as 'restless and active to such a degree, as might well excite the idea of its being the tabernacle of a demoniac spirit. His visage was beautiful even to effeminacy.'[89] Both figures too suggest a certain transgression of gender boundaries: Claverhouse's long ringlets and fine appearance find some repetition in the Master: 'upon one cheek he had a mole, not unbecoming; a large diamond sparkled on his hand; his clothes, although of the one hue, were of a French and foppish design; his ruffles, which he wore longer than common, of exquisite lace'.[90]

The figure of Claverhouse can also be read as an influence in a more abstract sense, exemplifying tensions between Highland and Lowland histories, between romance and realism, for he had, in a sense, two histories: as Chambers again comments:

> As, in Siberia, the traveller observes heat appreciated as the most excellent
> of things, while, in Guinea, it is looked upon as the grand enemy of human
> comfort, so is Dundee in the Highlands held as the greatest of all modern
> heroes, and in the Lowlands as the most barbarous of all brutes. It may
> seem strange that the *Bloody Claverse* of Ayrshire, should have become the
> Great Dundee of Athole. But the thing is by no means paradoxical. Dundee
> did not act upon feelings, or upon the ordinary motives and emotions of
> men. He acted upon a grand abstract principle, which he had established,
> like an idol, in the innermost shrine of his mind, and to which he was
> disposed to sacrifice all the natural sympathies ... He was inspired with
> as high a degree of religious fervour in his bloody deeds, as ever possessed
> the mind of the wildest enthusiast that sat for years among the wilds of
> Tweeddale.[91]

In Stevenson's novel the Master's ability to become all things to all men,
even seducing the stubborn Mackellar to his side, cannot be described
as the product of religious singlemindedness but the strength of feeling
he inspires – in both enmity and love – points to Stevenson's continuing
interest in the ways in which allegiances to a partisan perspective shape
understanding of the past and present.

Other shaping influences, however, apart from emotional pitch and
direct fertilisation as seen in the figure of Claverhouse, emerge from
the exchanges between Stevenson's reading in Covenanting history
and this post-Jacobite novel: from the outset *The Master of Ballantrae*
foregrounds the difficult nature of relationships with the past and raises
questions about ways in which narrative constructs history. When the
novel's main narrator Ephraim Mackellar, Steward in the House of the
old Master and observer of most of the action, arrives at the house of
Durrisdeer, he is surrounded by different elements of a Scottish past.
Led into the novel by ten-year old Patey Macmorland he is shown a
landscape invested with history:

> indeed, it would have taken any man, that cold morning, to hear all the
> old clashes of the country, and be shown all the places by the way where
> strange things had fallen out. I had tales of Claverhouse as we came through
> the bogs, and tales of the devil as we came over the top of the scaur. As we
> came in by the abbey I heard somewhat of the old monks, and more of the
> free-traders, who use its ruins for a magazine, landing for that cause within
> a cannon-shot of Durrisdeer.[92]

Prior to this, however, the novel's self-referential Preface (discarded by
Stevenson as being too like one of Scott's devices, before being reintroduced for the Edinburgh Edition) immediately highlights questions about
narrating the past.[93] Structured around an editorial joke, designed to
indicate the text's status as a form of 'history', it presents a first-person

narrative by a novelist newly returned to Edinburgh, meeting up with his old friend, the Edinburgh lawyer Mr Johnstone Thomson. (Johnstone and Thomson were the names adopted by Stevenson and Charles Baxter in a series of spoof correspondences, in Scots, based on personae they had invented in their youth.[94]) After celebrating their reunion, Mr Thomson produces the 'mystery' with which he honours his friend's arrival, the papers of the Durrisdeer family: '"The Durrisdeers!" cried I. "My dear fellow, these may be of the greatest interest. One of them was out in the '45; one had some strange passages with the devil … and there was an unexplained tragedy, I know not what, much later."' Thomson follows this with a narrative written as explanation of the papers, declaring: 'Here … is a novel ready to your hand: all you have to do is to work up the scenery, develop the characters, and improve the style', to which the editor responds: 'My dear fellow … they are just the three things that I would rather die than set my hand to. It shall be published as it stands.'[95] The authorial figure, therefore, declines to perform a role akin to that of the Covenanting historian Howie in offering an interpretative framework and embellishing its emotions. Nor will he produce the kind of 'history' offered by Stevenson's earlier self in *The Pentland Rising*: one which enhances scenery through poetic description, develops characters through interiority and embellishes style by making the language more dense and overtly textual. Instead, he is going to give us a 'bald' story, with no shaping 'artifice'. The Preface then already indicates a preference for the austere use of striking incident adopted by a narrator such as Patrick Walker.

The bald tale which follows, two brothers engaged in a lifelong feud over loyalty and love, leading eventually to their mutual destruction in the wilderness of North America, is presented through shifting narratives and an unevenness of genre.[96] Within the novel the 'shaping' role is played by the main narrator, the loyal servant of Henry Durie, that collector of documents, Ephraim Mackellar, a character who has been viewed with increasing critical suspicion as a figure of manipulative narratorial 'control', someone who seeks to conceal his own part in events and present a particular version of 'history'.[97] His role as narrator, however, might also be understood in relation to the different narrative modes Stevenson found within Covenanting literature. Mackellar would like to be the 'Howie' of this tale: to amplify emotions, to understand character, to draw moral lessons and to interpret for the reader. Like Howie, his interventions in the narrative aim to curtail any 'superstitious' element: for example, he describes as 'complete blunder' the assertion that the Master coincidentally speaks of Alison on the very day she is married. Supporting his narrative with self-enhancing asides which indicate the way in which moral benefit might be gained from the scenes of suffering he has described, his role appears to be that of educating the reader and containing the 'wilder' elements in the narrative.[98]

Yet for all his commitment to a moderate 'realism' and to interpretations which favour common sense and anti-superstitious rationality, Mackellar produces a far less coherent narrative than he would wish, composed of odd accounts, witness reports, unreliable narrators and dangerously allegorical tales told by the Master. Mackellar may attempt to control and interpret, but increasingly even the pieces of paper defeat him: he loses 'control' of dates and his journals become 'ill-redd up'.[99] In this respect Mackellar's narrative bears curious similarities to that of the Covenanting historians such as Wodrow and Walker who, in their determination to make the voices of those involved in events heard, often present curious mixtures of anecdotes, letters and reports of speeches. He becomes little more than a 'collector' of stories even if he does not possess a white pony and wander the countryside to collect his material. And while his interventions may seek to contain the flow of interpretations, they also fail to control the symbolic significance of the incidents themselves, as increasingly strange plot events – mysterious deaths and rebirths, journeys across continents, pirates, mutinies and buried treasure – acquire a resonance far beyond the novel's ostensible subject.

Mackellar also moves into non-realist modes of thinking. On the sudden and alarming return of the Master he writes: 'An old tale started up in my mind of a fairy wife (or perhaps only a wandering stranger), that came to the place of my fathers some generations back, and stayed the matter of a week, talking often in a tongue that signified nothing to the hearers; and went again, as she had come, under cloud of night, leaving not so much as a name behind her.'[100] And for all his 'rationality', Mackellar's narrative becomes increasingly 'prophetic':

> I sat by my taper, looking on the black panes of the window, where the storm appeared continually on the point of bursting in its entrance; and upon that empty field I beheld a perspective of consequences that made the hair to rise upon my scalp. The child corrupted, the home broken up, my master dead or worse than dead, my mistress plunged in desolation – all these I saw before me painted brightly on the darkness; and the outcry of the wind appeared to mock at my inaction.[101]

Prior to embarking on his voyage to the New World this oppressive envisioning of the future grows:

> And all the time, sleeping or waking, I beheld the same black perspective of approaching ruin; and the same pictures rose in my view, only now they were painted upon hillside mist. One, I remember, stood before me with the

colours of a true illusion. It showed me my lord seated at a table in a small room; his head, which was at first buried in his hands, he slowly raised, and turned upon me a countenance from which hope had fled ... it haunted and returned upon me half the voyage through.[102]

Although Mackellar might state: 'My pen is clear enough to tell a plain tale', the implications of his term require some thought: his 'plain' tale could signify the constructed transparency of a 'realist' text, yet it may also be a 'plain' tale in which events begin to 'speak' for themselves, to acquire less directly controllable symbolic significance as part of a larger narrative.[103] Through analogy with his own literary activities Mackellar suggests that the Master 'ate bread by the shedding of his comrade's blood as I do by the shedding of ink';[104] in its elision of blood and ink this image indicates a textual commitment to 'authenticity' of a visceral kind, linking Mackellar with the violence of action, rather than the passivity of reportage but also situating the act of writing itself within 'the cockpit of experience'.

In comparison with Stevenson's early writing in *The Pentland Rising*, it is evident that his focus had changed. Like Walker, rather than Howie, he kept the reader at a distance from 'characters', abandoning attempts at interiority and developing instead attention to significant detail, to what Bachelard calls the 'reverberating image'.[105] Incidents and places became key to the novel's systems of signification, as the blood-hued flag did in the tale of Arthur Murray. Rather than adopting an elaborately stylised narrative voice, which comes 'between words and things' while at the same time attempting to overcome that barrier to 'experience', he deliberately overplayed that distance by providing the reader with a series of clearly 'inadequate' narrators, narrators unable to control and smooth out the 'cockpit of experience'. Finally, rather than using a historically achieved overview, that convention of realism manifested in literary prolepsis and obvious in his techniques in *The Pentland Rising*, he both made clear the retrospective nature of the account and created a narrator susceptible to prophetic visions. In that deep division within the troubled narrative persona of Mackellar, striving towards the containment of a writer like Howie, but delivering instead the 'brute incident' found in Walker, Stevenson performed a Calvinistic scrutiny of the literary narrative and answered his own anxieties about the immediacy of the literary experience.

The plains of history

In May 1679 a group of ardent Presbyterians were plotting to murder Archbishop Sharp as a response to increasingly bitter persecution of the

Covenanters. The man they wanted to lead the attack, David Hackston, declined because he had a personal grudge against the Archbishop, and believed his own grievances would prevent the action being understood in terms of its wider religious and political significance. He, therefore, accompanied the murderers, partially disguised, but would not strike a blow. Nor, however, would he help the dying Archbishop. In an essay of 1888 Stevenson picked up on this incident in Scotland's complicated and bloody history of religious differences and talked of the hold it continued to have upon his imagination, a power partly attributable to the dramatic quality of the moment, but also to the indecipherability of its central figure: 'It is an old temptation with me, to pluck away that cloak and see the face – to open that bosom and to read the heart.'[106] No matter how much he read about Hackston, however, and despite the attempted narrative experiments with which 'the drawers of my youth were lumbered', he could get no further through writing or reading. Oscillating between a sense that he knew too much and the feeling that his knowledge was insufficient (a tension characteristic of all his dealings with the Covenanters), he was nevertheless forced to acknowledge that the power of the image is undiminished; Hackston sits, 'with his cloak about his mouth, inscrutable'.[107] In the image of Hackston of Rathillet that paradox of the 'literary' which obsessed Stevenson – the more vividly a writer attempts to render an event in detail, the more the systems of signification make themselves apparent, and the intensity of the experience is lost – was given dramatic realisation. As he recognised, the desire to pull the cloak away from the mouth of Hackston and thus see into his heart is the very thing that will reduce the intensity of that figure: 'I do not think he can have been a man entirely commonplace; but had he not thrown his cloak about his mouth, or had the witnesses forgot to chronicle the action, he would not thus have haunted the imagination of my boyhood, and today he would scarce delay me for a paragraph.'[108] For Hackston to speak would make him less 'speaking'. Likewise the power of Covenanting history, the delight that literature appeared to exercise upon Stevenson as a reader, is dependent upon its uninterpreted qualities, the jumble of voices, the brute incidents from the cockpit of experience. As a reader of both Walker and Howie, Stevenson encountered alternative responses to the distance between language and event; as a text, *The Master of Ballantrae* inhabits that space. There is a critical tendency to suggest that, while Stevenson's knowledge of Scottish history may have inspired him, his Presbyterian inheritance hampered his career as either novelist or historian.[109] And yet his literary vagabonding in that tradition produces an alternative paradigm for his aesthetic concerns, a frame for engagement with debates around language and mimesis, and, in Patrick

Walker, however peculiar his writing may have been, an example of textuality in which action predominates and meaning becomes immanent.

Coda: *Heathercat*

The fragment that gestures towards the novel *Heathercat*, sketched out in the bare bones of plot towards the end of Stevenson's life, and with only three chapters complete, finally brings that coalescence of textual strategies to the Covenanters as a subject in itself. In its first chapter the book draws attention to its sources through words that again refuse to efface themselves:

> The period of this tale is in the heat of the *killing-time*; the scene laid for the most part in solitary hills and morasses, haunted only by the so-called Mountain Wanderers, the dragoons that came in chase of them, the women that wept on their dead bodies, and the wild birds of the moorland that have cried there since the beginning.[110]

Emphasising the performative element of its material, through the sense of a tale oft-told expressed in a narrative voice that begins almost imperceptibly to drop back in time and in familiarity, the text acquires the rhythm of oral history: 'The Traquairs were always strong for the Covenant; for the King also, but the Covenant first; and it began to be ill days for Montroymont when the Bishops came in and the dragoons at the heels of them.'[111] By the end of the first chapter, Patrick Walker is being quoted at length, and the problems of interpretation made explicit through disparaging aside: 'I have never heard it claimed for Walker that he was either a just witness or an indulgent judge.'[112] In this effort, described as 'an attempt at a real historical novel', Stevenson may have found a form which could accommodate both readerly delight and the intensity of lived experience, through acknowledging the refusal of words to efface themselves by drawing attention to their status within the text. If so, it is unsurprising that this strategy emerged from that history which made the most demands upon his own partisan relationship to the past. As with his other projects, however, the race was never completed.[113]

Notes

1 Originally published as 'Contributions to the History of Fife: Random Memories', *Scribner's Magazine*, 4 (October 1888), 507–12, later as two essays, 'I. The Coast of Fife' and 'II. The Education of an Engineer', 'Random Memories', in *Further Memories*, Tusitala XXX, pp. 9–19, pp. 14–15. See also 'reams upon reams must have gone to the making of Rathillet'. 'My First Book: *Treasure Island*', Tusitala II, p. xxiii.

2 'A Humble Remonstrance', p. 134.

3 In writing *St Ives*, for example, he was discomfited to find, following a reading of Gille, *Mémoires d'un Conscrit de 1808*, much of the plot for his hero's escape invalidated by the Frenchman's details of prison life: 'How could I have dreamed the French prisoners were watched over like a female charity school, kept in a grotesque livery, and shaved twice a week? And I had made all my points on the idea that they were unshaved and clothed anyhow.' 24 or 25/4/94 to Colvin, *Letters*, vol. 8, p. 279. See also 17/4/94 to Charles Baxter, *ibid.*, p. 265 and n. 6.

4 8/12/79 to Gosse, *Letters*, vol. 3, p. 32.

5 22/9/73 to Frances Sitwell, *Letters*, vol. 1, p. 311. He spent so much effort researching the life of John Knox that he finally produced two different essays on the subject: see 5/9/74 to George Grove, *Letters*, vol. 2, p. 48. He had first given two papers on Knox to the Speculative Society, in November 1874 and January 1875 (Swearingen, *Prose Writings of Robert Louis Stevenson*, p. 8). The essays were published in *Macmillan's Magazine* in September and October 1875, and later included in *Familiar Studies of Men and Books* (1882). Tusitala XXVII, pp. 202–44 (Swearingen, *Prose Writings*, p. 16).

6 See E. J. Cowan, '"Intent upon my own race and place I wrote": Robert Louis Stevenson and Scottish History', in E. Cowan and D. Gifford (eds), *The Polar Twins* (Edinburgh: John Donald, 1999), pp. 187–214.

7 Mary Lascelles argues that it is a strong sense of family history, learned from the stories of his father, that produced the wider interest. *The Storyteller Retrieves the Past: Historical Fiction and Fictitious History in the Art of Scott, Stevenson, Kipling and Some Others* (Oxford: Clarendon Press, 1980).

8 See Noble on 'Highland History and Narrative Form in Scott and Stevenson', *Robert Louis Stevenson*, pp. 187–214.

9 See V. Smith, *Literary Culture and the Pacific: Nineteenth-century Textual Encounters* (Cambridge: Cambridge University Press, 1998).

10 'History for Children? This flows from my lessons to Austin: no book is any good. The best I have seen is Freeman's *Old English History* [E. A. Freeman 1869]; but his style is so rasping, and a child can learn more, if he's clever.' 24(26)/10/92 to Colvin, *Letters*, vol. 7, p. 182.

11 Menikoff, *Narrating Scotland*.

12 For example, although his knowledge of history (and Highland history in particular) was impressively detailed, to the extent that in 1881 he engaged in an acerbic correspondence in the *Stirling Observer* over various points of detail in local history (October 1881, *Letters*, vol. 3, pp. 234–5), what that white heat of reading about a Highland past most immediately produced in his 1881 retreat to Pitlochry was fiction: the short stories 'Thrawn Janet' and 'The Merry Men', and shortly afterwards, in Braemar, *Treasure Island*. All three are informed by a sense of the past and by Stevenson's own reading but consumption did not feed directly or immediately into production – although the understanding of Highland history and the aftermath of the Jacobite

rebellion serve their purpose in the writing of *Kidnapped*, *The Master of Ballantrae* and *Catriona*. As Menikoff argues, the impact of his studies in Highland history also has wider cultural and political implications.

13 Cowan, *The Polar Twins*, p. 191.

14 Simpson draws on Stevenson's own words, 'With all my romance, I am a realist and a prosaist, and a most fanatical lover of plain physical sensation, plainly and expressly rendered; hence my perils' (20/5/92 to Colvin, *Letters*, vol. 7, p. 284). 'Realism and Romance: Stevenson's Scottish Values', p. 234.

15 Noble, *Robert Louis Stevenson*, p. 178.

16 Jolly, *Henry James: History, Narrative, Fiction*, p. 3.

17 *Ibid.*, p.5.

18 See *ibid.*, pp. 222–3, but also S. Bann, *The Clothing of Clio: A Study of the Representation of History in Nineteenth-century Britain and France* (Cambridge: Cambridge University Press, 1984).

19 'A Humble Remonstrance', p. 135.

20 P. Ricoeur, *Hermeneutics and the Human Sciences*, ed. and trans. J. B. Thompson (Cambridge: Cambridge University Press, 1981), p. 149.

21 *Ibid.*

22 'A Humble Remonstrance', p. 136.

23 'Selections from His Notebook', Tusitala XXIX, p. 191.

24 ? Summer/71 to Maud Babington, *Letters*, vol. 1, p. 214.

25 Bann, *The Clothing of Clio*, p. 139.

26 For a stimulating and alternative reading of the dialectic between words and things in Stevenson, see P. Fielding, 'Words in Themselves: *Weir of Hermiston*', *Writing and Orality: Nationality, Culture and Nineteenth-century Scottish Fiction* (Oxford: Clarendon Press, 1996), pp. 179–97.

27 7/12/93, *Letters*, vol. 8, p. 205.

28 See I. B. Cowan, *The Scottish Covenanters 1660–1688* (London: Victor Gollancz, 1976).

29 'A Covenanting Story-book', 1868–69: Yale, Haverford College Library, unpublished. Notebook lists of short stories. See Swearingen, *Prose Writings of Robert Louis Stevenson*, p. 6.

30 8 March 1870, Swearingen, *Prose Writings*, p. 8.

31 See n. 5, letter to Frances Sitwell.

32 17/5/91 to George Saintsbury, *Letters*, vol. 7, pp. 125–6.

33 The significance of Scott's interest is a matter of some debate: the editors of one edition of *Old Mortality* suggest he saw it as uncontentious subject matter – 'It is unlikely that he thought the religious fanaticism depicted in *Old Morality* to be anything more than a historical fact, safely over and done with.' J. Stevenson and P. Davidson (eds), *Old Mortality* (Oxford: Oxford University Press, 1993), p. xxiii. Others argue that his representation of Covenanting history was politically active, as part of his containment of threats to the British constitution. A. Calder (ed.), *Old Mortality* (Harmondsworth: Penguin, 1975); D. Mack (ed.), *The Tale of Old Mortality* (Edinburgh: Edinburgh University Press, 1993). See also J. Currie, *History,*

Hagiography, and Fakestory: Representations of the Scottish Covenanters in Non-fictional and Fictional Texts from 1638 to 1835 (PhD thesis, University of Stirling, 1999), chapter 3.

34 See Currie, *History, Hagiography, and Fakestory*, p. 152.

35 7/5/91 to Saintsbury, *Letters*, vol. 7, pp. 125–6, written on receipt of essays in *English Literature 1780–1860* (1890), which included an essay on Hogg.

36 T. C. Smout, *A History of the Scottish People 1560–1830* (1969: London, Fontana Press, 1998), p. 218; Altick, *The Common Reader*, notes general interest in religious works with the early nineteenth-century religious revival (see chapter 5), while G. D. Henderson has identified Scottish evangelicalism of the period leading to renewed interest in the Covenanters. *Religious Life in Seventeenth-century Scotland* (Cambridge: Cambridge University Press, 1937). See also Swearingen, *The Early Literary Career*, p. 471.

37 Currie, *History, Hagiography, and Fakestory*, p. 244.

38 For detailed discussion of this see *ibid*.

39 'The Plague-Cellar', 1864, MS Princeton University Library: see Swearingen, *Prose Writings of Robert Louis Stevenson*, p. 3.

40 18/5/94, *Letters*, vol. 8, p. 284. A different version of this letter (which Booth and Mehew suggest may have been a garbled version from Crockett's memory) is quoted by Colvin in his Editorial Note on *Heathercat* produced for the Edinburgh Edition: 'I have made many notes for *Heathercat* but do not get much forrarder. For one thing, I am not inside these people yet. Wait three years and *I'll race you*. For another thing, I am not a keen partisan, and to write a good book you must be. The Society men were brave, dour-headed, strong-hearted men fighting a hard battle and fighting it hardly. That is about all the use I have for them.' Tusitala XVI, p. 167; see *Letters*, vol. 8, p. 286, n. 6.

41 13/8/94, *Letters*, vol. 8, p. 354.

42 Swearingen, *Early Literary Career*, pp. 472ff.

43 Swearingen, for example, points to Hyslop's poem 'The Cameronian's Dream' as fulfilling Stevenson's desire for the sensuous and picturesque use of detail. *Ibid.*, p. 482.

44 'My First Book *Treasure Island*', Tusitala II, p. xxiii. See also letter from Aunt Jane Whyte Balfour in Balfour's *Life*, vol. 1, pp. 67–8.

45 R. Wodrow, *The History of the Suffering of the Church of Scotland from the Restoration to the Revolution: collected from the public records, original manuscripts of that time, and other well-attested narratives*, 2 vols (Edinburgh: James Watson, 1721 and 1722; reprinted *With an original memoir of the author, extracts from his correspondence, a preliminary dissertation and notes by the Rev Robert Burns, Minister of St. George's Paisley*, 4 vols (Glasgow: Blackie and Son, 1836); J. Kirkton, *The Secret and True History of the Church of Scotland from the Restoration to the Year 1678 by the Rev James Kirkton, to which is added an account of the murder of Archbishop Sharp by James Russell, an actor therein, edited from the mss by Charles Kirkpatrick Sharpe esq.* (Edinburgh: Longman, Hurst, Rees, Orme and Brown, 1817). See Currie, *History, Hagiography, and Fakestory*,

chapter 5, for full discussion of Sharpe's editing of Kirkton and the effect of his paratextual insertions.

46 For a full and thoughtful analysis of Stevenson's Covenanting reading see also Swearingen, *Early Literary Career.*

47 Robert Wodrow went to Glasgow University in 1691, held office of librarian at college, displayed a talent for historical and bibliographical inquiry and developed an interest in antiquarianism. He was ordained minister of Eastwood parish in 1703.

48 William Ferguson, *Scotland 1689 to the Present* (London: Oliver and Boyd, 1968), p. 217; Thorbjörn Campbell, *Standing Witnesses: An Illustrated Guide to the Scottish Covenanters* (Edinburgh: Saltire Society, 1996), p. ix; Calder, Introduction, *Old Mortality*, p. 16. As Swearingen notes, however, Wodrow's account was a 'research diary' rather than a connected narrative prepared by him for publication. *Early Literary Career*, p. 489.

49 7/9/68 to his Mother, *Letters*, vol. 1, p. 144.

50 David Reid (ed.), *The Party-coloured Mind: Prose Relating to the Conflict of Church and State in Seventeenth-century Scotland* (Edinburgh: Scottish Academic Press, 1982), p. 130.

51 Wodrow, *The History of the Suffering of the Church of Scotland*, p. 28.

52 Reid, *The Party-coloured Mind*, p. 130.

53 Kirkton, *The Secret and True History of the Church of Scotland*, p. 240.

54 *The Pentland Rising* (Edinburgh: Andrew Elliott, 1866), 16 pp. Tusitala XXVIII, pp. 93–110, pp. 101–2.

55 'A Gossip on Romance', Tusitala, XXIX, p. 119.

56 *The Pentland Rising*, p. 103.

57 For a contrast with later work, see Menikoff's analysis of description 'made to serve atmosphere and emotion beyond all else', 'Introduction', *Robert Louis Stevenson's Kidnapped – or the Lad with the Silver Button* (California: Huntington Library Press, 1999), pp. xxiff.

58 Kirkton, *The Secret and True History of the Church of Scotland*, p. 247.

59 *The Pentland Rising*, p. 106.

60 18/5/94 to Charles Baxter, 'I would rather die than have *The Pentland Rising* foisted upon any reader as my idea of literature.' *Letters*, vol. 8, p. 289.

61 L. Edel and M. Wilson (eds), *Henry James Literary Criticism*, 2 vols (New York: Library of America, 1984), vol. 1, p. 1254, quoted in Jolly, *Henry James*, p. 25.

62 Late August/78 to his Mother, 'I shall ask you to send me at once: Patrick Walker's Lives which I possess and which I believe to be at Swanston – *Biographia Presbyteriana*, they are called – and Howie's Worthies, of which there are many editions. Send me one with most notes. For these I shall be much indebted, as I want them badly for work.', *Letters*, vol. 2, pp. 263–4. As noted (Anderson I, p. 180), Stevenson had a copy given to him by his father in 1869.

63 Swearingen, *Early Literary Career*, p. 592; at the beginning of chapter 4 in *Kidnapped*, David Balfour finds 'a chap-book (one of Patrick Walker's)' in his uncle's collection of books (Tusitala VI, p. 20).

64 P. Walker, *Biographia Presbyteriana* (1728), 2 vols (Edinburgh: D. Speare and J. Stevenson 1827); including *Some Remarkable Passages in the Life and Death of Mr Alexander Peden* (1728), p. vii. Stevenson's marked copy of *Biographia Presbyteriana* (1827) is in the Beinecke Library.

65 *Ibid.*, p. viii.

66 *Ibid.*, xiii.

67 See J. Currie, *History, Hagiography, and Fakestory.*

68 J. Howie, *Faithful Contendings Display'd: Being an historical relation of the state and actings of the suffering remnant in the Church of Scotland, who subsisted in select societies, and were united in general correspondence during the hottest time of the late persecution from the year 1681 to 1691* (Glasgow: John Bryce, 1780); *Biographia Scoticana* (Glasgow: John Bryce, 1779); *The Scots Worthies: Volume First Containing a Brief Historical Account of the most eminent Noblemen, Gentlemen, Ministers and Others who testified or suffered for the cause of Reformation in Scotland, from the beginning of the sixteenth century to the year 1688 originally compiled by John Howie of Lochgoin. Now revised, corrected and enlarged by A Clergyman of the Church of Scotland and enriched with a preface and notes by William M'Gavin esquire* (Glasgow: McPhun, 1829)

69 Cameron, *The Dictionary of Scottish Church History and Theology*, p. 414.

70 Calder, *Old Mortality*, p. 17.

71 8/9/78 to his Mother, 'Received *Scots Worthies*, without notes.' *Letters*, vol. 2, p. 267.

72 Howie, Original Preface, reprinted in 1829 edition, p. xxviii.

73 The Preface to 1829 edition notes: 'Common fame reports it as having been his practice to revisit from time to time the scenes of his early life, on which occasions he is said to have rendered himself somewhat conspicuous, being uniformly mounted on a little white poney' (p. viii). 'He himself says that he had travelled upwards of a thousand miles to collect and verify the traditions which he has recorded, many of which bear, it must be allowed, internal evidence of their wild mountain origin, and the reporter's boundless credulity ... The plain matter of fact style in which they are narrated, and the narrator's apparent self-conviction of their authenticity, add, however, no inconsiderable portion to their interest' (p. ix).

74 Walker's address to the Reader in 1725 edition of 'Remarkable Passages in the Life and Death of Mr Alexander Peden', reprinted in 1829 edition, p. v.

75 'Much controversy has been generated by this episode, and the Covenanters have been accused of surreptitious pathetic embroidery of the tale designed to blacken Claverhouse's name and heighten the sufferings of the Browns.' Campbell, *Standing Witnesses*, pp. 161–2.

76 Howie, *The Scots Worthies, Volume First*, p. 446.

77 *Ibid.*, pp. 443–57.

78 *Ibid.*, p. 453.

79 *Ibid.*, p. 455.

80 Walker, *Biographia Presbyteriana*, p. 72.

81 Claverhouse's own account of events (in a letter to the Duke of Queens-bury, 3 May 1685) was: 'I caused shoot him dead, which he suffered very inconcernedly', *Reports of the Royal Commission on Historical Manuscripts* (London, 1870), XV, part viii, p. 292, given in Campbell, *Standing Witnesses*, p. 207.

82 For an equally positive reading of Walker's influence, see Swearingen, *Early Literary Career*, pp. 493–6.

83 *The Master of Ballantrae*, *Scribner's Magazine*, 4–6, twelve monthly instal-ments November 1888 to October 1889; *The Master of Ballantrae: A Winter's Tale* (1889), Tusitala X.

84 Stevenson, in a letter to Charles Baxter, puzzled over this: 'I wonder why Henley thinks it grimy: grim it is, God knows; but sure not grimy: else I am the more deceived.' C.5/2/1890, *Letters*, vol. 2, p. 360.

85 Henley, 'The New Stevenson', *Scots Observer* 2: 47 (12 October 1889), 583–4, p. 583, reprinted in Maixner, *Critical Heritage*, p. 117.

86 *Treasure Island* is a particularly striking example of this, especially in the powerful and almost non-judgemental account of the death of the sailor killed from behind by Silver. *The Ebb-Tide* also presents chillingly detached accounts of violent deeds. On Stevenson and violence see Parfect, 'Hell's Dexterities'.

87 Walker, *Biographia Presbyteriana*, p. 72.

88 R. Chambers, *History of the Rebellions in Scotland under the Viscount of Dundee and the Earl of Mar in 1689 and 1715* (Edinburgh and London: Constable and Co.; Hurst, Chance and Co., 1829), p. 21.

89 *Ibid.*, pp. 21–2.

90 *The Master of Ballantrae*, Tusitala X, p. 71.

91 Chambers, *History of the Rebellions in Scotland*, pp. 99–100.

92 *The Master of Ballantrae*, p. 13.

93 In a later letter to Charles Baxter, Stevenson wrote: of 'the original plan of *The Master of Ballantrae* a sort of introduction describing my arrival in Edinburgh on a visit to yourself and your placing in my hands the papers of the story. I actually wrote it and then condemned the idea as being a little too like Scott, I suppose.' 18/5/94, *Letters*, vol. 8, p. 290.

94 See, for example, letters exchanged between October and December 1883.

95 *The Master of Ballantrae*, p. xxii.

96 C. Mills, '*The Master of Ballantrae*: An Experiment with Genre', Noble, *Robert Louis Stevenson*, pp. 118–33.

97 See: C. Craig, *Out of History: Narrative Paradigms in Scottish and English Culture* (Edinburgh: Polygon, 1996); Fielding, *Writing and Orality: Nation-ality, Culture and Nineteenth-century Scottish Fiction*; D. Gifford, 'Steven-son and Scottish Fiction: The Importance of *The Master of Ballantrae*', in J. Calder (ed.), *Stevenson and Victorian Scotland* (Edinburgh: Edinburgh University Press, 1981), pp. 62–87; Lascelles, *The Story-teller Retrieves the Past*.

98 Following the Chevalier Burke's account of a series of incidents of unremit-ting savagery on the part of the Master, he notes: 'I have refrained from

comments on any of his extraordinary (and in my eyes) immoral opinions, for I know him to be jealous of respect. But his version of the quarrel is really more than I can reproduce; for I knew the Master myself, and a man more insusceptible of fear is not conceivable. I regret this oversight of the Chevalier's, and all the more because the tenor of his narrative (set aside a few flourishes) strikes me as highly ingenuous.' *The Master of Ballantrae*, p. 58.

99 'It is a strange thing that I should be at a stick for a date – the date, besides, of an incident that changed the very nature of my life, and sent us all into foreign lands. But the truth is, I was stricken out of all my habitudes, and find my journals very ill redd-up, the day not indicated sometimes for a week or two together, and the whole fashion of the thing like that of a man near desperate.' *Ibid.*, p. 137.

100 *Ibid.*, pp. 137–8.

101 *Ibid.*, p. 158.

102 *Ibid.*, p. 160.

103 *Ibid.*, p. 21.

104 *Ibid.*, p. 117.

105 'Through the brilliance of an image, the distant past resounds with echoes, and it is hard to know at what depth these echoes will reverberate and die away.' G. Bachelard, *The Poetics of Space*, trans. M. Jolas (1958; Boston: Beacon Press, 1994), p. xvi.

106 'The Coast of Fife' in 'Random Memories', *Further Memories*, Tusitala XXX, pp. 9–19, p. 14.

107 *Ibid.*, p. 15.

108 *Ibid.*

109 K. G. Simpson, 'Realism and Romance: Stevenson's Scottish Values'.

110 *Heathercat*: first mentioned in July 1893, but Stevenson is thought not to have worked on the novel after the summer of 1894. Tusitala XVI, pp. 141–64, p. 143.

111 *Ibid.*, p. 144.

112 *Ibid.*, p. 147.

113 For Stevenson this kind of story was always associated with his plans to write 'history', even when he talked of writing what would become the first part of *Heathercat* – 'The Killing-Time', as he described it: 'alas the thought! ... an attempt at a real historical novel to present a whole field of time' into which he would pour 'all my weary reading as a boy'. 17/6/94 to Bob Stevenson, *Letters*, vol. 8, p. 306.

6

Textual haunting:
Stevenson and Dumas

Since then I have been going to and fro at very brief intervals in my favourite book; and I have now just risen from my last (let me call it my fifth) perusal, having liked it better and admired it more seriously than ever.[1]

When I think of rereading I often turn to a metaphor of haunting. First, there are texts that haunt us, that cannot and will not be forgotten … that urge us to reread them, to make them present to our mind again and again. Second, there are texts that haunt other texts, in the sense that they appear in them as expected or unexpected visitors … Textual haunting, in this second sense, is just one instance – but a very important one – of the larger phenomenon of intertextuality. The third meaning of my metaphor suggests that it is we, active readers, who are haunting the texts.[2]

Stevenson frequently revisited his childhood reading experiences, identifying in them a primary and activating engagement with the text from which changing patterns in his own literary development emerged. In 'A Gossip on a Novel of Dumas's', one of his most moving essays about a reading journey, the different stages of reading and rereading became a springboard for reflections not only on the psychic pull of narrative desire but on the relationship between genres and historical moments, developing through this dynamic an analysis of pleasure which also informed his fiction.[3] This chapter focuses on that essay as one of Stevenson's most productive intertextual performances, examining first the deployment of Dumas as the basis for an extended exploration of the relationship between reading and rereading, but developing from that an analysis of Stevenson's own individualistic understanding of the romance genre.[4] Rereading Stevenson's own textual revisitings further clarifies his perceptions of chivalric romance and his own contributions to fiction of chivalry and adventure.

In his analysis of rereading, suggestively delineated above as a process of textual haunting, the reading theorist Matei Calinescu moves away from the emphasis of earlier analysts such as Roman Ingarden who stressed the importance, for literary critics, of the first reading, that reading which 'decides in large measure whether one will succeed in a correct apprehension of the work at all'.[5] Inclining to a Barthian emphasis on 'plural readings of a plural text' as the more revealing and characteristic mode of textual engagement, Calinescu also challenges the established distinction between intensive and extensive reading models, suggesting that different groups and individuals carry out particular practices in certain situations.[6] Citing Stevenson as a case in point, he notes that he defends the Gospel of St Matthew as an exciting read but only when it is read, not like the Bible – in an intense, repeated search for meaning, characteristic of intensive reading – but (as he described in 'Books Which Have Influenced Me') 'freshly like a book, not droningly and dully like a portion of the Bible'.[7] Rereading for Stevenson, however, was not only a process of literary revitalisation but also a key subject of scrutiny in his explorations of literary consumption. In his attentiveness to the complexity of revisited texts, Stevenson anticipated both Barthes and Calinescu in their theorisation of difference within reading positions but also engaged with the specific dynamics of a genre that was enjoying a revival in his own time.

In essays such as 'Child's Play', 'The Lantern-Bearers', 'Popular Authors' and '*Rosa Quo Locorum*', as if in confirmation of Calinescu's observation that, 'Assuming that the apprenticeship of literacy is over, the child reader or the older (re) readers as *roles* can appear successively or simultaneously, earlier or later in one's reading life'[8], Stevenson performed a manoeuvre whereby he could appear as an unsophisticated, unmediated 'general' reader, while simultaneously offering an analysis of such engagements from the perspective of the more detached man of letters, both nostalgic for his earlier engagement but also coolly observant of its mechanics. 'A Gossip on a Novel of Dumas's', however, set out a more complicated layering of reading experiences, as Stevenson detailed the many times he had returned to the *Vicomte de Bragelonne*. A performative analysis of the act of reading, this short essay also produced a text which ensured that the reader will seek a return to the words of not one but two writers.

Deceptively simple in its enthusiasm, seductive in its delightful 'plot', 'A Gossip on a Novel of Dumas's' is characteristic of Stevenson's essays on fiction in being underpinned by a highly sophisticated structure which allowed him to play out and reconcile a number of different roles as writer, reader and critic. By taking a personal narrative as a point of entry into wider psychological and aesthetic issues, the essay not only addressed key questions about the relationship between reader, writer and text, but also, in its focus on Dumas, the great purveyor of romance, raised further speculations about the nature of the genre and its place at the end of the nineteenth century. Through its reading of textual revisiting, this chapter explores further dimensions of Stevenson's theoretical analysis of reading involvement and its pleasures by a detailed discussion of one short essay, but also extends understanding of his complicated relationship with the romance form through analysis of the relationship between changes in the literary milieu and the discourses of adventure romance and through consideration of Stevenson's own endeavours in the genre, in particular with the late and unfinished novel *St Ives*.

Reading Dumas: a revivification

While Ricoeur asserts that the exchanges of writer and reader cannot be compared to dialogue, as other hermeneuticists such as Gadamer have asserted, some kind of relationship is nevertheless established between the activities of reading and writing.[9] For Stevenson, as we have seen with Covenanting histories, not only did texts speak to him, but he also sought to speak back to them. Again it is Bachelard who describes the reader–writer relationship in terms closest to that which Stevenson appeared to envisage. With those texts we admire, and reread, Bachelard suggests, we become, in a sense, ghost writers through the very act of reading: 'In this admiration, which goes beyond the passivity of contemplative attitudes, the joy of reading appears to be the reflection of the joy of writing, as though the reader were the writer's ghost.'[10] Moreover, he notes, when those texts that we most admire, that we feel most engagement with and sympathy for, are also those that we recognise as flawed, the relationship is further complicated. It becomes, in a way, 'liberated', because the dynamic whereby reading becomes a means both of nurturing and repressing the desire to write is subtly altered: 'All readers who have a certain passion for reading, nurture and repress, through reading, the desire to become a writer. When the page we have just read is too near perfection, our modesty suppresses this desire. But it reappears nevertheless.'[11] Describing the style of Alexandre Dumas, in the novel of his he most loved, Stevenson talked of it as being 'with every fault, yet never tedious; with no merit, yet inimitably right'.[12] Both the work and the authorial figure of Dumas, with all their flaws, may be seen then as performing exactly that function for Stevenson described by Bachelard, repressing yet nurturing the desire to write, engaging the reader is a complex process of admiration and estrangement. In turn, Stevenson's essay becomes a force for activating readerly desire.

The essay itself was written in 1887, after what Furnas described as a 'foul winter' for Stevenson: his father was declining in health and he was coming to terms with the death of family friend and mentor Fleeming

Jenkin.[13] It reflected a general and long-standing admiration of Dumas; as he admitted to Henley, whom he had urged to write a biography of the author: 'Dumas I have read and re-read too often.'[14] The French novelist was a frequent point of reference in essays and letters; in January and February 1886, when Henley and Stevenson were planning a collection entitled *Masterpieces of Prose Narrative*, most of Stevenson's letters to Henley are dominated by his agonising over which piece of Dumas to include in the anthology.[15] It was clearly important to him that Dumas should be well represented; remembering an article George Saintsbury had written eight years earlier for the *Fortnightly Review*, he went so far as to write for advice on the matter.[16] Stevenson loved the writer for a number of reasons: he figured large (in every sense) in Stevenson's imagination, both as a literary model and as a person. As Henry James, noted, 'It is … my impression that he prefers the author of *The Three Musketeers* to any novelist except Mr George Meredith. I should go so far as to suspect that his ideal of the delightful work of fiction would be the adventures of Monte Cristo related by the author of *Richard Feverel*.'[17]

Stevenson, of course, was not alone in his admiration: Saintsbury had written equally positively about Dumas in the essay in the *Fortnightly*. Acknowledging that he has been a site of conflicting opinions, and the subject of debate because of his collaborative work, Saintsbury nevertheless praised Dumas for his handling of incident: 'The authorities at the disposal of this author or his own fertile imagination usually supply him with an inexhaustible supply of moving incidents, and these he connects together as well as may be by the expedience of making the same personages figure in all or both of them.'[18] In terms which are echoed in Stevenson's defence of action and incident as opposed to character exploration, in 'A Gossip on Romance' and 'A Humble Remonstrance', he noted that Dumas 'does not attempt to give us complicated or intricate studies of character, but his men and women are curiously adapted to their purpose and curiously lifelike of their kind'.[19] Both Henley in his 1883 article on the erection of a monument to Dumas in Paris, and Saintsbury in his later writing on the historical novel in 1895, also stressed Dumas's readerly qualities: Henley wrote of him as 'a novelist read wherever novels are read', and Saintsbury noted the nature of the involvement he demanded: 'His rapid and absorbing current of narrative gives no time for any strictly intellectual exertion on the part of either writer or reader.'[20]

The focus of Stevenson's particular admiration was that novel he had read again and again, and to which he devoted his essay on Dumas: the *Vicomte de Bragelonne*. The more famous romance, *The Three Musketeers*, was first serialised in *Le Siècle* 1843–44 and the Musketeers saga was then continued in a number of volumes. Under the title of *Dix Ans Plus Tard, ou Le Vicomte de Bragelonne* (1847–50) Stevenson appears here to refer to the last three Musketeer novels, now better known as the *Vicomte de Bragelonne, Louise de la Vallière* and *The Man in the Iron Mask*.[21] What made that final Musketeers adventure, serialised between October 1847 and January 1850, such a significant site for rereading? What ghostly writing activity did this novel promote in Stevenson? And, remembering De Certeau's observation that 'Barthes reads Proust in Stendhal's text; the viewer reads the landscape of his childhood in the evening news', if we look for Dumas in Stevenson, what can we see of Stevenson in Dumas?[22]

In the course of the 1887 essay Stevenson made clear what he admired about Dumas as a man and a professional writer: his amazing energy, rate of production, appetite for success and for life. As a novelist, Dumas's handling of plot, protagonists and dramatic incident, and his rather variable success in creating female characters (a problem he was all too familiar with himself), also drew Stevenson. At several points in the essay, therefore, he adopted a comparative approach, positioning himself very much as an author writing about a fellow 'craftsman', a tactic which is most clearly manifested in his aside on this troublesome business of delineating heroines:

> Authors, at least, know it well; a heroine will too often start the trick of 'getting ugly'; and no disease is more difficult to cure. I said authors; but indeed I had a side eye to one author in particular, with whose works I am very well acquainted, though I cannot read them, and who has spent many vigils in this cause, sitting beside his ailing puppets and (like a magician) wearying his art to restore them to youth and beauty.[23]

This technique of increasingly overt reference to his own status, both as a writer and as author of the essay, was a common one for Stevenson in his essays, most obvious in 'A Chapter on Dreams'. Coexisting, however, with this explicit acknowledgement of his own 'writerly' interest was Stevenson's fabrication of himself as a reader: the essay consistently played upon these two different levels of response. And, as with most of Stevenson's literary essays, this also contained a narrative within the disquisition; here it is the story of how Louis, the young reader, forms an acquaintance with the book and his different experiences in subsequent revisiting of it. Engagement with the novel is thus situated in relation not only to his own experiences as a writer but also to key moments in his development as a reader: it was, for example, through depiction of scenes from the novel on dessert plates in a hotel in Nice that he first made acquaintance with the Musketeers story, immediately establishing for his readers associations of Dumas with the more pleasure-oriented atmosphere of southern France, with holiday, perhaps even with the delights of pudding.[24] But he was already, he admits, familiar with the name of D'Artagnan through reading a novel of Miss Yonge's. The novel in question has been identified as *The Young Stepmother*, in which one of the younger male characters is found reading 'one of the worst and most fascinating of Dumas's romances', becomes terrified that his father will find out, and is advised that 'there are some exciting pleasures that we must turn our backs on resolutely. I think this book is one of them.'[25] This image of transgressive pleasure must surely have spoken to Stevenson, not unfamiliar with a censorious paternal presence. When he described acquiring a copy himself there is again an undercurrent of alterity and the illicit in it being 'one of those pirated editions that swarmed at that time out of Brussels, and ran to such a troop of neat and dwarfish versions'.[26] Reading the Musketeers' adventures is, from the outset, identified with gratification and transgression.

Stevenson did not, however, include in his recollections the comments made in a letter to Bob Stevenson in 1866:

> I have read *Bragelonne*. The conversations are certainly wonderful, but the strength of the plot is frittered away and the whole story is lengthened out to a most unconscionable and dreary extent. The strength of Porthos, and the furiously acute intellects of Aramis and D'Artagnan are singularly overdone. There are too many conversations in which the latter braves the King, and, when he has thoroughly failed in his object, succeeds all at once by shamming that he is going to stick himself, or throwing up his situation.[27]

While still testament to the degree of active engagement the book produced, this more critical insight was not part of the essay's narrative of 'reconstructed' readings. It is also ironic, given the representation of the book as beloved but dangerous, that the defence Stevenson offered in the latter part of the essay for his (perhaps surprising) enthusiasm, is the model of morality it provides. A morality which may not appeal to everyone, but nevertheless offers a model of 'truthfulness', is to be found in D'Artagnan in particular: 'his conscience is void of all refinement whether for good or evil; but the whole man rings true like a good sovereign'.[28] Of course, as with his highly 'moral' list of reading in 'Books Which Have Influenced Me' such rectitude need not be taken at face value, but from this defensive strategy it is evident that Stevenson felt the need to claim an educative value for the book. Nevertheless, however flawed his writing may be, however solid its morality, Dumas was predominantly exciting, dangerous, 'other'. While Stevenson's ambivalences towards pleasure may surface in the articulation of 'moral value', it is the desire for dangerous involvement and excitement that the novel most clearly fulfilled in his initial readings and that is acknowledged in both textual and paratextual associations with transgression.

The next reading recollected in the essay pulled the novel more firmly towards Stevenson's own personal and domestic environment: reading it alone while in a cottage in the Pentlands, the book is described as part of the comforts of home, along with dog, slippers and warmth, which await him on his return from the cold countryside. But even within this domestic interior, he described experiencing a kind of spatial bifurcation, one familiar to any reader moving between fictional location and the place of reading:

> I would rise from my book and pull the blind aside, and see the snow and the glittering hollies chequer a Scotch garden, and the winter moonlight brighten the white hills. Thence I would turn again to that crowded and sunny field of life in which it was so easy to forget myself, my cares, and my surroundings: a place busy as a city, bright as a theatre, thronged with memorable faces, and sounding with delightful speech.[29]

Although the polarities of moonlight and sunlight, silence and noise, solitude and throng, reflection and performance, are clearly set out, the comforting explanation of 'forgetting himself' and his cares through reading appears inadequate as a means of accounting for that striking sense of disruption and dislocation described, by which the world of the novel brought into being, in chiaroscuro imagery, a more sharply etched and more alienating world of the reader. The writer becomes 'lost in a book' to such an extent that he views the world outside his book as in some ways more 'unheimlich' and less 'real' than the fictional world to which he returns.

Stevenson's interest was once again directed towards the nature of involvement and absorption offered by reading that, as we have seen, increasingly became the focus of psychologists, phenomenologists and literary critics. It was also to engage the sociologist Erving Goffman, who in his influential study *Frame Analysis*, emphasises the 'mediated' nature of all experience:

> It should be stressed that the matter of being carried away into something – in a word, engrossment – does not provide us with a means of distinguishing strips of untransformed activity from transformed ones: a reader's involvement in an episode from a novel is in the relevant sense the same as his involvement in a strip of 'actual' experience.[30]

Stevenson, in his cameo of winter reading, presents a vivid performance of just such a process of involvement. In his more obviously literary engagement with narrative analysis, the reading theorist Wolfgang Iser also talks of what he calls 'entanglement' in a text: this, he suggests, carries several effects simultaneously:

> While we are caught up in a text, we do not at first know what is happening to us. That is why we often feel the need to talk about books we have read – not in order to gain some distance from them so much as to find out what it is that we were entangled in … The more 'present' the text is to us, the more our habitual selves – at least for the duration of the read – recede into the 'past' … This does not mean, however, that these criteria of our past experience disappear altogether. On the contrary, our past still remains our experience, but what happens now is that it begins to interact with the as yet unfamiliar presence of the text. [31]

Drawing on John Dewey's ideas from *Art as Experience*, Iser sees the conjunction of new and old as a 'recreation in which the present impulsion gets form and solidity while the old, the "stored" material is literally revived, given new life and purpose through having to meet a new situation'.[32] But through an awareness of discrepancies in these *Gestalten*, Iser suggests, the reader is also detached from his or her own participation in the text: 'The ability to perceive oneself during the process of participation is an essential quality of the aesthetic experience; an observer finds himself in a strange halfway position: he is involved, and he watches himself being involved.'[33] In this section of the essay, through a complicated negotiation of the present of the text with a number of his past reading selves, Stevenson enacted for his readers that very process of engagement and observation of engagement, of participation and detachment described by Iser: the novel becomes part of his familiar world, but also makes that world – through the activity of reading – other. More importantly the essay provided the reader with access to that doubled perspective too: we actively engage with two fictionalised worlds – the world of Stevenson's early life and that of Dumas's novel – while simultaneously reflecting on the processes of engagement. Writing about reading Dumas allowed Stevenson both to become an 'innocent' reader again and to view with detachment his earlier reading self; that other reading self is, however, already a selective and fictionalised one, expressing a wholehearted enthusiasm not entirely supported by his more critical comments to Bob. In creating a narrative whereby pleasures could be experientially acknowledged but also intellectually dissected, Stevenson found a structure in which his own Calvinist-inflected anxieties about pleasure and the necessary scrutiny of the reading process could be accommodated. This framework in turn propels both him and his readers into a performative understanding of reading dynamics articulated in more abstract terms by later theorists. This striking moment also forced both Stevenson and his readers to confront the different temporalities of reading, as past and present 'experiences' intersect and multiply.

From this point on the essay also moved towards complicating the relationship between reader, writer, text and critic in terms of ownership. After his early engagement, Stevenson informed the reader, he had returned to the book often, and has just 'risen from my last (let me call it my fifth) perusal, having liked it better and admired it more seriously than ever'.[34] The relationship, however, had changed again: from being either a writerly compatriot of the author, or an avid reader of the text, Stevenson now presented himself as being 'read' by this novel: 'Perhaps I have a sense of ownership, being so well known in these six volumes. Perhaps I think that d'Artagnan delights to have me read of him, and Louis Quatorze is gratified, and Fouquet throws me a look, and Aramis, although he knows I do not love him, yet plays to me with his best graces, as to an old patron of the show.'[35] So while Stevenson possesses the book he is also a possession of it; he has become, he appears to suggest, its ideal reader – not just an implied reader but a figure closer to Riffaterre's super reader – for whom the characters perform at their best.[36] He is the point at which these characters are most themselves, offering coherence to the novel, a reinforcement of identity. Any more thinking along such lines, he observed, and he would be like George IV at the Battle of Waterloo and 'may come to fancy the *Vicomte* one of the first, and Heaven knows the best, of my own works'.[37] (George IV liked to claim that it was through his efforts that Napoleon was defeated.) In his joy of reading Stevenson had indeed been transformed into the reader as the 'writer's ghost'.

With this role constructed, Stevenson then enumerated the values of the novel, of the character of D'Artagnan, and of the 'ventripotent mulatto' Dumas himself, before concluding that one of the novel's most striking features is the way in which it educates by anticipating the end of life, seeing beyond the present moment to failed ideals, to the death of friends: 'to read this well is to anticipate experience'. (And Stevenson, as he has demonstrated, reads well.) Looking forward himself, the essay does not go 'beyond' the novel towards 'experience' but ends instead, in a further temporal twist, with anticipation of another reading, a reading that will lead forward to into a world of familiar romance but also fresh possibilities: 'Yet a sixth time, dearest d'Artagnan, we shall kidnap Monk and take horse together for Belle Isle.'[38] The piece closes therefore with the novel still open for rereading, returning us – revived as it were – to it and away from the author of the essay.

There is however another complex process of revivification being enacted. The central relationship between writer and reader has frequently been depicted in terms of life and death: Ricoeur writes: 'to read a book is to consider the author as already dead, and the book as posthumous. For it is when the author is dead that the relation to the book becomes complete and, as it were, intact'; while Alberto Manguel states: 'The primordial relationship between writer and reader presents a wonderful paradox: in creating the role of the reader, the writer also decrees the writer's death, since in order for a text to be finished, the writer must withdraw, cease to exist.'[39] In this essay, by describing his consumption – and continued, active consumption – of the *Vicomte de Bragelonne* – Stevenson was repeating, enacting again and again, that closure of writing, that 'death' of the author, of which Manguel and Ricoeur speak. In two respects the essay revives, gives life: it recreates for us D'Artagnan, and what he is for Stevenson – 'none love I so wholly' – and while we read D'Artagnan stands before us again, animated not only by the character invested in him by his author but by the virtues accorded, read into him, by the literary persona of Stevenson. Dumas, too, was 'brought to life', a figure taken out of his text, placed again on what the essay calls 'the battlefield of life', and invested with all the qualities – 'the great eater, worker, earner and waster, the man of much and witty laughter, the man of the great heart and alas! of the doubtful honesty' – that no portrait has yet done justice to.[40] Yet in the very act of 'reading' D'Artagnan, Stevenson was also writing the death of Dumas as author and, in putting words on the page depicting Dumas, was enacting his own 'death' by giving life to his readers. Dumas, being read, and Stevenson, writer of our text, both die before us. While the nature of this process is never fully articulated, it is suggestively alluded to by the novel under discussion, for the *Vicomte de Bragelonne* is a novel explicitly about the death of friends, the breaking of bonds, and the letting go of outmoded beliefs and ideals. It is also, unusually, a novel in which the eponymous hero is no hero but, because he is 'boring', a blank for the reader: 'I may be said to have passed the best years of my life in these six volumes and my acquaintance with Raoul has never gone beyond a bow.'[41] As such, that blank space becomes in a site which the dynamics of reading and writing, recovery and loss can be played out. In its final gesture, 'yet once more, dearest d'Artagnan', Stevenson's essay attempts a return to the role of reader, yet the words fix the narrative voice as writer, and liberate us into being his readers – and at the same time, the ghosts of his writer. The essay succeeded therefore in delineating the relationship between different reading selves, but also allowed Stevenson a defensively analytic scrutiny of his own 'involvement' with the seductive pleasures of Dumas.

Reading nostalgia

That momentary break from reading in the Pentlands brings into play another dimension of Stevenson's relationship with Dumas's text: in the narrative recollection of experience there is a powerful element of nostalgia, of returning to the past, revisiting the reading pleasures it contained, pleasures which were less informed by his own literariness ('I understood but little of the merits of the book') and somehow more 'innocent'.[42] Pleasure, as we have seen, was for Stevenson linked with notions of transgression, but in this essay 'innocence' was linked with the past, and pleasure imbued with the shadow of loss. It was nostalgia that formed part of the appeal of Dumas, a figure whom he referred to in his letters as 'Old Dumas' (as opposed to the 'Master Balzac').[43] Nostalgia is also a central feature of this part of the Musketeers series: Stevenson loved the *Vicomte de Bragelonne* in particular (rather than earlier tales) because in that novel the Musketeers are old, placed in a new and changing society, clinging to what are increasingly seen as outmoded values: 'Upon the crowded, noisy life of this long tale, evening gradually falls; and the lights are extinguished, and the heroes pass away one by one.'[44] As Stevenson came to terms with the death of his friend and mentor, Fleeming Jenkin, and with the imminent death of his own father, such words must have carried personal resonance. But the negotiations between past and present reading selves, different moments of experienced pleasure and the nature of love and loss in reading itself also suggest that such notions of loss interact with wider literary concerns. In his analysis of Dumas, in his letters about the novels he had been reading, and in his own fiction, there emerges an attempt to understand the dynamics of the romance genre through that frame of intersecting temporalities, past and present desires and experiences that he worked out in the tale of rereading the Musketeers.[45]

If 'A Gossip on a Novel of Dumas's' served to demonstrate the significance attached to rereading by Stevenson and enacts a engagement with its theoretical implications, his choice of Dumas and this particular novel was also significant in terms of the emergence of a new literary culture and the position of romance towards the end of the century. While Stevenson was looking back upon an earlier reading self, there were also gestures towards a wider literary past. Nostalgia in the essay operates not just in the association with a literary figure who played a part in Stevenson's youth, but also in the construction of Dumas as an 'excessive' writer, less 'cautious' in his profession than the denizens of Stevenson's literary milieu, belonging to an older and more exciting world: 'Chastity is not near his heart; nor, yet, to his own sore cost, that virtue of frugality which is the armour of the artist.'[46] Dumas was both more 'productive' but also less 'professional' in his profligacy than Stevenson's fellow writers. This contrast between an instinctively prolific, naturally popular creativity and a market-driven pragmatism is, as Stevenson noted, played out in the novel between the characters of Fouquet, the charismatic, generous, yet corrupt, superintendent of finance, and Colbert, his rigidly calculating replacement. (Stevenson's observation on the depiction of Fouquet – 'Dumas saw something of himself and drew the portrait more tenderly' – implicitly suggests a way of reading his own representation of Dumas.) Both Fouquet and Dumas become, in Stevenson's eyes, victims of a new commercial world in which restraint and calculation were imposed upon vitality and creativity. When he wrote to Saintsbury to discuss the inclusion of Dumas in *Masterpieces of Prose Narrative* his tone was of regret: 'For is it not sad to consider that Dumas, the most untranslatable of men, has fallen (except for a small fragment translated by yourself in the *Fortnightly)* into the hands of mere browsing, moonlit, penny-a-lining sheep, and the forlorn "promontory goats" of Grub Street – or café?'[47] Dumas also represented the pleasures of romance which, because of their association with 'popular' taste, had fallen from high literary status. Such fiction, nevertheless, Stevenson argued, related to central needs and desires, recognisable from his own experience as set out a few years earlier in his letter to Henley when he expressed his desire for a romance that no-one would write for him: 'Dumas I have read and re-read too often; Scott, too, and I am short. I want to hear swords clash ... O my sighings after romance, or even Skeltery, and O! the weary age which will produce me neither.'[48] His sense that the 'weary age' had moved beyond fulfilling such desires was articulated more fully in his representation of Dumas.

If romance as a genre appeared to belong increasingly to the past, the language of romance was still in evidence, present even in the context of literary criticism, although here too it was becoming representative of a lost past. Within the literary establishment the decorous tones of Gosse, Besant and Saintsbury, who stressed the gentlemanly obligations of the critic to be fair-minded, were being replaced by a sterner and more calculating code of professionalism and scholarship. Indeed, even John Churton Collins, vehement in his attack on Gosse and what he saw as the dilettantism of the literary establishment, found his critique of Gosse (adopted very much to serve his own ends in arguing for a School of English at Oxford) caught in this shifting terminology within literary criticism codes.[49] Defending himself against the charge of a personal attack on Gosse he claimed that a similarly severe approach to Swinburne was not intended to be read (and indeed was not read) in 'personal' terms: 'I have yet to learn that Mr Swinburne considers me "no gentleman" or complains of "mortal wounds given by an estranged".'[50] Andrew Lang, predictably, extended the application of chivalric imagery in criticism when he deployed it to describe polarities within the contemporary novel: fiction was 'a shield with two sides, the silver and the golden: the study of manners and of character, on one hand; on the other, the description of adventure, the delight of romantic narrative'.[51] The discourse lingers, for in 1915, the critic William L. Phelps reflects how 'when the giant Realism had got the spirit of English fiction safely locked in her dungeon, the young knightly figure of Stevenson arrived to release her'.[52] In critical terminology then chivalric romance becomes an expression of regret for a less professional, more 'human' engagement with literature that Dumas, in his enthusiasm, also represented.

The 'young knightly figure of Stevenson', however, while hailed as the defender of romance, did not see romance in quite the same terms as his contemporaries. It is important, therefore, to distinguish between the ways in which Stevenson discussed romance and how his fellow revivalists talked of it and between his discussions of romance as a reader and his own forays into that genre. Saintsbury perceived a programme of resurrection for the romance evident in Stevenson's writing: with Haggard, 'both writers have deliberately reverted to the simpler instead of the more complicated kind of novel, and have pitched away minute manners-painting and refined character analysis'.[53] Both Saintsbury and Haggard also stressed the universal and organic dimensions of the romance as a form: Saintsbury noted that 'the incidents and the broad and poetic features of character on which the romance relies, are not matters which change at all. They are always the same, with a sameness of nature, not of convention' while Haggard began his essay on romance by asserting that 'the love of romance is probably coeval with the existence of humanity', suggesting that 'it flourishes as strongly in the barbarian as in the cultured breast'.[54] Lang too claimed that 'It is now undeniable that the love of adventure, and of mystery, and of a good fight lingers in the minds of men and women' and was, likewise, keen to stress that 'There is, there can be, no Romantic School. Any clever man or woman may elaborate a realistic novel according to the rules … But Romance bloweth where she listeth.'[55] Nicholas Daly, in his project to reassess the supposed divisions between modernism and romance, picks up on this language of sameness and universality, noting the theorisation of romance as a form of primitivism, 'appealing to a basic appetite for narrative incident'.[56] In the emphasis he gave to the brute incident Stevenson would appear to share this interest in centralising reading experiences. There are, however, some differences: in his theorisation of romance Stevenson presented it as representing a paradigmatic reading experience, but not one that is necessarily 'timeless' or 'primitive': rather it is specifically aligned with boyish response. Moreover, as the essay on Dumas suggested, his response to the form was always shaped by an understanding of the commercial context in which it operated: he saw its more recent and popular incarnations as overdetermined by market pressures so that even Dumas is tainted by the 'Grub Street' effect. Most interestingly, his fascination with Dumas, his taste in other fictions of romance, and his own literary activities in the genre suggest a recognition that chivalric romance, rather than being 'timeless', embodied in its very form an acknowledgement of temporality. The gap between past and present, shifting states of engagement in the reading experience, becomes for Stevenson part of its appeal.[57]

Reviving romance

In his own reading Stevenson was always seeking romance that would fulfil his expectations. In 1886 he was hopeful of George Bernard Shaw's effort in the genre, *Cashel Byron's Profession*:

> It is all mad, mad, and deliriously delightful; the author has a taste in chivalry like Walter Scott's or Dumas's, and then he daubs in little bits of socialism; he soars away on the wings of the romantic griphon – even the gryphon, as he cleaves air, shouting with laughter at the nature of the quest – and I believe in his heart he thinks he is laboring in a quarry of solid granite realism.
>
> It is this that makes me – the most hardened adviser now extant – stand back and hold my peace. If Mr Shaw is below five and twenty, let him go his path; if he is thirty, he had best be told that he is a romantic, and pursue romance with his eyes open; – or perhaps, he knows it; – God knows! – my brain is softened.
>
> It is HORRID FUN.[58]

Shaw, who had much fun in later editions of the novel with the judgement that the book is '1 part Charles Reade: 1 part Henry James or some kindred author, badly assimilated; ½ part Disraeli (perhaps unconscious): 1½ parts struggling, overlaid original talent; 1 part blooming gaseous folly', did not, of course, answer Stevenson's hopes.[59] Nor did a more likely candidate, Arthur Conan Doyle. In 1893, Stevenson responded critically to his most recent novel:

> Have read *The Refugees* ... You have reached a trifle wide perhaps; too *many* celebrities? ... The devil of all that first part is that you see old Dumas; yet your Louis XIV is *distinctly good*. I am much interested with this book, which fulfills a good deal and promises more. Question: How far a Historical Novel should be wholly episodic? I incline to that view, with trembling.[60]

The writer who seemed most successful in satisfying Stevenson's desire for romance in those latter years was the popular and prolific author Stanley J. Weyman. In April 1893, Stevenson wrote to him personally – 'I must write to congratulate you on the first chapter of your new novel in *Longman's*. I never read a better first chapter, and I never want to read a better.'[61] He subsequently praised both *A Gentleman of France* and Weyman's next novel, *Under the Red Robe* (1894):

> Seriously, I have a heavy debt of gratitude to acknowledge. Reading becomes daily a more and more ungrateful task. Of a hundred books that I take up, perhaps not forty are finished, certainly not fifteen are read to an end with the least relish. Of books that I have appreciated this year, novels and otherwise, I can remember only three – Forbes-Mitchell, *Reminiscences*, *La Rôtisserie de la Reine Pédauque* by Anatole France, and *Cicero* by Gaston Boissier. And now I feel that I have a continual promise of pleasure in your writing.[62]

Weyman was also a regular feature on his written requests for books to be sent from home to Samoa.[63]

By the time he was praising Weyman so enthusiastically, Stevenson had moved into an increasingly practical and less romantic approach to his own fiction. In reflections on 'The Beach of Falesá', he acknowledged his own movement away from romance in the direction of realism, although he worried about the commercial implications of this: 'As to whether anyone else will read it, I have no guess.'[64] He expressed similar doubts about the palatability of *The Ebb-Tide*, that 'most grim and gloomy tale',[65] and wrote to his mother: 'I believe you will think it vile; though it does end in a conversion. It is a tale that will make you ready to throw up … Yet I think it has a certain merit too; if the public will accept so gross a business, of which I am doubtful.'[66] Nevertheless by this stage he was relatively nuanced in situating of his own work in terms of the realism/romance opposition and could claim that 'The Beach of Falesá' carried 'the smell and look' of the South Seas without being carried away by romance.[67] Writing to Colvin of the difficulty of the 'love yarn' dimension to *Catriona*, he was also confident enough to joke about it and note: 'with all my romance, I am realist and a prosaist, and a most fanatical lover of plain physical sensations plainly and expressly rendered; hence my perils'.[68] It would appear then that he was not unduly troubled by his own movement into 'realism' or by the demands being made upon him by the romantic revivalists to save the genre.

His acclaim for Stanley Weyman is significant, however, as further evidence of his implicit recognition that romance as a form, while offering a paradigmatic reading experience, is linked with the dynamics between past and present, presence and absence. If Stevenson's essay on

Dumas (prompted by negotiation with his father's decline) was, in both tone and choice of text, engaged with the idea of ageing, so too was Weyman's novel. Although Phelps, who had embraced the figure of the young knight Stevenson, also found in Weyman 'a glorious relief from tiresome party politics and pharisaical reformers in London' in 'the rush for the dark street, the clash of swords, the parry and thrust – we're off!', *A Gentleman of France* carries a more sombre note which echoes that of the *Vicomte de Bragelonne*.[69] Like Dumas it focuses on an ageing hero and, again, by implication, the decline of chivalric codes. The perception of D'Artagnan and, to an extent, his compatriots is that they no longer belong to their times but operate according to an unfashionable chivalric ethic. While Dumas still conveys approval for the qualities exemplified by the Musketeers – 'that which is actually good never alters', says Aramis of Athos – the series drives not only towards the dramatic death of Porthos in the grotto of Locmaria but also that of Athos when he hears of the death of his son, Raoul. Although the past may be associated with a golden age of youth – D'Artagnan says, when reminiscing, 'it was a good time, seeing that it is always a good time when we are young' – the death of Raoul suggests that such values are not to be carried over by the young into the present.[70]

Weyman's novel has a more positive conclusion than *The Man in the Iron Mask* but even more explicitly takes outmoded heroism as its focus. The Sieur de Marsac, narrator and central character in the novel's adventures, is, at its opening, a ragged figure, without horses or fine clothes, just turned forty, poverty-stricken and mocked at court. This unlikely figure is then rehabilitated into a chivalric role through a series of adventures, often winning through chance rather than stratagem, but nevertheless regaining his position, fortune and love of a fair lady by the novel's conclusion. Yet his own sense of representing antiquated codes (even in the setting of France in the 1580s) finds echoes in other characters in the novel. The King of Navarre, for example, is equally nostalgic about his own opportunities for adventure:

> I swear to God, I would I were in your shoes, sir. To strike a blow or two with no care of it. To take to the road with a good horse, and a good sword and see what fortune would send. To be rid of all this statecraft and protocolling, and never to issue another declaration in the world, but just to be for once A Gentleman of France, with all to win and nothing to lose save the love of my lady.[71]

By this point in the 1890s there is therefore explicit recognition that the conventions of chivalric romance, handled with ease and apparent conviction earlier in the century – in Scott's *Ivanhoe*, for example, in which there is no ironic questioning of the role – can no longer be accepted. In his novel Weyman, like Stevenson, acknowledged – and attempted to fulfil – the desire for that genre but the elegiac nature of the novel's plot problematises the context of such reading desires while simultaneously appearing to assuage them.

Writing romance

In his own fiction, Stevenson had adhered more closely to the conventions of the genre, although it also emerged as increasingly under stress in his writing. *Kidnapped* (1886) permitted its swashbuckler, Alan Breck, to be contained by the cautious and doubting figure of David Balfour, wryly questioning the veracity of his tales: 'much as I admired his courage, I was always in danger of smiling at his vanity'.[72] But David's safe arrival 'into port', at 'the very doors of the British Linen Company's Bank', is also accompanied by Alan's departure to 'keep to the country'. The novel, moreover, allowed adventures aplenty when the heroes 'take to the road'. The generic ambivalence present emerges therefore only at the boundaries of the text. *Catriona* (1893), in its testing of the association of masculinity and heroism, adopts a more challenging approach to the genre. In his dedication to Charles Baxter, Stevenson explicitly located the novel as occupying that space between their idealistic youth and his present perspective; the book might, he hopes, still appeal to 'some long-legged, hot-headed youth' who will 'repeat today our dreams and wanderings of so many years ago'.[73] Much of the rhetoric of chivalric action in the novel belongs to the ageing and venial James More, father of the heroine Catriona, ever-ready with talk of fellow soldiers and brave deeds, but all too happy to shift allegiance when needed: 'I would harken to his swaggering talk (of arms, and "an old soldier", and "a poor Highland gentleman", and "the strength of my country and my friends") as I might to the babblings of a parrot.'[74] The absurdity of 'parrot' discourse is further reinforced by one of David Balfour's greatest triumphs in the novel when he stands stock still and allows the young Highland buck who challenges him, to spin the sword out of his hands three times, causing the latter's extreme bewilderment and eventual acceptance of a new definition of bravery: '"Pe tamned if I touch you!" he cried, and asked me bitterly what right I had to stand up before "shentlemans" when I did not know the back of a sword from the front of it … "But to stand up there – and you ken naething of the fence! – the way that you did, I declare it was peyond me."'[75] And while there are romantic elements to the adventures of David and Catriona, failure to save the wrongly accused James of the Glens produces a weary resignation in David:

Innocent men have perished before James, and are like to keep on perishing (in spite of all our wisdom) till the end of time. And till the end of time young folk (who are not yet used with the duplicity of life and men) will struggle as I did, and make heroical resolves, and take long risks; and the course of events will push them upon the one side and go on like a marching army.[76]

In the meantime, Alan Breck, who ignited the action in *Kidnapped*, spends a considerable part of the novel in hiding, making up songs about the deer, the heather and ancient chiefs, but with no one to hear or to see his skills at knucklebones: as he complains 'it's a poor piece of business playing with naebody to admire ye'.[77] The audience for romance seems to have disappeared.

In Stevenson's oeuvre *Weir of Hermiston* was still to come, with a return to a very different kind of romance, the wildness of Scotland's austere ballads, but as he worked on *Weir*, Stevenson also engaged with another serious reconstruction of historical romance.[78] His perceptions of *St Ives* indicated more turbulence and doubt than his excursions into realism. This unfinished work was dictated to Belle Strong in 1893 and 1894, and is narrated by a French prisoner imprisoned in Edinburgh Castle. Once again Stevenson's research on the topic was so prodigious as to become inhibiting.[79] In terms of the form, however, he appeared to grow increasingly uneasy: in January 1892 he reconciled himself to it when writing to Colvin by drawing on the wise words of his own fictional creation: 'It is *merely* a story of adventure, rambling along; but that is perhaps the guard that "sets my genius best", as Alan might have said.'[80] By the following year he is slightly less positive: 'St Ives is unintellectual, and except as an adventure novel, dull. But the adventures seem to me sound and pretty probable.'[81] But in a letter to Bob in June 1894 he is defiant but critical: 'the present book Saint Ives, is nothing – it is in no style, in particular, a tissue of adventures, the central character not very well done, no philosophic pith under the year, and in short, if people will read it, that's all I ask – and if they won't, damn them! I like doing it though; and if you asked me why!'[82] A couple of months later he is in such despair that Colvin thought it might have been best to 'let it slide': 'I'm as sick of the dammed thing as ever anyone can be; it's a rudderless hulk, it's a pagoda, and you can just feel – or I can feel – that it might have been a pleasant story, it had been only blessed at baptism.'[83] The novel was never finished by Stevenson, but completed instead, with some accuracy of tone, by Arthur Quiller-Couch.[84]

The novel, with its combination of aristocratic adventuring and picaresque, moving uneasily in location between Scotland, England and France, was recognised as an oddity on publication in 1897. As one critic, describing the plot as a 'panorama of improbabilities', noted, 'this book bears the mark of a fagged mind on almost every page of it. It is largely reminiscent of other works of the same writer ... while he was occupied in writing "St Ives" his mind had lost its power of fresh combination.'[85] *St Ives*, however, can be read also as a product of Stevenson's sense of romance as a form which is in itself imbued with a recognition of the past. Shaped by the clash of adventuring ideals and political realities, so accurately represented in *Bragelonne*, the form becomes explicitly attuned to nostalgia, mimetic of its author's recognition that loss, experienced in leaving the world of fiction, is also paradigmatic of both the genre and the reading experience.

While *St Ives* adheres to the basic romance format – imprisoned soldier of lost aristocratic origins, who falls in love, escapes and encounters a series of adventures, unusual travelling companions and incidents en route – the first-person narrative permits some elements of self-mockery. The central adventurer, St Ives, jests about his ability to make large romantic gestures which cost him dear and at times even explicitly acknowledges the ridiculous aspects of the genre: describing the adventures of the runaway couple he notes: 'the whole business had been such a "hurrah-boys" from the beginning, and had gone off in the fifth act so like a melodrama'.[86] The purchase, when in flight from his enemies, of a large claret-coloured chaise as a means of concealment also becomes the subject of mockery as another misplaced grand gesture, and in discussions with a innkeeper who might buy it, he alludes to Ann Radcliffe's 1791 archetype of the genre by describing their story as 'having too much of the Romance of the Forest about it'.[87] Even the caricature Edinburgh landlady, Mrs McRankine, is permitted to describe herself in her youth in terms of a mock romantic heroine: '"I mind I had a green gown, passementit, that was thocht to become me to admiration. I was nae just exactly what ye would ca' bonny; but I was pale, penetratin', and interestin'."'[88] The interplay between youth and age, past heroism and present reality, also underpins the novel's concerns: St Ives is amused by the boy, Rowley's, admiration for him:

> There came to me from my own boyhood memories of certain passionate admirations long passed away, and the objects of them long discredited or dead. I remembered how anxious I had been to serve those fleeting heroes, how readily I told myself I would have died for *them*, how much greater and handsomer than life they had appeared. And looking in the mirror, it seemed to me that I read the face of Rowley, like an echo or a ghost, by the light of my own youth.[89]

Ghosts walk in this novel, as they do in the *Vicomte de Bragelonne*. Rowley may look with admiration on St Ives, who consistently identifies himself as more mature than the young bloods he encounters (including the members of the university of Cramond who in their absurd boyish enthusiasms and riotous behaviour clearly refer back to Stevenson's own youth), but St Ives gazes with fear upon the face of maturity revealed in the cynicism of his dying uncle. The warning St Ives is given by the Edinburgh lawyer, Mr Robbie, coming towards the close of his adventuring, also suggests that it has a limited timespan: 'take up with no more drovers, or rovers, or tinkers, but enjoy the naitural pleesures for which your age, your wealth, your intelligence, and … your appearance so completely fit you'.[90] Although the villain of the novel, the Viscount St Yves, is never fully realised as a character, he is depicted in terms which simultaneously follow the conventions of the form, acknowledge their ridiculous elements and mourn their passing. Mocked from the first by St Ives as an exaggerated figure – 'of a pictorial, exuberant style of beauty, all attitude, profile and impudence; a man whom I could see in fancy parade'[91] – the Viscount is also scorned by the English lawyer, Romaine: all the Viscount has gathered over the years is 'a prodigious accumulation of trash – stays, I dare say, and power puffs, and such effeminate idiocy'.[92] Romaine, however, also expresses a sympathetic reluctance to see him destroyed, 'to break anything so big and figurative, as though he were a big porcelain pot or a big picture of high price'.[93] Within the novel there is a sense that its author recognises the limitations of, but also regrets breaking, those fictional forms that belong to the past but are still impressively 'big and figurative'.

The romance form at the end of the nineteenth century has been critically understood as gratifying certain desires of the time: 'the special quality of romance which satisfied the needs of late-Victorian society, we may conclude, was its simple avowal of an existence of absolute truths which could pacify a large number of potentially disaffected people'.[94] Alternatively, it has been viewed as a form which allowed the negotiations of social change: it 'provided the narratives and figures that enabled late Victorian middle-class culture to successfully accommodate certain historical changes, notably modernising processes'.[95] Certainly much of the fiction that was produced would appear to serve this purpose, appealing to a wider readership. Arguing that romance writing in the last years of the nineteenth century should not be understood as 'popular' culture in terms of production associated with subordinated people in their own interest out of resources that also, contradictorily, serve the economic interests of the dominant class, but rather as a 'popular dominant culture' which is not representative of 'high' or 'official' culture', Nicholas Daly notes of writers such as Stoker, Haggard and Du Maurier that 'The work that they produced would have been read by a broad section of the middle class, but it would probably have been thought of as "light" literature rather than as anything more demanding or rewarding (the reception of R. L. Stevenson may be seen as a partial exception in this respect.)'.[96] Daly's identification of Stevenson as offering readers something slightly more complicated in his fiction might also be extended to his understanding of romance itself. As critics have argued Stevenson's critical and popular success not only situates him in a different position from other writers of masculine romance at the time but also forms the basis for an interrogation of existing literary mappings of the relationships between modernism, popular fiction, aestheticism and the marketplace.[97] His deployment of this popular genre also, however, demands a reassessment of the dynamics of the romance-reading experience itself.

Stevenson's enthusiasm for romance in his reading and his productions within this genre could be read in terms of that pattern of arrested development which has been so powerfully used to situate him within particular critical contexts, especially if romance is viewed as a form popular with the young because it provides the familiarity of repetition and the comfort of order emerging from chaos.[98] In his understanding of romance – or the best of that form as it appears in a writer like Dumas – Stevenson, however, acknowledged that fulfilment of the desiring self was contextualised by the transience of reading: the experience can be intense in its immediacy, but is also always moving towards the loss of that intensity when we emerge out of the book at the point of closure. Romance might fulfil a desire for order but also sharpens, by its very temporality, our sense of disorder. Reading romance thus epitomises the dynamics of reading pleasure which are both intense and reassuring but also inevitably transient.

Stevenson's interest in romance, as manifested in his essay on Dumas, thus becomes on one level an acknowledgement of loss of childhood, an explicitly expressed regret for the past, and for past readings in which the reader's trust and engagement is immediate and unmediated. In that sense there may indeed be a desire to 'suspend' development, maturation, social responsibility in his embrace of the genre. On another level, however, his essay works with a recognition that the purity of the romance genre is always inherently limited. Stevenson's choice of the final Musketeers adventures for his favourite site of rereading makes explicit the temporal intersections of past and present within the genre, more finely poised in that romance that in his own, overly determined wake for the form in *St Ives*. At the same time as it examines the temporalities of the reading process, configured around that estranging moment when the reader looks up and away from the book and into the dark night, the essay confronts the elegiac nature of that most transformative model of reading. If the reader always lurks as the writer's ghost when Stevenson writes Dumas, romance, as he saw it, was also haunted by its own inevitable bereavements.

Notes

1 Stevenson, 'A Gossip on a Novel of Dumas's', *Memories and Portraits*, Tusitala XXIX, p. 112.

2 M. Calinescu, *Rereading* (New Haven and London: Yale University Press, 1993), pp. xi–xii.

3 Written in the spring of 1887 and included in *Memories and Portraits*, November 1887.

4 A version of the early parts of this chapter appeared in *Journal of Stevenson Studies*, 1 (2004), 60–75.

5 Calinescu, *Rereading*, pp. xi–xii; R. Ingarden, *The Cognition of the Literary Work of Art* (Evanston, IL: Northwestern University Press, 1973), p. 145.

6 'nothing says that this same text will please us a second time; it is a friable pleasure, split by mood, habit, circumstance, a precarious pleasure (obtained by a silent prayer addressed to the Desire for ease, and which that Desire can revoke.' Barthes, *The Pleasure of the Text*, p. 52.

7 'Books Which Have Influenced Me', Tusitala XXVIII, pp. 62–8, p. 64.

8 Calinescu, *Rereading*, p. 99.

9 Ricoeur, *Hermeneutics and the Human Sciences*, p. 146. Gadamer writes: 'In interpreting, the questions a text puts to us can be understood only when the text, conversely, is understood as an answer to a question.' *Truth and Method*, trans. J. Weinsheimer and D. G. Marshall; second, revised edition (London: Continuum 1975; 1989; 2004), p. 578.

10 Bachelard, *The Poetics of Space*, p. xxvi.

11 *Ibid*.

12 'A Gossip on a Novel of Dumas's', p. 114.

13 Written between autumn 1885 and summer 1887, his tribute to Jenkin was published as *A Memoir of Fleeming Jenkin* in January 1888. It is difficult to date the essay on Dumas. Swearingen suggests spring or early summer of 1887. There is no mention of it in the list of essays originally to be included in *Memories and Portraits*, although it appears on a second list submitted after 28 July. The collection was published on 21 November 1887. See A. Nash, 'Two Unpublished Letters of Robert Louis Stevenson', *Notes and Queries*, 245:3 (2000), 334–6. Furnas comments: 'That was a foul winter of 1886–7. Jenkin had died in June 1885, but work on the *Memoir* kept death in Louis's mind. Thomas Stevenson's condition was flagrantly worsening.' *Voyage to Windward*, p. 259. Stevenson's father died in May 1887.

14 ? June/84, *Letters*, vol. 4, p. 307.

15 See *Letters*, vol. 5: Letters 1524, 1539, 1544, 1545, 1546.

16 2/2/86, *Letters*, vol. 5, pp. 193–4, referring to an article by Saintsbury, 'Alexandre Dumas', *Fortnightly Review*, 1 October 1878, 527–42. Henley

had also written an article describing Dumas as a 'master of modern art' in the *Saturday Review*, 56:1463 (10 November 1883), 594–5.

17 H. James, 'Robert Louis Stevenson', *Century Magazine*, 35 (April 1888), 869–79, p. 877. Written in 1887 and shown to Stevenson in the autumn.

18 Saintsbury, *Fortnightly Review*, p. 531.

19 *Ibid.*

20 Henley, *Saturday Review*, p. 594; Saintsbury, 'The Historical Novel, Scott and Dumas' in *Essays in English Literature 1780–1860*, second series (London: J. M. Dent and Co., 1895), p. 352.

21 Alexandre Dumas, *The Three Musketeers*; *Twenty Years After*; *Vicomte de Bragelonne*; *Louise de la Vallière*; *The Man in the Iron Mask* (World Classics edition, ed. David Coward, following 1857 Routledge English translations) (Oxford: Oxford University Press, 1991–5).

22 De Certeau, *The Practice of Everyday Life*, p. xxi

23 'A Gossip on a Novel of Dumas's', p. 113.

24 'My acquaintance with the *Vicomte* began, somewhat indirectly, in the year of grace 1863, when I had the advantage of studying certain illustrated dessert plates in a hotel at Nice' (p. 111). The association of French literature with pleasure might also be read into his dislike of Zola and (continuing culinary metaphors), 'the rancid' school of realism: 'To afford a popular flavour and attract the mob, he adds a steady currrent of what I may be allowed to call the rancid', 'A Note on Realism', p. 70.

25 C. M. Yonge, *The Young Stepmother* (1857–60), chapter IV.

26 Of course, as Saintsbury notes, Dumas himself was disparaged in terms which identified him as 'other'. 'I find that under the title of Dumas that "his crisp hair and thick lips bear testimony to his African origin, a testimony confirmed by the savage voluptuousness and barbaric taste of his innumerable compositions." 'Alexandre Dumas', p. 527.

27 November/66 to Bob Stevenson, *Letters*, vol. 1, p. 112.

28 'A Gossip on a Novel of Dumas's', p. 117.

29 *Ibid.*, pp. 112–13.

30 E. Goffman, *Frame Analysis: An Essay on the Organisation of Experience* (Harmondsworth: Penguin, 1975), p. 346. See also William James on *Ivanhoe*: W. James, *Principles of Psychology*, vol. 2 (New York: Dover, 1950), pp. 292–3.

31 W. Iser, *The Act of Reading, a Theory of Aesthetic Response* (London: Routledge and Kegan Paul, 1987), pp. 131–2.

32 *Ibid.*, p. 132, quoting J. Dewey, *Art as Experience* (New York: Capricorn Books, 1959), p. 60).

33 *Ibid.*, p. 134.

34 'A Gossip on a Novel of Dumas's', p. 112.

35 *Ibid.*, p. 112.

36 See M. Riffaterre, 'Describing Poetic Structures: Two Approaches to Baudelaire's "Les Chats"', in J. P. Tompkins (ed.), *Reader-Response Criticism: From Formalism to Post-Structuralism* (Baltimore and London: Johns Hopkins University Press, 1980), pp. 26–40.

37 'A Gossip on a Novel of Dumas's', p. 112.

38 *Ibid.*, p. 118.

39 Ricoeur, *Hermeneutics and the Human Sciences*, p. 147; Manguel, *A History of Reading*, p. 179.

40 'A Gossip on a Novel of Dumas's', p. 115.

41 *Ibid.*, p. 112.

42 *Ibid.*, p. 111.

43 This I think is a term of endearment, and not simply a distinction of 'Dumas père'.

44 'A Gossip on a Novel of Dumas's', p. 118.

45 Farr also identifies that characteristic nostalgia in Stevenson's essays, understanding it in terms of a suspension within the development into adult masculinity. 'Surpassing the Love of Women'.

46 'A Gossip on a Novel of Dumas's', p. 116.

47 2/2/86, *Letters*, vol. 5, pp. 193–4.

48 ? June/84, *Letters*, vol. 4, p. 307.

49 See Palmer, *The Rise of English Studies*, p. 90.

50 See running debate in *Athenaeum*, November 1886.

51 A. Lang, 'Realism and Romance', *Contemporary Review*, 52 (November 1887), 683–93, p. 684.

52 W. L. Phelps, *The Advance of the English Novel* (London: John Murray 1919), p. 135, cited in N. Daly, *Modernism, Romance and the Fin de Siècle: Popular Fiction and British Culture 1880–1914* (Cambridge: Cambridge University Press, 1999), p. 17.

53 'The Present State of the Novel I' *Fortnightly Review*, 42 (1887), 410–17, p. 415.

54 *Ibid.*, pp. 415–16; H. Rider Haggard, 'About Fiction', *Contemporary Review*, 51 (February, 1887), 172–80, p. 172.

55 Lang, 'Realism and Romance', p. 692; p. 691.

56 Daly, *Modernism, Romance and the Fin de Siècle*, p. 24.

57 Daly also argues that the term 'romantic revival' is in several respects a misnomer, and in some respects was in fact a 'distinctively modern phenomenon'. *Ibid.*, p. 9.

58 c. 9/3/86 to William Archer, *Letters*, vol. 5, pp. 225.

59 G. B. Shaw, *Cashel Bryon's Profession* (1886), first published with Shaw's Preface 1901; rev. edition (London: Constable and Co. Ltd., 1932).

60 23/8/93 to Arthur Conan Doyle, *Letters*, vol. 8, p. 155. *The Refugee: A Tale of Two Continents* (Leipzig: Bernard Tauchnitz, 1893).

61 5/4/93 to Stanley J. Weyman, *Letters*, vol. 8, p. 49. *A Gentleman of France* was serialised between January and December 1893. *Under the Red Robe* (Leipzig: Bernard Tauchnitz, 1894).

62 7/7/94 to Stanley J. Weyman, *Letters*, vol. 8, pp. 315–16.

63 14/8/93: requests S. J. Weyman, *The New Rector* (Leipzig: Heinemann and Balesteir, 1891); 18/5/94 requests S. J. Weyman, *Under the Red Robe*; 6/11/94 requests S. J. Weyman, *My Lady Rotha: A Romance* (Leipzig: Bernard Tauchnitz, 1894).

64 28/9/91 to Colvin, *Letters,* vol. 7, p. 161.

65 17/2/93 to Baxter, *Letters,* vol. 8, p. 29.

66 21/5/93, *Letters,* vol. 8, p. 79.

67 'It is the first realistic South Sea story; I mean with real South Sea character and details of life; everybody else who has tried, that I have seen, got carried away by the romance and ended in a kind of sugar candy sham epic, and the whole effect was lost ... Now I have got the smell and look of the thing a good deal. You will know more about the South Seas after you have read my little tale, than if you had read a library.' 28/9/91 to Colvin, *Letters,* vol. 7, p. 161.

68 18/5/92, *Letters,* vol. 7, p. 284.

69 S. J. Weyman, *A Gentleman of France: being the memoirs of Gaston de Bonne, Sieur de Marsac* (London: Longman's, 1894).

70 Coward (ed.), *The Man in the Iron Mask,* p. 3; p. 569.

71 Weyman, *A Gentleman of France,* p. 23.

72 *Kidnapped,* Tusitala VI, p. 70.

73 *Catriona,* Tusitala VII, p. xix

74 *Ibid.,* pp. 247–8. For a different aspect of 'parrot' discourse in relation to *Treasure Island,* see Sandison, *Robert Louis Stevenson and the Appearance of Modernism,* chapter 2.

75 *Catriona,* originally entitled *David Balfour.* Serialised *Atalanta,* December 1892 to September 1893. Published as *Catriona: A Sequel to 'Kidapped' Being Memories of the Further Adventures of David Balfour at Home and Abroad* (1893); Tusitala VII, pp. 70–1.

76 *Ibid.,* p. 187.

77 *Ibid.,* p. 101.

78 '*St. Ives* was written entirely to dictation; not continuously but at intervals, in conjunction with *Hermiston.* My husband would work on one book until he was tired or his mood changed, when he would take up the other.' Prefatory Note by Mrs R. L. Stevenson, *St Ives being the Adventures of a French prisoner in England,* Tusitala XV, p. xi.

79 24/4/94 to Colvin, *Letters,* vol. 8, p. 279. See also *Letters,* vol. 8, p. 20 requesting books on fashion and manners 1810–20 and especially 1814 – the setting for both *St Ives* and *Hermiston.*

80 Dec./Jan./92, *Letters,* vol. 7, p. 465.

81 Sept./93 to Colvin, *Letters,* vol. 8, p. 157.

82 17/6/94, *Letters,* vol. 8, p. 306.

83 8/9/94, *Letters,* vol. 8, p. 357.

84 'St Ives: The Adventures of a French Prisoner in England', serialised *Pall Mall Magazine,* November 1896 to November 1897; chapters 31–6 by Sir Arthur T. Quiller-Couch. See Swearingen, *Prose Writings of Robert Louis Stevenson,* pp. 181–3.

85 J. Jacobs, Unsigned review, *Atheneum,* 3651 (16 October 1897), 518–19, reprinted in Maxiner, *Critical Heritage,* pp. 485–6.

86 *St Ives,* Tusitala XV, p. 217.

87 *Ibid.,* p. 222.

88 *Ibid.*, p. 258.
89 *Ibid.*, pp. 149–50.
90 *Ibid.*, p. 257.
91 *Ibid.*, pp. 171–2.
92 *Ibid.*, p. 184.
93 *Ibid.*, p. 166.
94 W. R. Katz, *Rider Haggard and the Fiction of Empire: A Critical Study of British Imperial Fiction* (Cambridge: Cambridge University Press, 1987), p. 32.
95 N. Daly, *Modernism, Romance and the Fin de Siècle*, p. 24.
96 *Ibid.*, p. 6.
97 See Ambrosini and Farr.
98 In theorising the young reader's engagement with romance Appleyard suggests that a main reward in reading fictional stories at a young age is satisfying the need to imagine oneself as the figure who can take centre stage and solve the problems of a chaotic world. *Becoming a Reader*, pp. 59–60.

7

Trading texts: Stevenson and the popular

> What were these villains after but money? What do they care for but
> money? For what would they risk their rascal carcases but money?[1]

The story of *Treasure Island's* creation is well known: on holiday in
Braemar in 1881, closeted with his stepson Lloyd Osbourne in a period
of bad weather, Stevenson produced a treasure map at Lloyd's request,
then began a yarn to accompany it. While he was reading the tale to the
boy and to his own father, the household received a visitor, Dr Japp,
who listened to the story and was so impressed that he carried away the
manuscript and passed it on to his friend Mr Henderson, the editor of
Young Folks.[2] In *Young Folks* it was subsequently published.[3]

In 1900, six years after Stevenson's death, a curious spat took place
in the pages of *The Academy*. Stevenson's friend (and the inspiration,
in both his disability and his force of character, for Long John Silver)
W. E. Henley, wrote an article for the *North American Review*, later
reported in *The Academy*, which suggested that the 'gold' of *Treasure
Island* was not fully appreciated by its readers, so much as it was recognised by other writers who realised its value and had therefore made it
'currency' by debasing it through imitation in their own popular fictions.[4]
The tale, when first published, was not a great commercial success, but
other writers recognised its worth and – through their imitations – a
wider public learned to become more responsive to Stevenson's novel.
The reading public, Henley suggested, might be compared to a set of
Japanese boxes: 'one inside the other, the larger containing the lesser
throughout the series', and this is why 'a good writer ... is very often
felt to some extent a great way outside the limits of the particular public
which happens to be his'.[5] Musing upon his own particular example of
this phenomenon, the publication of *Treasure Island*, Henley speculated
about the fate of the *Young Folks* editor, James Henderson, whom he
believed might be dead.

The Academy's plea for information on this subject elicited a response
the following week from Robert Leighton, an editor of *Young Folks*

in 1885, who confirmed Henley's point that *Treasure Island* was not a great commercial success, (less so, in fact, than *The Black Arrow*), helpfully noted that James Henderson *was* still alive, but then complicated the narrative by adding the detail that Mr Henderson (introduced to Stevenson by their mutual friend Dr Japp) 'offered to take a story from the young Scotsman, and, as indicating the kind of story he desired for *Young Folks*, he gave to Stevenson copies of the paper containing a serial by Charles E. Pearce – a treasure-hunting story entitled *Billy Bo's'n*'.[6] Leighton continues: 'In his "My First Book" article in *The Idler*, Stevenson seems to suggest that "Treasure Island" was already formed and planned in his mind prior to the time at which it was thought of as a serial for *Young Folks*; but there is evidence that in *Billy Bo's'n* he found and adopted many suggestions and incidents for his own narrative.' Leighton's version of events, suggesting that Stevenson was inspired by a 'popular' story, quite reversed Henley's reading of *Treasure Island* as encouraging weaker imitators who then educated public taste into an appreciation of a novel which Henley sees as properly belonging to the realm of art. Leighton's account, by contrast, suggested that the 'gold' of *Treasure Island* emerged from a debased 'currency'.

His assertion provoked an immediate response. Firstly, and perhaps predictably, Stevenson's friend and (initially) his official biographer, Sidney Colvin, wrote to the journal protesting against this version of events and enclosing an account by Dr Japp, 'in his own words', of the production of *Treasure Island* which confirmed Stevenson's version and argued that '*Treasure Island* was written absolutely for the sake of writing it, and in conformity with the ideas suggested by the map which R.L.S. had elaborately drawn and coloured ... so that the statement that he found and adopted many incidents from *Billy Bo's'n* is thus wholly met and disposed of'.[7] The main thrust in Japp's account of the process of placing *Treasure Island* with *Young Folks* was to stress the importance of his personal connection and friendship with both Stevenson and Henderson, in direct contrast to the emphasis on the commercial context, and hierarchies of editors and writers which emerged from Leighton's letter. He also stressed Stevenson's 'originality' in contrast to Leighton's depiction of Stevenson as an apprentice who was not only guided by Henderson but needed to be shown the dubious literary merits of *Billy Bo's'n* as a model.

Leighton's intervention was followed a week later by a letter from James Henderson, supporting Japp and endorsing his statement that Henderson's first meeting with Stevenson took place after the proofs had been corrected.[8] The voice of the (clearly living and therefore suitably authenticated) Henderson appears to have put an end to the dispute and the demon raised by Leighton was safely put back within its own set of Japanese boxes.

The speed and vehemence with which Leighton's suggestion was disposed of suggests that this whole contretemps raised difficult questions about relationships between popular fiction and original art, between the commercial and the pleasurable dimension of literature, between writing as a 'trade' and writing as an act of creative inspiration. Moreover, the alacrity with which Stevenson's friends sprung to his defence after his death demonstrates their own awareness that he occupied a particularly precarious position in relation to such issues. Yet, as was often the case, with Stevenson's defenders, they also underestimated his own complicated and complicating role within these debates. As earlier chapters of this book demonstrate, Stevenson had anxieties of his own to resolve about public admiration and 'the popular', both in terms of his own position as a writer and in his role as reader. The powerful image of writer as prostitute functioned as a trope through which he could play out those elements of transgression and debasement associated on the one hand with the consuming desires fulfilled by fiction and on the other with the guilty pleasures of pandering to public taste. While the paradigmatic model of the child reader could, as we have seen, go some way towards theorising Stevenson's own position on the pleasures of reading and indeed help resolve aesthetic tensions in the realism/romance debate, it offered little purchase on specific anxieties about the trade in desires with which a successful author must engage. In many of his letters and essays Stevenson addressed the question of 'writing as a trade': what impact does the need to earn a living through his craft have on a writer's work; what distinguishes serious artistic endeavour from popular fiction aimed at the commercial market; how might the circulation of a text through that market affect its status?[9] Stevenson's questions around authenticity and seriousness were highly representative of his time with its concerns over the increasing professionalisation of the author and the resultant reconfiguration of aesthetics, but also particular and personal in their subtle negotiations of such tensions. This chapter examines Stevenson's literary manoeuvres in relation to this tricky business of producing texts for public consumption. It begins with a paratextual exploration of *Treasure Island*, showing how Stevenson as author 'traded' texts to establish his own literary authority and to allay his own anxieties about his profession, before moving into a discussion of his late (and to many minds unsuccessful) novel *The Wrecker*, co-written with Lloyd Osbourne, as a revealing intervention into debates on the nature of artistic production.

Valuing the popular

The post-publication spat over *Treasure Island* is indicative of contemporaneous concerns over the 'popular'. In his image of 'gold', namely, artistic quality, passing unrecognised until it was transformed into copper, thus turned into 'currency' and debased through imitation, Henley established a dichotomy between 'art', expressed in familiar terms of purity of form and originality of content, and the 'trade', the economic exchange, of writing. The subsequent argument in *The Academy* over *Billy Bo's'n* reveals how much was at stake here, how much was invested in the need to prove Stevenson was not influenced by a popular text: that his work was original. Stevenson, moreover, had to be kept separate from the commercial processes of publication which function within a recognisable economy of exchange and imitation, an economy which legitimises both mass production and plagiarism. The debate operated within the classic demarcations of high and low by which art is defined: Henley's metaphor of coinage allowed him to work with a recognisable polarisation of the authentically unique (the gold) and the inauthentically repetitive (the copper currency) as normative categories in the separation of high and low culture. The contribution by Stevenson's other defenders, which proved that Stevenson produced the novel in an 'unfettered' context, for his own pleasure rather than with any eye to a commercial market, likewise drew upon the same binaries. As Frow notes of contemporary popular culture: 'the terms in which the emancipation and universalisation of the category of art come to be cast are those of a distinction between works founded in freedom and internal necessity, on the one hand, and in unfreedom and external economic necessity on the other'.[10] In the fight over the source of *Treasure Island*, such oppositions are specifically translated into the changing literary commercial context of the time, played out as defence of the creative processes which differentiate high art as the work of an inspired individual from the commercial production of made-to-measure fictions in a context of shared responsibilities and contributions.

Revealing as the arguments about *Treasure Island* after the author's death are, Stevenson's own manoeuvrings around the opposition of originality and imitation during his lifetime are equally significant.[11] Apart from the abhorrence which met the suggestion that *Billy Bo's'n* may have been an influence on *Treasure Island*, what is most striking about the correspondence in *The Academy* is the way in which Stevenson's essay 'My First Book' was invoked as a source of authority.[12] This compelling narrative, first published in *The Idler* and written a considerable time after the creation of *Treasure Island*, has been subsequently questioned in its details, but, taken as a piece of writing rather than an authentication of sources, this essay demonstrates Stevenson's own ambivalent and ambiguous take on this business of popularity and originality.[13]

In his account of the creation of *Treasure Island* Stevenson can be seen as working within two very different aesthetic modes, two different regimes of value.[14] In his narrative he created a romantic picture of coming to Pitlochry 'in the fated year', transferring to Braemar on health grounds, sharing his cottage with a schoolboy home from the holidays; 'And now admire the finger of predestination ...' he dramatically admonished: the map was duly drawn, the story famously begun, 'on a chill September morning'. Chance dictated the course of events; inspiration was inevitable and almost beyond his control. This is the version Japp and Colvin embraced; this is the part of the essay they recalled. It is from this point in the essay, however, that the retrospective and analytic nature of Stevenson's narrative takes over: he cannot remember, he wrote, having sat down to write a story with more complacency but, in looking back, he had to embark upon 'a painful chapter' for 'stolen waters are proverbially sweet'. There follows a confession of his dismay at later discovering the sources that had influenced him in his apparently spontaneous writing of the tale: some were fairly minor – the parrot taken from *Robinson Crusoe*, the stockade from *Masterman Ready*. Others were more painful to discover: rereading Washington Irving's *Tales of a Traveller* he recognised the source material for the character of Billy Bones. Yet, although he goes on to itemise traces of Johnson's *Buccaneers*, Poe, Defoe and Kingsley's *At Last*, at the time of writing, he informs the reader, ownership was assured: 'it seemed to belong to me like my right eye'.[15] The essay, therefore, while acknowledging possible sources of plagiarism, and repetition of published material, also made claims for the apparent originality and innocence of the writer. *Treasure Island* is still, he suggested, different from these sources and arose from individual inspiration: the 'cultural value' of the novel was indeed being calculated in terms of opposition to other texts, set apart by its breaking of expectations, by the way it complicated rather than simplified. In other words it was being defined by the familiar strategies deployed to separate high culture from the popular. Yet, simultaneously, Stevenson provided an alternative reading, one which securely located the text in a pattern of familiarity and repetition, the very source of 'popular' pleasures: his narrative demonstrated how well known the elements of his own yarn were. *Treasure Island* in Stevenson's own account was thus categorised not only as dependent upon a range of other well-known tales, and therefore firmly within an identifiably popular genre, but also as distinctive and 'original'. The originality, moreover, is brought to the fore not only by the narrative of inspirational processes and innocent plagiarism but also through the meta-perspective revealed in the author's ability to review his own influences. This latter element fixed him in a 'high' literary context, while also claiming his familiarity with the 'low' of his sources. While Stevenson with this double-voiced discourse may seem, therefore, to situate his text within two different regimes of value, a hierarchy is clearly operating in which the inevitability of his 'high' cultural instincts are asserted, while his 'low' cultural sources are contained and their influence (while acknowledged) is diffused through the process of sophisticated identification.

'Popular Authors'

Not that the sources acknowledged in *The Idler* essay were really that 'low'; much lower, of course, were the other tales of piracy and adventure upon the high seas which Stevenson would have had access to through *Cassell's Family Paper* and in the works of certain other 'Popular Authors' whom he discussed in his 1888 essay of that name.[16] Although these authors were not mentioned in his reflection on the creation of *Treasure Island*, they too are implicated in a process of exchange, if the essay 'Popular Authors' is read in conjunction with *Treasure Island*.

Written while he was trapped in the wilderness of Saranac Lake in the Adirondacks over the autumn, winter and spring of 1887–88, 'Popular Authors' was part of the series of essays commissioned by *Scribner's Magazine*. Although produced through economic necessity, the writing of 'Popular Authors' gave Stevenson a range of pleasures, as it became both a process of recollection and a reconstruction of his childhood reading. Calling from his isolation for books half-remembered from his youth, he could, through the heroic efforts of Edward Burlinghame, Scribner's editor, to procure his reading lists, re-enact the pleasures of immersion in those tales that had thrilled him as a boy. Deliberately capitalising the names of now obscure populists, so that their fame might be rewarded – 'In this paper I propose to put the authors' names in capital letters; the most of them have not much hope of durable renown; their day is past, the poor dogs – they begin swiftly to be forgotten'[17] – Stevenson had much fun in giving serious and immortalising attention to ephemeral hacks. But the essay also became a highly sophisticated and wickedly parodic exploration of the nature of literary hierarchies and of the different demands of the literary marketplace. Stevenson's discourse in this essay is again double-voiced – and occupying a dual role: as a writer he articulated the dynamics of the marketplace but presented himself above such ephemeral hacks as Bracebridge Hemming who were more fully constrained by it; as a reader he is represented as both the passionate re-enactor of his early enthusiasms and an older and wiser critic of them.

Two aspects of Stevenson's concern with popular fiction emerge from this essay. One is an acute awareness of the exigencies of the commercial market. Writing at a time when pressures on the literary marketplace were rapidly changing, which saw the emergence of a new university-educated class of authors and when the criteria for 'good' literature were increasingly contested, Stevenson occupied an unusual position. Claimed as part of the re-masculinisation of the romance novel, yet accused of belles-lettristic mannerisms, he was also producing material serialised in popular magazines of the day. It was, therefore, with some insider authority that he talked of the commercial environment in which such authors as the famous Pierce Egan and Bracebridge Hemming operated. He could, however, also speak from the position of essayist and man of letters, part of a specific literary coterie. From that 'higher' perspective his attention, and the second focus of the essay, is on the nature of textual desire: the ways in which reading may create aspirations, produce false expectations or offer imaginary fulfilment. In both aspects of the essay, however, Stevenson's double-voiced discourse remained: he analysed remembered readings but also recreated his earlier enthusiasm; he described his dealing with the commercial world but also stood outside it. By presenting himself as both writer and a reader of popular fictions, a victim of these inspirational texts and a perpetrator of them, he could both admit and distance himself from both the imaginative and economic desires that market represented.

Tom Holt's Log

To return to *Treasure Island* however, and this business of originality and imitation, the essay presents further complications. 'Popular Authors' opens with an anecdote about an emigrant meeting up with a sailor, late at night on the deck of an Atlantic liner. Which book, the writer enquires of the hand, most gives a true picture of a sailor's life? '"Well", returns the other, with great deliberation and emphasis, "there is *one*; that is *just* a sailor's life. You know all about it, if you know that."'[18] The book is then revealed as *Tom Holt's Log* by the prolific novelist W. Stephens Hayward. This is the story that will send a young boy to sea; indeed, even once he has experienced life at sea and learnt the bitterness of its reality, a part of him will still structure his longings in the terms of his youthful reading for, as the essay continues:

> He cannot realise, he cannot make a tale of his own life; which crumbles
> in discrete impressions even as he lives it … It is not this that he considers

in his rare hours of rumination, but that other life, which was all lit up for him by the humble talent of a Hayward – that other life which, God knows, perhaps he still believes that he is leading – the life of Tom Holt.[19]

In his reference to *Tom Holt's Log* Stevenson's double-voiced discourse was again based upon occlusion and omission, trading texts in such a way as again to reinforce his own cultural authority. For although *Tom Holt's Log* was absent from Stevenson's litany of sea stories that relate to *Treasure Island*, the text is similar in several respects. A first-person narrative, with early sections of the book written from memory and the remainder compiled from a journal of daily events, with insertions of ship's log material, it, like many other nineteenth-century yarns, follows a young boy in a series of extraordinary adventures at sea.[20] It also includes a striking parallel with *Treasure Island* in the moment at which Tom Holt finds himself alone at sea, when everyone else has been swept off the boat and drowned in a water-spout storm. Like Jim, taking control of the *Hispaniola* after the fight with Israel Hands, he becomes master of all he surveys: 'No other eye than mine saw the bosom of the great blue ocean; from the ship, far away to the horizon, rising and falling with a slow solemn swell, or with the waves crested with foam – I was alone.'[21] Whether Stevenson had read or only heard of this novel that might have influenced *Treasure Island*, it received no mention in the carefully constructed admission of plagiarism presented in *The Idler* essay.[22]

One feature of *Tom Holt's Log* pertinent to both essays is its self-referentiality: as a boy Tom struggles with his mother's restrictions on his choice of reading – reading material which shapes his choice of career:

> Among the books which in my leisure hours I read with avidity, there were many relating to travels, discoveries and adventures of such men as Captain Cook, Francis Drake, Mungo Park, and many others.
>
> By degrees there grew in my breast an ardent longing to see more of the world than was contained within our island. But when I spoke of such a wish, my mother always replied discouragingly, and, so to say, threw cold water on the idea, declaring that the books I had read gave highly coloured and untrue accounts of the lives of those men whom I looked upon as fortunate heroes, and that the hardships and mishaps they endured more than compensated for the fame they gained and the pleasures of exploring foreign countries.
>
> I was a dutiful son, and did not always attempt to argue with my mother. But nevertheless the thoughts which reading about the adventures of others had instilled into my breast were not driven away, and as I grew in years the desire to travel and see the world increased.[23]

While Tom goes on to have a series of amazing adventures during his life at sea, the fantasy fulfilment offered by such narratives is both emphasised and warned against in the maternal voice at the beginning of the narrative. The fantasies themselves are, moreover, of so obvious a kind in terms of colonial and sexual power they that can be read only half-seriously. Tom, for example, has various ordeals to suffer when his isolated ship becomes inhabited by native women who insist on flaunting their bodies: 'I could not prevail upon them to wear a single thing beyond a cotton dress. As for stocking or any underclothings ... they utterly scorned them. Then, too, they had a wonderful fondness for the water and, somewhat to my embarrassment, would frequently throw off their loose dresses, wrap a piece of calico round them, and leap into the sea.'[24]

Tom Holt's Log, however, was not alone within the genre in alerting the reader to the relationship between fiction/desire and fact/experience and the implications of this for their engagement with the reading material before them. Even *Peter the Whaler* by W. H. G. Kingston contains a disquisition on the dangers of engaging too easily with what one reads about: 'I must warn my young friends, that although the adventures that I went through may be found very interesting to read about, they would discover the reality to be very full of pain and wretchedness were they subjected to it.'[25] Still more notable in this respect is the earlier and influential text, R. M. Ballantyne's *The Coral Island* (1858) in which the validity of reading books is much debated among the three boys marooned on the island. Jack Martin's knowledge that is necessary to survival is gleaned, he claims, entirely from his reading, but Peterkin Gay is highly suspicious of literary activity: 'I've seen lots o' fellows that were *always* poring over books, and when they came to try to *do* anything they were no better than baboons.'[26] Here leisured reading is presented in opposition to the useful acquisition of knowledge which permits the holding of colonial power. But, as Fiona McCulloch has argued, in destabilising the dichotomy of fact and fiction in the text, the novel begin to question 'the very validity of such truths by staging itself as a colonial story or sea yarn to excite its own boy readers'.[27]

So, this supposedly simplistic fiction, *Tom Holt's Log*, which Stevenson presented himself as viewing with external authority, pitying those, like the sailor, who take it too literally, was, like others of its genre, a text that explicitly articulated the nature of narrative desire – or at least acknowledged the shaping influence of early reading in structuring fantasies. Yet in 'Popular Authors' it is displayed as a novel to which the naive reader might (indeed did) respond but to which the sophisticated author can adopt a patronising evaluation, both of the text and, more significantly, of the processes of identification itself. Dismissed within the context of this essay, excluded from the much-discussed list of sources for *Treasure Island* in another essay, *Tom Holt's Log* occupies an ambiguous position within Stevenson's musings on the popular. Although beginning and ending with references to it, 'Popular Authors' does not dwell upon the novel but instead recounts in some detail another Hayward production, *The Twenty Captains*, as that best remembered by Stevenson: *Tom Holt's Log*, by comparison, is not such 'high-flying folly', nor 'half so entertaining'.[28] In the brief description given, Stevenson chose to 'recall' only one episode from the beginning of the novel in which Tom is presented with a 'small scale version of a ship', although the reader is encouraged to share his wonder that 'this was the work that an actual tarry seaman recommended for a picture of his own existence!' A degree of misrepresentation might be detected in Stevenson's depiction of the novel (if he had by this stage read it), not only passing over the more dramatic scenes from its latter sections but making no reference to the book's own potentially 'metafictional' moments. It is possible that a similar reading might be extended to its omission of *Tom Holt's Log* in the many sources cited as examples of inadvertent plagiarisms in the writing of *Treasure Island*.

Valuing reading

It is of course difficult to say for certain that Stevenson had read *Tom Holt's Log*, rather than being told about it by his seaman friend, but, even if that were his only encounter with the text, it has further significance in this complicated process of exchanges being traced here.[29] The recorded conversation took place aboard the *Devonia*, when Stevenson was sailing to New York in August 1879, on his way to meet Fanny Osbourne in California. On this voyage Stevenson encountered a more wide-ranging articulation of class-based perspectives on culture than he had hitherto experienced. Although sailing second-class, he had access to and contact with steerage passengers as well as the seamen on board, and their various attitudes clearly stimulated his thoughts on the function of fiction and the nature of the creative process. In particular he was struck by the outlook of 'Mackay', a small Scotsman, 'hot bigot' and engineer by trade, with whom Stevenson debated the value of literature. Perhaps because of resonances with his own 'family of engineers', Mackay's complaint that 'Literary men … were more highly paid than artisans; yet the artisan made threshing-machines and butter-churns, and the man of letters, except in the way of a few useful handbooks, made nothing worth the while. He produced a mere fancy article' struck Stevenson forcefully.[30] Unable to push Mackay into anything more than an admission that 'he had taken pleasure in reading books otherwise, to his view insignificant', Stevenson is led into speculation on the relationship between

Scottish culture and this 'mechanistic' attitude. If Mackay had been an English peasant, he suggests, this opposition to anything beyond the functional would perhaps have been understandable; but Mackay 'had most of the elements of a liberal education'.[31] He had also, however, been brought up 'in the midst of hot-house piety.' From this Stevenson concluded: 'One thing, indeed, is not to be learned in Scotland, and that is the way to be happy. Yet that is the whole of culture, and perhaps two thirds of morality.'[32]

Stevenson's own position is very much against that of Mackay. Although in other writings he may have shared elements of his anxiety about the production of 'mere fancy articles', here he presented himself in opposition to such thinking. Evaluations of the relationship between labour and taste are evident in other cultural exchanges on board the *Devonia*: Stevenson saw himself as different from those of his own class who perused only newspapers, interested in 'information for its own sake', but also from workmen who paid more attention but were not 'willing or careful thinkers', therefore falling short of Stevenson's definition of culture – 'the nicety with which we can perceive relations in that field, whether great or small'.[33] Workmen, moreover, further complicated definitions of 'work' and 'leisure' for, he noted with surprise, the average workman will candidly admit to idleness: they may labour for five hours but then pass the rest of the day doing nothing, while 'I have known men do hard literary work all morning, and then undergo quite as much physical fatigue by way of relief as satisfied this powerful frontiersman for the day'.[34] Although rejecting Mackay's utilitarian approach, Stevenson was still eager to stress the real labour involved in literary production and the capacity for toil, physical and intellectual, evidenced in its practitioners. On the other hand, workers encountered on board ship proved themselves to be good 'talkers', which led him to speculate that 'the less literary class show always better in narration' because although their use of detail may be dry, the 'thoughts, hopes and fears of which the workman's life is built lie nearer to necessity and nature. They are more immediate to human life.'[35] In terms which echo his enthusiasm for the 'partisan' writings of Covenanting historians and his own literary ambitions to encapsulate the brute energy of life, he argued that there was 'more adventure' in the life of a working man because 'human life is presented to you naked and verging to its lowest terms'.[36] From such anecdotes of the voyage, it is clear that Stevenson was engaged in a project of mapping responses to culture according to class hierarchies, national and political contexts. Animated as he was by this meshing of economic, social and aesthetic speculations, a heightened awareness of the politics of pleasure emerged. It is unsurprising, therefore, that a casual conversation with a seaman about his early reading should later be produced as an example of fiction's complicated relationship to the immediacies and necessities of life.

Writing as a trade

By the time 'Popular Authors' was written Stevenson had considerable personal experience of the relationship between trade and fiction and made several interventions on the subject. As we have seen, 'The Morality of the Profession of Letters' (1881) confronted James Payn's assertion that it was the business of the writer to tailor production to the demands of the literary marketplace, while his later venture into this territory, 'A Letter to a Young Gentleman' (1888), also refined his definitions of pleasure in relation to productivity.[37] His experiences in America, where he was both fêted and commodified as an author in the most public way possible but also exploited by the circulation of illegal copies of his works, gave him more practical experience of the dynamics of the marketplace. 'A Letter to a Young Gentleman' shows Stevenson struggling to reconcile a range of different positions within the art and trade dichotomy. While the essay consistently talks of art as a trade, its author also clings to a certain mystification of the artistic process. Many young people, he asserted, will be drawn to the creative arts because they are most attracted to the 'hot chase of experience' and only the representation of that experience in art seems sufficiently intense to satisfy them. (Stevenson's own attempts to capture the immediacy of Covenanting partisanship would seem to echo this ambition.) Such, however, is not the indication of true 'vocation'. That, he argued, belongs only to those who are born with the 'impulse to create words'. He then proceeded to distinguish between the direct returns that might be expected of this occupation as a 'trade', which would be small, and the 'wage of the life' which could be 'incalculably great'. For the artist then, the pleasure of the task is the main reward, combined with the training achieved by remaining true to the ideal of an aesthetic standard. Such fidelity could only be compromised by the artist saying 'it will do': 'three or four pot-boilers are enough at times (above all at wrong times) to falsify a talent'.[38] At this point, however, Stevenson changed direction and turned his attention towards the public: too many artists, he argued, turn their art inwards and forgot the need to please. 'The first duty in this world is for a man is to pay his way; when that is quite accomplished he may plunge into what eccentricity he likes; but emphatically not till then. Till then, he must pay assiduous court to the bourgeois who carries the purse.'[39] Echoes of Stevenson's own position as a 'young gentleman', dependent on his father, may be heard in these words, but it also suggests a perception of the avant-garde as luxury and as a warning against art that is self-indulgently interior. As if to gesture towards his former assertions about 'true' vocation, he noted that only in those with lesser talent will this need to compromise do any damage. Yet popularity, he continued, is ephemeral so: 'If you adopt an art to be your trade, weed your mind at the outset of all desire for money.'[40] While in this redefining of the ideas of a 'career' and a 'trade', Stevenson might appear to be engaged in a typical aesthetic emphasis which conceals monetary and social classification, his insistence that for the artist 'return' must be judged in quite different terms also suggests a peculiarly Scottish combination of creative pleasure and self-discipline. No less severe in its tone than fellow-passenger Mackay's condemnation of useless literary endeavours, Stevenson's recommendation for literary dedication combined high aesthetic aspiration and a commercial work ethic. But, as if in defiance of both, his 1888 essay also clings to the idea that, however fickle the public might prove, the artist should aim to give it pleasure: it is the concept of pleasure, always underpinning Stevenson's own activities as writer and reader, that is deployed to challenge the 'purposeless' nature of art, because even a 'Mackay' has to admit that at times he reads for enjoyment. From his critical writings it would appear that Stevenson had to perform as many changes of tack in steering a satisfactory course between trade and art as his friends performed after his death to acknowledge the popularity but justify the quality of *Treasure Island*.

The Wrecker

Many years later Lloyd Osbourne and Stevenson were again marooned together, their boat stuck in Apemama in the South Seas: to pass the time they again concocted a tale. This time the tale became *The Wrecker*, another narrative about sailors, books and commerce and perhaps Stevenson's most interesting exploration of the relationship between trade and art.

Finally completed in Samoa, 1891, this novel too has a narrative about its creation.[41] This time it was by Lloyd Osbourne, who stressed the simple joy of production, unmotivated by commercial concern: 'It was exhilarating to work with Stevenson' he wrote, 'he was so appreciative, so humorous – brought such gaiety, *camaraderie*, and goodwill to our joint task. We never had a single disagreement as the book ran its course; it was a pastime, not a task, and I'm sure no reader ever enjoyed it as much as we did.'[42] Osbourne positioned himself and Stevenson as leisured seekers after pleasure: the book was not written for material gain, only to entertain the writers; pleasure was to be found in the 'unfettered' nature of the pursuit. As Henley later struggled to free Stevenson from links to the commercial context and establish his artistic originality, so Osbourne strove to maintain the writing process as pastime not trade. *The Wrecker* nevertheless again shows Stevenson's own discourse as double-voiced, gesturing towards the thriller form which the tale takes, yet conveying his own repulsion at the 'insincerity and shallowness of tone' associated with such fiction.[43] Once again his literary manoeuvring involved a simultaneous declaration of popular influences and affirmation of his distance from them. Yet through both its subject matter and its own narrative version of a set of Japanese boxes, *The Wrecker* directly confronted the relationship between trade and text.[44] A *Künstlerroman*, a sea-story, a tale structured around economics and sharp practice, this is a novel preoccupied with questions of taste and authenticity.

Loudon Dodd, an American of Scots descent, who has been given a sound 'commercial education' by his father, nevertheless abandons the world of trade and commerce to follow his artistic ambitions as a sculptor in Paris. There he meets up with fellow American James Pinkerton, who has given up his rather dubious but successful commercial enterprises in the States to acquire art and culture in Europe. 'What is most wanted in my age and country? More culture, and more art, I said; and I chose the best place, saved my money, and came here to get them.'[45] Changes in their personal fortune necessitating a return to America, Dodd and Pinkerton become involved in various money-making enterprises, including the speculative purchase of a wreck, the *Flying Scud*, which they believe, because of the mysterious circumstances surrounding it and the high value for which it is sold, to be carrying an illegal cargo of opiates. Dodd is engaged to sail to the wreck and dismantle it to discover its secret cargo; as the ship is torn apart and the mystery of the wreck deepens, he discovers no treasure, but unearths the tale at its heart. The crew rescued from the *Flying Scud* was not, in fact, its real crew but the crew of another vessel, the *Currency Lass*, who had been rescued by the *Flying Scud* and, when forced to sacrifice much of their hard-earned wealth on board to their greedy rescuers, had slaughtered the crew of the *Scud*, and taken their places. For Dodd the most interesting aspect of this story is the identity of a mysterious crew member who turns out to be a man called Norris Carthew, scion of a wealthy English family cast off into the world of trade and labour through the disapproval of his father. Fearful of identification, Carthew has since fled back to England and his inheritance. Hoping to blackmail him, Dodd follows him to England, accompanied by the shyster lawyer Bellairs, who has staked his own interest in events after initially being commissioned by Carthew to purchase the *Scud*. The similarity of their circumstances – a disapproving father, dilettante aspirations, sea-faring adventures – draws Dodd into greater sympathy with Carthew however, and by the end of the story (and beginning of the novel) Dodd arrives in the Marquesas in a yacht splendidly furnished by the capital of his new business partner, Carthew. In its interest in connections between culture and commerce, between old moralities and new worlds, *The Wrecker* follows in the pattern of other late nineteenth-century colonial texts, but the framework in which it is set is very much Stevenson's own.

The novel's questions, 'about the material base of aesthetic pursuits and the value of artistic enterprise as measured against forms of manual activity', arose repeatedly in Stevenson's explorations of literature and might be linked to a more general utilitarian emphasis in Victorian defence of the novelist's art as being also a craft.[46] In the explicitly metafictional framework, and its attention not just to dichotomies of art and craft but to the relationship between trade and taste, Stevenson's inflection, however, is both representative of a particular structure of feeling and also clearly related to the work of that other Scottish writer R. M. Ballantyne. As we have seen, *The Coral Island* participates in the fracturing of a fact/fiction binary, but also extends its destabilising of oppositions into the dichotomy of trade and piracy: Ralph Rover is told that the schooner on which he is taken prisoner is a trader but it is later redefined as a pirate vessel in the sense that 'she trades when she can't take by force, but she takes by force, when she can, in preference'.[47] As McCulloch has argued, 'the text introduces legitimate and illegitimate trade, not as binary opposites, but as two faces of the same coin'.[48] The definition is further complicated by coming from a pirate himself. The link between trading – exchange – and piracy – taking by force – seems also, however, to be translatable into authorship, not just in terms of the bootleg copying of his work which so exercised Stevenson in America, but also in the ways in which pleasure might be traded between author and reader: an agreed exchange of currency or a plundering of the text over which the producer has no control.

Such connections are immediately drawn to the reader's attention in the prologue to *The Wrecker*, in which inhabitants of a South Seas port assemble to greet the owner of a yacht that has just sailed into their waters. Going on board to greet the newcomer, the Englishman, Havens, is not only surprised to recognise the occupant of the main cabin, Loudon Dodd, but also astonished at his surroundings. Dodd explains that such luxury is paid for by his sleeping partner: 'His money, my taste ... The black walnut bookshelves are Old English; the books are all mine – mostly Renaissance French. You should see how the beachcombers wilt away when they go round them looking for a change of Seaside Library novels. The mirrors are genuine Venice; that's a good piece in the corner.'[49] Claiming that he is interested only in art, Dodd dismisses Havens's queries about her financial viability, by protesting that all the money comes from his partner and he brings only 'the want of business habits'. Later, however, ashore in the club he admits to having being involved in smuggling opium, underwriting, buying wrecks and blackmail, all of which lead to Havens's demanding a full account of the tale: 'Here follows the yarn of Loudon Dodd, not as he told it to his friend but as he subsequently wrote it.'[50] The yacht, sailing into the story, therefore epitomises the peculiar conjunction between art, taste, trade, pleasure and criminality that the novel explores. It also serves as a metafictional reflection upon the text's own mannered complexity; as Havens remarks: 'she is too big for the trade, to my taste; and then you carry so much style'.[51] In *The Wrecker* Stevenson's concerns about the relationship between worthy labour and the purveyance of fantasy are played out, but his anxieties about 'style' and 'truth', as potentially contradictory aspects of the written word, also inform the novel, part of his exploration of what it means to produce, in the words of his earlier sea-faring companion Mackay, 'a mere fancy article'.

In its structure *The Wrecker* vagabonds its way through a number of different worlds and outlooks. Geographically, its wandering narrative traverses the old culture of Europe, the new commercial world of the United States and the more confusing environment of the South Seas. Old Europe is most obviously represented by the scenes in Paris which for Dodd functions as the centre of 'art', but also by a rural England already commodified for the New World visitor: 'In short, Stallbridge-Minster was one of those towns which appear to be maintained by England for the instruction and delight of the American rambler; to which he seems guided by an instinct not less surprising than the setter's; and which he visits and quits with equal enthusiasm.'[52] The novel further juxtaposes two different centres of cultural trading: the United States as a centre of cultural investment in which history can be bought or traded and art invested in, and the South Seas in which one culture trades its commodities with another, but in which those functioning in this liminal world have a tenuous hold on their own cultural positioning. Operating through a network of contrasts and an emphasis on difference, the novel nevertheless gradually pulls these worlds closer together in order to assess the cultural and economic connections underpinning their relationship:

> To a stranger, this conversation will at first seem scarcely brilliant; but he will soon catch the tone; and by the time he shall have moved a year or so in the island world, and come across a good number of the schooners,

so that every captain's name calls up a figure in pyjamas or white duck, and becomes used to a certain laxity of moral tone which prevails ... on smuggling, ship-scuttling, barratry, piracy, the labour trade, and other kindred fields of human activity, he will find Polynesia no less amusing and no less instructive than Pall Mall or Paris.[53]

As the narrator comments, the South Seas offers glimpses of a new, yet also familiar, global configuration.

Likewise, although the two main characters in the early parts of the adventure, Loudon Dodd and James Pinkerton, appear initially to represent radically different attitudes, it is their underlying similarity that leads them through their escapades. Dodd, the son of an American entrepreneur, is forced into an education which should teach him the rules of commerce and the 'value' of money; instead, he maintains a resolute distance from such practicalities, insisting instead (ironically through a financial metaphor), 'I never cared a cent for anything but art, and never shall.'[54] Pinkerton, coming from a much poorer and less settled background, with no educating and feeding hand to bite, is the product of a far more eclectic cultural milieu: 'As he tramped the Western States and Territories, taking tin-types, the boy was continually getting hold of books, good, bad and indifferent, popular and abstruse, from the novels of Sylvanus Cobb to Euclid's Elements, both of which I found (to my almost equal wonder) he had managed to peruse.'[55] Pinkerton, moreover, directs his self-education to the acquisition of culture and financial success, his aim being 'to get culture and money with both hands and with the same irrational fervour'. Rather than aspiring to art for its own sake, or for his own sake, as the indulgent Dodd does, he seeks to enhance his country, to benefit the public sphere through his endeavours. Dodd and Pinkerton appear to present very different examples of the formation of taste; indeed they might be said to represent the distinction between what Bourdieu terms the 'aesthetic gaze' and the 'naive gaze'.[56] Loudon, epitomising the former, prioritises style and the mode of representation, a habitus acquired through the distance from material necessity and which operates through distinction from the social group. Pinkerton, by contrast, could be understood (at this stage of events) in terms of the 'naive regard' which stresses the common or shared experience and which refuses to make aesthetic judgement independent of moral approval or disapproval. This difference is manifested by an incident early in the novel, in which Dodd and Pinkerton visit an unpleasant French artist; both perceive him to be a ruffian because of his physical abuse of a discarded mistress, but while Pinkerton (unable to speak French) asks Dodd to voice his moral outrage, Dodd translates his moral disapproval into '*Monsieur se sent mal au coeur d'avoir trop regardé votre croute*' because aesthetic criticism was 'the only thing that he could feel'.[57]

As their friendship and speculative ventures develop, such differences become less distinct. Dodd (through Pinkerton) becomes involved in a series of adventures in which the categories he had adhered to with such enthusiasm and conviction as a young man, become disrupted. In Paris, for example, Pinkerton develops particular talents – for buying furnishings, sizing up property etc. – which propel him into the realm of 'taste', albeit on limited terms: 'although he would never be a connoisseur, he was already something of an expert. The things themselves left him as near as may be cold; but he had a joy of his own in understanding how to buy and sell them.'[58] Even this distinction between good taste and expert knowledge is put under pressure when Dodd realises that for Pinkerton the dealings of the money market provide the intensity of art – they are his romance:

> In the same spirit as a schoolboy, deep in Mayne Reid, handles a dummy gun and crawls among imaginary forests, Pinkerton sped through Kearney Street upon his daily business, representing to himself a highly coloured part in life's performance, and happy for hours if he should have chanced to brush against a millionaire. Reality was his romance; he gloried to be thus engaged; he wallowed in his business. Suppose a man to dig up a galleon on the Coromandel coast, his rakish schooner keeping the while an offing under easy sail, and he, by the blaze of a great fire of wreckwood, to measure ingots by the bucketful on the uproarious beach: such a one might realise a greater material spoil; he should have no more profit of romance than Pinkerton when he cast up his weekly balance-sheet in a bald office. Every dollar gained was like something brought ashore from a mysterious deep; every venture made was like a diver's plunge.[59]

(The image used to describe Pinkerton's financial endeavours – 'No dollar slept in his possession; rather he kept all simultaneously flying like a conjurer with oranges' – also echoes the terms Stevenson had used to depict the writer in his 1884 'long and peculiarly solemn paper on the technical elements of style in literature'.[60]) On the other hand, as Dodd's own situation becomes financially precarious and he takes on the advertising side of Pinkerton's business in San Francisco, he is forced to use his 'talents' both to stage the famous Hebdomadary picnics and to assess the art work for the business, looking at pictures, 'thenceforward, not with the eye of the artist, but the dealer'.[61] Drawing to our attention the increasingly fine line between such distinctions as 'expert/connoisseur' and 'artist/dealer', the novel takes the process of complication one stage further when action moves into the South Seas. Dodd has already stated that in the bars of San Francisco can be found types similar to those encountered by Stevenson on the *Devonia*: 'full men besides, though not by reading, but by strong experience; and for days together I could hear their yarns with an unfading pleasure. All had indeed some touch of the poetic; for the beachcomber, when not a mere ruffian, is the poor relation of the artist'.[62] But it is only when Dodd and his ambiguous captain, Nares, reach the wreck of the *Flying Scud* that categorisation becomes even more confusing as they are confronted with the reading matter left on the wreck:

> The books were the first to engage our notice. These were rather numerous (as Nares contemptuously put it) 'for a lime-juicer' … There were Findlay's five directories of the world – all broken-backed, as is usual with Findlay, and all marked and scribbled over with corrections and additions – several books of navigation, a signal code, and an Admiralty book of a sort of orange hue, called *Islands of the Eastern Pacific Ocean, Vol. III*, which appeared from its imprint to be the latest authority, and showed marks of frequent consultation in the passages about the French Frigate Shoals, the Harman, Cure, Pearl and Hermes reefs, Lisiansky Island, Ocean Island, and the place where we then lay – Brooks or Midway. A volume of Macaulay's *Essays* and a shilling Shakespeare led the van of the *belles-lettres*; the rest were novels: several Miss Braddons – of course, *Aurora Floyd*, which has penetrated to every isle of the Pacific, a good many cheap detective books, *Rob Roy*, Auerbach's *Auf Der Höhe* in the German, and a prize temperance story, pillaged (to judge by the stamp) from an Anglo-Indian circulating library.[63]

The only book, however, that the cabin should contain, *Hoyt's Pacific Directory* (which the captain alleges misinformed him and led to the wreck of his boat) is, significantly, missing.

The whole plot of the novel, indeed, hinges on the extent to which Dodd and Nares can successfully 'read' the contents of the ship: 'That's the trouble with this brig racket; any one can make half a dozen theories for sixty or seventy per cent. of it; but when they're made, there's always a fathom or two of slack hanging out of the other end.'[64] Believing at its auction that raised bidding indicated the promise of opium, Pinkerton and Dodd misinterpret the 'value' of *Flying Scud*, thinking it held a hidden cargo. The true 'value' represented in that auction, however, is the involvement of Carthew in the villainy aboard that ship. It is only by reading the contents that Nares and Dodd can find the leads towards a different kind of financial gain – through blackmail. Nares can decipher the signs of seamanship to decide that something untoward has happened, while Dodd detects the presence of a cultivated man on board, not only through the books but also by the discovery of a palette knife and a Winsor and Newton pencil – 'and a BBB at that. A palette knife and a

BBB on a tramp brig! It's against the laws of nature.'[65] Dodd, by making this assessment, also of course defines himself: the process of classification classifies the classifier.

Strangest of all in its blurring of aesthetic, moral and economic categories is the final part of the novel in which Loudon Dodd, wealthy once again, follows the sleazy lawyer Bellairs to England in an attempt to prevent him from blackmailing the guilty but also 'honourable' Carthew, a figure who in his failure to live up to expectations suggests similarities not only with Dodd but with Stevenson: in his youth he had

> developed a taste for low pleasures and bad company … and when he was near twenty, and might have been expected to display at least some rudiments of the family gravity, rambled the country over with a knapsack, making sketches and keeping company in wayside inns. He had no pride about him, I was told; he would sit down with any man.[66]

Meeting in England, the unlikely pair perform a cultural tour of the country – the one with his high artistic standards, the other reading *Werther* without having heard of Goethe, evidence of a spontaneous response to the literary and artistic which, although extreme, sentimental and 'a thought ridiculous', was genuine in its tastes. Although Dodd maintains a supercilious amusement at Bellairs's incredulity, reinforcing the cultural stereotype that lower-class readers have less complicated reading strategies, Dodd and Bellairs both perform as American tourists, 'travelling with a design of self-improvement'. And it is Dodd who undertakes the less 'literary' and more utilitarian course, finding his 'self-improvement' in detective work on stamp albums or filling in idle hours with 'useful' reading: with *Whitakers Almanac*, for example, he 'obtained in fifty minutes more information than I have yet been able to use'.[67]

The Wrecker thus makes explicit the author's fascination with diverse aesthetic responses, encountered so vividly in his own sea-faring experiences on the *Devonia*, as the significance attached to different kinds of texts becomes increasingly and explicitly complicated. Even the rough seamen involved in the dreadful events upon the *Flying Scud* are to be found debating the nature of literary realism: Wicks, the captain involved in the massacre, is unhappy with the 'real' log on the ship because it seems so unlikely: '"it doesn't look like real life, that's all I can say", returned Wicks. "It's the way it was though", argued Carthew. "So it is, and what the better are we for that if it doesn't look so", cried the captain, sounding unwonted depths of art criticism.'[68] In such knowing references the text also draws the reader into confronting hierarchies of taste and discrimination, and to thinking about our own pleasure in literary consumption. Questions around the quality of our reading are explicitly flagged in the novel when the narrator asks for alternative interpretations of the material presented: 'Here at last was the end of my discoveries; I learned no more till I learned all; and my reader has the evidence complete. Is he more astute than I was? Or, like me, does he give it up?'[69] (They are also raised by the textual apparatus, when Stevenson dedicates the novel to Will Low, who had himself published a response to Stevenson's 'Daughter of Joy' piece, adding in the Epilogue that this strange novel 'full of details of our barbaric manners and unstable morals' is pledged to Low because he is 'a man interested in all problems of art, even the most vulgar'.[70])

If *The Wrecker* foregrounds such concerns paratextually, it also presents a challenge to aesthetic criteria in its form. In its 'preferred' shape – not that of a mystery or thriller because in those genres 'the mind of the reader, always bent to pick up clues, receives no impression of reality or life … and the book remains enthralling but insignificant' – the novel is both intriguing and exasperating in its slipping between continents and character groups, its intermingling of genres, in the movement between *Künstlerroman*, adventure yarn and Conradian confrontation with otherness.[71] Subplots and incidents which seem to lead nowhere in relation to the main narrative present a particular challenge to the reader, slowing the action and constraining reading pleasures. Yet it is through such apparently tedious passages that the novel pushes further in its questions about the point and pleasures of consumption. At an early stage in the novel Loudon Dodd relates the curious series of events which brought him into contact with Pinkerton. Having drunk too much of a very fine Roussillon wine one night, he is unable to find his room within his lodging house, which appears to have stretched from its four-flight original to a building which contains at least thirteen flights of stairs. Eventually, finding himself 'three stories higher than the roof', he approaches the room of a young lady whose door is open and she takes him back to his room, in a house which still seems two or three times its size. The following day, with the house returned to normal dimensions, he is unable to locate her, but suddenly sees her in the street approaching the art gallery, with a young man (who turns out to be Pinkerton) carrying her drawing board. But Pinkerton, it transpires, has only the most casual acquaintance with this lady, and she is never mentioned again. The narrative therefore has completely different key points to those which we might expect: the strange power of the wine, the shifting house, the romantic figure of the young lady are not, in themselves, significant and we never return to the house, the wine or the lady: only Pinkerton remains as a key character and the incident functions as 'an excellent example of the Blind Man's Buff that we call life'.[72] But this minor incident remains paradigmatic of the novel's narrative pattern, whereby the aesthetic pleasure of recounting a tale – or of reading it – is privileged over the exchange of a moral 'nugget' of truth from the tale. The incident is both compelling and ultimately 'useless': a 'mere article of fancy'. A similar sense of frustration might be experienced at the end of the novel: the main narrator, Loudon Dodd, doesn't finish his own tale, but hands over to Carthew's 'yarn', which is then followed, but it is left to the Epilogue and a 'fabricated' Stevenson, who knows both Havens and Dodd so is within the fiction but can also comment on publication and genre from an external position, to conclude the tale.

In its hybridity of form, in its self-referentiality, in its confusing juxtapositions of moral and aesthetic criteria, *The Wrecker* forces us to become discriminating readers, engaging with the questions that beset Stevenson in his own thinking about the nature of literary production and textual pleasure. While in several respects it engages with broad questions about the relationship between taste, enjoyment and class, its interest can be understood as emerging directly from Stevenson's own personal configuration of concerns and his recognition, epitomised in the 'writer as prostitute' image, that neither the production nor the consumption of textual pleasure is without a price.

This understanding that 'freedom' of aesthetic irresponsibility has to be bought in one way or another is further illustrated by two minor figures in the novel, the 'Stennis boys', who, in their 'artistic' and vagabonding aspirations might be read as a parody of Bob and Louis in their own early adventures:

> They had come from London, it appeared, a week before with nothing but great-coats and tooth-brushes. No baggage – there was the secret of existence. It was expensive to be sure; for every time you had to comb your hair, a barber must be paid, and every time you changed your linen, one shirt must be bought and another thrown away; but anything was better (argued these young gentlemen) than to be the slaves of haversacks.[73]

Their emphasis upon the shedding of worldly goods, the need to be driven by pleasure alone (both underpinned by their access to material wealth), echoes Lloyd Osbourne's own representation of writing *The Wrecker* with Louis. 'It was a pastime, not a task.'[74] In the novel itself however, in contrast to his sophisticated negotiations in essay form, Stevenson confronted the workings of libidinal, textual and monetary economies in which the currency of his fiction had to operate. Although in his literary theory, his writings on romance and on reading Stevenson may have found ways of responding to Calvinist-inflected anxieties about the consumption and creation of the written word, the fact that 'articles of fancy' offer stylistic delight and psychological pleasure but must exist within the material contexts of labour and trade continued to pose problems; for him literary production could never be simply 'pastime' or wholly 'task'.

Notes

1 *Treasure Island*, Tusitala II, p. 42. An earlier version of the first part of this chapter was published as 'Trading Texts: Negotiations of the Professional and the Popular in the Case of *Treasure Island*', in R. Ambrosini and R. Dury (eds), *Robert Louis Stevenson: Writer of Boundaries* (Madison: University of Wisconsin Press, 2006), pp. 60–9.

2 See A. Japp, *Robert Louis Stevenson, a Record, an Estimate and a Memorial*, (London: T. Werner Laurie, 1905); see also Furnas, *Voyage to Windward*; W. R. Katz, 'Introduction', *Treasure Island* (Edinburgh: Edinburgh University Press, 1998), pp. xix–xli.

3 On the significance of this form of publication see J. A. Pierce, 'The Belle Lettrist and the People's Publisher; or, the Context of *Treasure Island*'s First-form Publication', *Victorian Periodicals Review*, 31:4 (1998), 356–68.

4 W. E. Henley, 'Some Novels of 1899', *North American Review*, 170:519 (February 1900), 253–62; reported in *The Academy*, 1451 (24 February 1900), 156.

5 *Ibid.*, p. 156.

6 R. Leighton, 'Stevenson's Beginnings', *The Academy*, 1452 (3 March 1900), 189.

7 A. H. Japp, *The Academy*, 1453 (10 March 1900), 209–10, p. 210.

8 J. Henderson, *The Academy*, 1454 (17 March 1900), 237–8.

9 See, for example, 'The Morality of the Profession of Letters', *Fortnightly Review*, 157 (1881), 513–20, *Essays Literary and Critical*, Tusitala XXVIII, pp. 51–60; 'Letter to a Young Gentleman Who Proposes to Embrace the Career of Art', *Scribner's Magazine*, 4 (1888), 377–81, *Across the Plains* (1892); Tusitala XXVIII, pp. 1–11; 'On the Choice of a Profession', *Scribner's Magazine*, 57 (1915), 66–9, Tusitala XXVIII, pp. 12–19. On the professionalisation of authorship see: Keating, *The Haunted Study*; McDonald, *British Literary Culture and Publishing Practice 1880–1914*; J. Sutherland, *Victorian Fiction: Writers, Publishers, Readers* (London: Macmillan, 1995).

10 Frow, *Cultural Studies and Cultural Value*, p. 18.

11 For a related discussion of pleasure see S. Arata, 'Stevenson, Morris and the Value of Idleness', in Ambrosini and Dury (eds), *Robert Louis Stevenson: Writer of Boundaries*, pp. 3–12.

12 'My First Book' was written in spring/summer 1893, and appeared in *The Idler*, VI (1894), 2–11, and in *My First Book*, ed. Jerome K. Jerome (London: Chatto and Windus, 1894), pp. 297–309. Tusitala II, pp. xxiii–xxxi.

13 Katz (ed.), *Treasure Island*, pp. xxix–xxxiii.

14 Frow has a particularly helpful discussion of the concept of 'regimes of value'

in *Cultural Studies and Cultural Value*, chapter 4.

15 'My First Book', p. xxvii.

16 Written in February/March 1888; *Scribner's Magazine*, 4 (July 1888), 122–8; Tusitala XXVIII, pp. 20–32. For a useful discussion of *Cassell's Family Paper* see Swearingen, *Early Literary Career*, pp. 122–8.

17 'Popular Authors', p. 20.

18 *Ibid.*, p. 20.

19 *Ibid.*, p. 32.

20 W. S. Hayward, *Tom Holt's Log: A Tale of the Deep Sea* (London: C. H. Clarke, 1868).

21 *Tom Holt's Log*, p. 1. This motif, of the hero 'marooned' on the ship, captured into roles of captain and crew, and engaged in struggle of self against elements, is not confined to *Tom Holt's Log* and *Treasure Island*: it can also be found in William Clark Russell's *A Sailor's Sweetheart* (1880), another novel omitted as a source for *Treasure Island* but mentioned in 'A Gossip on Romance', in which a chapter entitled 'The Lonely Deep' explores similar themes. Ballantyne's earlier novel *The Coral Island* also contains a scene in which Ralph Rover return to the Island, alone on board ship. 'Alone! In the midst of the wide Pacific, having a most imperfect knowledge of navigation, and in a schooner requiring at least eight men as her proper crew' (R. M. Ballantyne, *The Coral Island: A Tale of the Pacific Ocean* (London: T. Nelson and Sons, 1858), p. 344). Stevenson's text, of course, differs considerably from these possible sources in its subtle exploration of the moral psychological impact of isolation and confrontation, while also omitting the many pages describing the practicalities of navigation and Crusoe-like details of surprising survival tactics to be found in other fictions.

22 Swearingen suggests that he had not read the book at the time of the *Devonia* voyage, although he comments on it in a passage in *The Amateur Emigrant*, later deleted: 'it is either excellent or downright penny trash. There seems to be no medium in the taste of the unliterary class; mediocrity must tremble for its judgement; either strong, lively matter solidly handled, or mere ink and banditti forms its literary diet.' See *Prose Writings of Robert Louis Stevenson*, p. 124; R. G. Swearingen, *The Amateur Emigrant, with Some First Impressions of America*, 2 vols (Ashland, OR: L. Osborne, 1976–77, I, p. 80; J. D. Hart (ed.), *From Scotland to Silverado* (Cambridge, MA: Belknap Press of Harvard University Press, 1966), p. 75.

23 *Tom Holt's Log*, pp. 3–4.

24 *Ibid.*, pp. 252–3. On colonial adventure see: P. Brantlinger, *Rule of Darkness: British Literature and Imperialism 1830–1914* (Ithaca and London: Cornell University Press, 1988); J. Bristow, *Empire Boys: Adventures in a Man's World* (London: Unwin Hyman, 1991).

25 W. H. G. Kingston, *Peter the Whaler* (1873) p. 9.

26 *The Coral Island*, p. 39.

27 F. McCulloch, '"The Broken Telescope": Misrepresentation in *The Coral Island*'. *Children's Literature Association Quarterly*, 25:3 (2000), 137–45, p. 142.

28 'Popular Authors', p. 23.
29 It does not appear to be in either library or auction catalogues of his books. See also n. 20.
30 'The Amateur Emigrant', written September 1879 to June 1880 (originally Part I 'The Emigrant Ship'). Tusitala XVIII, pp. 1–150, p. 29. (For full publishing history see Swearingen, *Prose Writings of Robert Louis Stevenson*, pp. 42–5.)
31 *Ibid.*, p. 30.
32 *Ibid.*, p. 31.
33 *Ibid.*, p. 61.
34 *Ibid.*, p. 62.
35 *Ibid.*, pp. 64–5
36 *Ibid.*, p. 65.
37 'On the Choice of a Profession', which follows this in *Essays Literary and Critical*, Tusitala XXVIII, pp. 2–19, was, explained Lloyd Osbourne, first supposed to be a draft for 'Letter to a Young Gentleman' but was, in fact, a separate piece. Stevenson had submitted an essay on a similar topic to Leslie Stephen at the *Cornhill* in January 1879. Swearingen, *Prose Writings of Robert Louis Stevenson*, p. 39.
38 'Letter to a Young Gentleman', *Scribner's Magazine*, 4 (September 1888), 377–81; Tusitala XXVIII, pp. 3–11, p. 7.
39 *Ibid.*, pp. 7–8.
40 *Ibid.*, p. 10.
41 *The Wrecker*, written summer 1889 to November 1891. Published in *Scribner's Magazine*, 10–12, August 1891 to July 1892; *The Wrecker* (New York: Charles Scribner's Sons, 1892), Tusitala XII. See Swearingen, *Prose Writings of Robert Louis Stevenson*, pp. 130–4.
42 Tusitala XII, p. ix.
43 'We had long ago been at once attracted and repelled by that very modern form of police novel or mystery story, which consists in beginning your yarn anywhere but at the beginning, and finishing it anywhere but at the end; attracted by its peculiar interest when done; repelled by that appearance of insincerity and shallowness of tone, which seems its inevitable drawback' (pp. 404–5).
44 For a reading of the real trade to which the novel alludes, see G. Hirsch, 'The Commercial World of *The Wrecker*', *Journal of Stevenson Studies*, 2 (2005), 70–97. On art theory in relation to economics see W. Gray, 'Stevenson's "Auld Alliance": France, Art Theory and the Breath of Money in *The Wrecker*', *Scottish Studies Review*, 3:2 (2002), 54–65.
45 *The Wrecker*, p. 42.
46 Smith, *Literary Culture and the Pacific*, p. 151.
47 Ballantyne, *The Coral Island*, p. 278.
48 McCulloch, '"The Broken Telescope": Misrepresentation in *The Coral Island*', p. 141.
49 *The Wrecker*, p. 6.
50 *Ibid.*, p. 14.

51 *Ibid.*, p. 8.
52 *Ibid.*, p. 291.
53 *Ibid.*, p. 10.
54 *Ibid.*, p. 15.
55 *Ibid.*, p. 41.
56 As Bourdieu notes, 'It is in the relationship between the two capacities which define the habitus, the capacity to produce classifiable products and works, and the capacity to differentiate and appreciate these practices and products (taste), that the represented social world, i.e. the space of life-styles, is constituted.' *Distinction*, p. 170.
57 'The gentleman is sick at his stomach from having looked too long at your daub', *The Wrecker*, p. 40.
58 *Ibid.*, p. 58.
59 *Ibid.*, p. 92.
60 'The conjurer juggles with two oranges, and our pleasure in beholding him springs from this, that neither is for an instant overlooked or sacrificed. So with the writer.' 'On Style in Literature: Its Technical Elements', *The Contemporary Review*, 47 (April 1885); 'On Some Technical Elements of Style in Literature', *Essays Literary and Critical*, Tusitala XXVIII, pp. 33–50, p. 36.
61 *The Wrecker*, p. 96.
62 *Ibid.*, p. 123.
63 *Ibid.*, p. 214.
64 *Ibid.*, p. 215.
65 *Ibid.*, p. 212.
66 *Ibid.*, p. 305.
67 *Ibid.*, p. 293.
68 *Ibid.*, p. 390.
69 *Ibid.*, p. 260.
70 See also reading of this in Richard Ambrosini, 'R. L. Stevenson and the Ethical Value of Writing for the Market', *Journal of Stevenson Studies*, 1 (2004), 24–41. Stephen Arata in his paper 'Observing *The Wrecker*', given at 'Stevenson and Conrad: Writers of Land and Sea' (Edinburgh, 2004), suggests that the frequent use of 'tableaux' in the novel offers moments of stasis in which the reader can observe the story and relates this to the novel's alertness to the deployment of genre in narrative.
71 *The Wrecker*, p. 405.
72 *Ibid.*, p. 36.
73 *Ibid.*, p. 56.
74 Lloyd Osbourne, 'Stevenson at Forty', Tusitala XII, p. ix.

8

Conclusion

Of all books these are the least wearisome to read and the richest in matter; the course of roads and rivers, the contour-lines and the forests in the maps – the reefs, soundings, anchors, sailing-marks, and little pilot-pictures in the charts.[1]

In tracing out Stevenson's reading practices and their relationship to his theoretical interventions this book itself has vagabonded through the side-roads of his writing. Mapping out the textual exchanges between a range of his writings and the cultural climate in which they developed, it has argued that a particular combination of personal response and cultural formation shaped by Scottish Calvinism and emerging both as reaction against, and internalisation of, a specific world view pushed him towards his insights on romance, realism, textual involvement and the purveying of literary pleasure. In both his self-representation as literary vagrant and in the idiosyncratic nature of his excursions, the interplay between the reading experiences of a particular reader, the culturally determined strategies of figuring a reading role and the historically shaped formation of reading positions are revealed. In this particular instance the configuration produced is that of an illuminating theorist of reading and an experimental adventurer in fictional genres. The production of that figure also, however, suggests that in understanding both 'real' readers and the interpretative frameworks through which we conceptualise reading processes an attentiveness to cultural, historical and national specificity is essential. The textual inscription of Stevenson as reader emerges from personal biography, from belief formations within a particular culture and from the discursive constructions of literary debate at a specific moment in time. If Stevenson developed a phenomenological analysis of reading that appeared ahead of his time, it was as a result of the particular dynamic which created a self-scrutinising reader, defiantly, yet anxiously, asserting the pleasures of literary consumption. It was perhaps inevitable that others, emerging from rather different configurations, were puzzled by this figure, as both writer and reader, and sought to explain him as eternal boy, escapist, dilettante, lost genius, saviour of romance.

A review in *The Bookman* of *Catriona*, published in 1893, reveals exactly this clashing of perspectives. 'There is in the book one source of delight', comments the reviewer, 'of which the Southerner cannot avail himself – the topographical nomenclature.' This love of the repetition of local names is, he suggests, an idiosyncrasy of North Angles and Celtic Highlanders and 'the book abounds in them'. For this reason, he concludes, the book 'will find most favour north of the Tweed, where David's itinerary can not only be traced but its innumerable halting places and landmarks pronounced with loving cacophony.'[2] The reviewer attributes to an unthinking national trait in Stevenson a characteristic of the book that was in fact the subject of philosophical scrutiny on the part of the author. From his early essay 'The Philosophy of Nomenclature', originally published in *Edinburgh University Magazine* in February 1871, Stevenson had been fascinated with what would now be termed processes of signification, and the ways in which the signifier can carry an excess of gratification not served by the signified.[3] It is a subject he returns to in essays and in his note book: in '*Rosa Quo Locorum*', for example, he writes that for the child 'words are very live to him, phrases that imply a picture eloquent beyond their value'.[4] In 'The Ideal House' he suggested that there should be a 'map table, groaning under a collection of large-scale maps and charts'. Not only because 'Of all books these are the least wearisome to read and the richest in matter' but also because 'in both, the bead-roll of names, make them of all printed matter the most fit to stimulate and satisfy the fancy'.[5] The year after *Catriona*'s publication he had requested Sir Herbert Maxwell's study of *Scottish Land Names*, published after his Rhind Lectures on the subject given in 1893, and later corresponded with him about the origins of the name Stevenson.[6] Nevertheless, the reviewer is in a sense correct in attributing Stevenson's fascination with place names to a particular national identity, for in 'naming' Stevenson found the most extreme example of the power, the seductiveness and the problematic tension between word and referent that was an inevitable focus of his attention given the complex of forces at play in his own cultural formation. Reading, for Stevenson, offered neither a purely indulgent escape into another world nor an insistent engagement with the real world: rather the processes of reading themselves become paradigmatic of imaginative contradictions and human longings: to return to that dominant metaphor, in books as in travel, 'the line of the road leads the eye forth with the vague sense of desire up to the green limits of the horizon'.[7]

Notes

1 'The Ideal House', Tusitala XXV, pp. 190–5, pp. 193–4.
2 'New Books', '*Catriona*', *The Bookman*, October 1893, 18–19, p. 19.
3 'The Philosophy of Nomenclature', '*College Papers*, V (originally printed in *Edinburgh University Magazine*, April 1871; *Virginibus Puerisque and Other Essays in Belles Lettres*, Tustiala XXV, pp. 159–62.
4 '*Rosa Quo Locorum*', Tusitala XXX, pp. 1–8, p. 2.
5 'The Ideal House', p. 194.
6 Sir Herbert Maxwell, *Scottish Land Names: Their Origin and Meaning* (Edinburgh: William Blackwood and Sons, 1894; based on Rhind Lectures in Archaeology, given in 1893). See 18/6/94 to Charles Baxter, *Letters*, vol. 8, p. 308; 10/9/94 to Sir Herbert Maxwell, *Letters*, vol. 8, p. 367; 1/12/94 to Sir Herbert Maxwell, *Letters*, vol. 8, p. 396.
7 'Roads', first published in the *Portfolio*, November 1873, Tusitala XXV, pp. 183–9, p. 188.

Bibliography

Stevenson's works

The Works of Robert Louis Stevenson, Tusitala edition, 35 vols (London: William Heinemann Ltd, 1923–24).

B. A. Booth and E. Mehew (eds), *The Letters of Robert Louis Stevenson*, 8 vols (New Haven: Yale University Press, 1994–95).

Reference works

Allibone, S. A., *A Critical Dictionary of English Literature and British and American Authors* (2 vols) (Philadelphia: Childs and Peterson, 1859); *Supplement* (Philadelphia: J. B. Lippincott and Co., 1891).

Hammond, J. R., *A Robert Louis Stevenson Chronology* (Basingstoke: Macmillan, 1997).

Maixner, P., *Robert Louis Stevenson: The Critical Heritage* (London, Boston and Henley: Routledge and Kegan Paul, 1981).

Sadleir, M. *XIX Century Fiction: A Bibliographic Record Based on His Own Collection*, 2 vols (Cambridge: Cambridge University Press, 1951).

Swearingen, R. G., *The Prose Writings of Robert Louis Stevenson* (London: Macmillan, 1980).

Wolff, R. L. *Nineteenth-century Fiction: A Bibliographic Catalogue Based on the Collection Formed by Robert Lee Wolff* (New York: Garland, 1982).

Stevenson's library

Advocates Library Borrowing Records 1875–80, National Library of Scotland, FR277; FR278.

The Anderson Auction Company Catalogue, Autograph Letters, Original Manuscripts, Books, and South Sea Curios from the Library of the

Late Robert Louis Stevenson Part I (New York: 1914); Part II (New York: 1915).

Brown, N. M., 'Ex Libris RLS: Much Travelled Books', *Scottish Book Collector*, 4:7 (1994), 5–8.

——'Le Ona's Library', *Scottish Book Collector*, 4:8 (1994), 5–8.

—— 'A Wreck of Books', *Scottish Book Collector*, 4:10 (1995), 7–9.

—— 'Picking over the Bohns: Stevenson's Vailima Library', *Scottish Book Collector*, 5:1 (1995), 19–21.

—— 'Stevenson's Scottish Books', *Scottish Book Collector*, 5:3 (1996), 15–18.

——'RLS Bibliopest', *Scottish Book Collector*, 5:6 (1996), 27–30.

—— 'RLS, Frail Warrior', *Scottish Book Collector*, 5:7 (1996), 25–9.

—— 'The French Collection: RLS's Vailima Library', *Scottish Book Collector*, 5:9 (1997), 22–5.

Mahaffy, A. W., 'A Visit to the Library of R. L. Stevenson, at Vailima, Samoa', *The Spectator*, 30 November 1895, 762–3.

McKay, G. L., *A Stevenson Library: Catalogue of a Collection of Writings By and About Robert Louis Stevenson Formed by Edwin J. Beinecke*, 6 vols (New Haven: Yale University Library, 1951–64).

Swearingen, R. G., *The Early Literary Career of Robert Louis Stevenson 1850–1881: A Bibliographical Study*, Vol. 2, PhD Dissertation (Yale University, 1970).

Wainwright, A. D., *Robert Louis Stevenson: A Catalogue of the Henry E. Gerstly Collection, the Stevenson Section of the Morris L. Parrish Collection of Victorian Novelists and Items from other Collections* (The Department of Rare Books and Special Collections of the Princeton University Library: Princeton: Princeton University Library, 1971).

Editions

Calder, A. (ed.), *Robert Louis Stevenson: Selected Poems* (Harmondsworth: Penguin, 1998).

Gelder, K. (ed.), *Robert Louis Stevenson: The Scottish Stories and Essays* (Edinburgh: Edinburgh University Press, 1989).

Hart, J. D. (ed.), *From Scotland to Silverado* (Cambridge, MA: Belknap Press of Harvard University Press, 1966).

Katz, W. R. (ed.), *Treasure Island* (Edinburgh: Edinburgh University Press, 1998).

Lewis, R. C. (ed.), *The Collected Poems of Robert Louis Stevenson* (Edinburgh: Edinburgh University Press, 2003).

Menikoff, B. (ed.), *Robert Louis Stevenson's Kidnapped – or the Lad with*

the Silver Button (San Marino: Huntington Library Press, 1999).
Norquay, G. (ed.), *R. L. Stevenson on Fiction: An Anthology of Literary and Critical Essays* (Edinburgh: Edinburgh University Press, 1999).
Robert Louis Stevenson: A Bookman Extra Number (London: Hodder and Stoughton, 1913).
Swearingen, R. G. (ed.), *The Amateur Emigrant, with Some First Impressions of America*, 2 vols (Ashland, OR: L. Osborne, 1976–77).

Periodical articles and essays

Barrie J. M., 'Brought Back from Elysium', *Contemporary Review*, 57 (June 1890), 846–54.
—— 'Robert Louis Stevenson', *Gavin Ogilvy; An Edinburgh Eleven: Pencil Portraits from College Life* (Edinburgh: Hodder and Stoughton, 1894); *An Edinburgh Eleven* (Edinburgh: Hodder and Stoughton, 1929), pp. 111–22.
Besant, W., *The Art of Fiction: A Lecture delivered at the Royal Institution on Friday evening, April 25, 1884* (London: Chatto and Windus, 1884).
Collins J. C., 'English Literature at the Universities', *Quarterly Review*, 163 (October 1886), 289–329.
Collins, W., 'The Unknown Public', *Household Words*, 439 (21 August 1858), 217–22.
Gosse, E., 'The Influence of Democracy on Literature', *Contemporary Review*, 59 (April 1891), 523–36.
Haggard, H. R., 'About Fiction', *Contemporary Review*, 51 (February 1887), 172–80.
Harrison, F. 'On the Choice of Books', *Fortnightly Review* n.s., 25 (April 1879), 497.
Henderson, J., 'Stevenson's Beginnings', *The Academy*, 1454 (17 March 1900), 237–8.
Henley, W. E., 'Alexandre Dumas', *Saturday Review*, 56:1463 (10 November 1883), 594–5.
—— 'The New Stevenson', *Scots Observer*, 2:47 (12 October 1889), 583–4.
—— 'Some Novels of 1899', *North American Review*, 170:519 (February 1900), 253–62; reported in *The Academy*, 1451 (24 February 1900), 156.
Hillebrand, K., 'About Old and New Novels', *Contemporary Review*, 45 (March 1884), 399–402.
James, H., 'The Art of Fiction', *Longman's Magazine*, 4 (September 1884), 502–21.

—— 'Robert Louis Stevenson', *Century Magazine*, 35 (April 1888), 869–79.

Japp, A. H., 'Stevenson's Beginnings', *The Academy*, 1453 (10 March 1900), 209–10.

Lang A., 'Romanticism and Realism', *Saturday Review*, 8 November 1894, 615–16.

—— 'Realism and Romance', *Contemporary Review*, 52 (November 1887), 683–93.

Le Gallienne, R., *The Academy*, 1045 (14 May 1892), 462–4.

Leighton, R., 'Stevenson's Beginnings', *The Academy*, 1452 (3 March 1900), 189.

Lubbock, Sir J., 'On Reading', *Morning Advertiser*, 11 January 1886, 2.

—— 'On the Pleasure of Reading', *Contemporary Review*, 49 (February 1886), 240–51.

Saintsbury, G., Review of *Malcolm*, *The Academy*, 140 (9 January 1875), 34–5.

—— 'Alexandre Dumas', *Fortnightly Review*, 1 October 1878, 527–42.

—— 'The Present State of the Novel I', *Fortnightly Review*, 42 (September 1887), 410–17.

—— 'The Present State of the Novel II', *Fortnightly Review*, 43 (January 1888), 112–23.

—— 'The Historical Novel II – Scott and Dumas', *Essays in English Literature 1780–1860*, Second Series (London: J. M. Dent and Co., 1895).

—— 'The Present State of Criticism', *A History of Criticism and Literary Taste in Europe*, 3 vols, vol. 3 (Edinburgh and London: William Blackwood and Sons, 1904), pp. 603–10.

Tilley, A., 'The New School of Fiction', *National Review*, 1 (April 1883), 257–68.

Unsigned., 'The Modern Novel', *Saturday Review*, 11 November 1882, 633–4.

—— 'Sir John Lubbock's Liberal Education', *Pall Mall Gazette*, 11 January 1886, 4.

—— 'The Best Hundred Books', *Pall Mall Gazette*, 2 February 1886, 1–2.

—— 'To Read or Not to Read', *Pall Mall Gazette*, 8 February 1886, 11.

—— 'The Choice of Books: A Lecture by Mr J. R. Lowell', *Pall Mall Gazette*, 11 February 1886, 11.

—— 'Carlyle on the Best Books', *Pall Mall Gazette*, 17 February 1886, 1–2.

—— 'How to Speak, How to Read and How to Think: Report of a Lecture given by Mr Goschen to students attending the London Society for the Extension of University Teaching', *Pall Mall Gazette*, 1 March 1886, 11.

—— 'The Cheapening of Poetry', *National Observer*, 5 (1892), 624–5.

—— 'Robert Louis Stevenson', *Saturday Review*, 22 December 1894, 675–6.

Wells, H. G., 'The Lost Stevenson', *Saturday Review*, 81 (13 June 1896), 603–4; reprinted in P. Parrinder and R. M. Philmus, *H. G. Wells's Literary Criticism* (Brighton: Harvester Press, 1980), pp. 99–103.

—— 'The Contemporary Novel', *An Englishman Looks at the World* (1914), pp. 148–69; reprinted in P. Parrinder and R. M. Philmus, *H. G. Wells's Literary Criticism* (Brighton: Harvester Press, 1980), pp. 192–205.

General bibliography

Aikman, J., *Annals of the Persecution in Scotland from the Restoration to the Revolution* (Edinburgh: Hugh Paton, 1842).

Altick, R. D., *The English Common Reader: A Social History of the Mass Reading Public, 1800–1900* (Chicago and London: Chicago University Press, 1957).

—— *Victorian Studies in Scarlet* (London: J. M. Dent, 1972).

Ambrosini, R., 'R. L. Stevenson and the Ethical Value of Writing for the Market', *Journal of Stevenson Studies*, 1 (2004), 24–41.

Ambrosini R. and R. Dury (eds), *Robert Louis Stevenson: Writer of Boundaries* (Madison: University of Wisconsin Press, 2006).

Amigoni, D., *The English Novel and Prose Narrative* (Edinburgh: Edinburgh University Press, 2000).

Anderson, C., 'No Single Key: The Fiction of Robert Louis Stevenson and Italo Calvino', in J. J. Simon and A. Sinner (eds), *English Studies 3: Proceedings of the Third Conference on the Literature of Region and Nation* (Luxembourg: Publications du Centre Universitaire de Luxembourg, 1991), pp. 15–34.

Angus, D., 'Robert Louis Stevenson: The Secret Sources', *Studies in Scottish Literature*, 27 (1993), 81–91.

Appleyard, J. A., *Becoming a Reader: The Experience of Fiction from Childhood to Adulthood* (Cambridge: Cambridge University Press, 1990).

Arata, S., 'Stevenson Reading', *Journal of Stevenson Studies*, 1 (2004), 192–200.

—— 'Observing *The Wrecker*', conference paper 'Stevenson and Conrad: Writers of Land and Sea', Second International Stevenson Conference, Edinburgh, 2004.

Bachelard, G., *The Poetics of Space*, trans. M. Jolas (1958; Boston: Beacon Press, 1994).

—— *The Poetics of Reverie: Childhood, Language and the Cosmos*, trans. D. Russell (1960; Boston: Beacon Press, 1969).

Balderston, D., *Borges' Frame of Reference: the Strange Case of Robert Louis Stevenson*, PhD thesis, University of Princeton, 1981; Ann Arbor, MI: University Microfilms.

Baldick, C., *The Social Mission of English Criticism* (Oxford: Clarendon Press, 1983).

Balfour, G., *The Life of Robert Louis Stevenson*, 2 vols, vol. 1 (London: Methuen, 1901).

Ballantyne, R. M., *The Coral Island: A Tale of the Pacific Ocean* (London: T. Nelson and Sons, 1858).

Bann, S., *The Clothing of Clio: A Study of the Representation of History in Nineteenth-century Britain and France* (Cambridge: Cambridge University Press, 1984).

Barthes, R., *S/Z*, trans. R. Miller (New York: Hill and Wang, 1974).

—— *The Pleasure of the Text*, trans. R.Miller (New York: Hill and Wang, 1975).

—— *The Rustle of Language*, trans. R. Howard (Oxford: Basil Blackwell, 1986).

Bell, I., *Robert Louis Stevenson: Dreams of Exile* (London: Headline, 1993).

Benedict, P., *Christ's Church Purely Reformed: A Social History of Calvinism* (New Haven and London: Yale University Press, 2002).

Bennett, A., *Readers and Reading* (London and New York: Longman, 1995).

Besant, W., *The Pen and the Book* (London: Thomas Burleigh, 1899).

Beveridge C. and R. Turnbull, *Scotland After Enlightenment* (Edinburgh: Polygon, 1997).

Blake, A., *Reading Victorian Fiction: The Cultural Context and Ideological Content of the Nineteenth-century Novel* (London: Macmillan, 1989).

Bloom, H., *The Anxiety of Influence: A Theory of Poetry* (New York: Oxford University Press, 1973).

Bourdieu, P., *Distinction: A Social Critique of the Judgement of Taste*, trans. R. Nice (London: Routledge and Kegan Paul, 1986).

Brantlinger, P., *Rule of Darkness: British Literature and Imperialism 1830–1914* (Ithaca and London: Cornell University Press, 1988).

—— *The Reading Lesson: The Threat of Mass Literacy in Nineteenth-century British Fiction* (Bloomington and Indianapolis: Indiana University Press, 1998).

Brearley M. and D. Doust, *The Ashes Retained* (London: Hodder and Stoughton, 1979).

Bristow, J., *Empire Boys: Adventures in a Man's World* (London: Unwin Hyman, 1991).

Burnet, G., *The History of My Own Time*, 2 vols (London: Thomas Ward, 1724–34).

Calder, A., 'Byron and Scotland', *Cencrastus*, 15 (1984), 21–4.

Calder, J., *RLS: A Life Study* (London: Hamish Hamilton, 1980).

—— (ed.), *Stevenson and Victorian Scotland* (Edinburgh: Edinburgh University Press, 1981).

Caldwell, E. N., *Last Witness for Robert Louis Stevenson* (Norman: University of Oklahoma Press, 1960).

Calinescu, M., *Rereading* (New Haven and London: Yale University Press, 1993).

Calvin, J., *Institutes of the Christian Religion*, ed. J. T. MacNeill; trans. F. L. Battles, 2 vols (London: SCM Press, 1961).

Calvino, I., *I nostri antenati* (*Our Ancestors*) trans. I. Quigley (London: Picador, 1980).

Cameron, N. M. de S. (ed.), *The Dictionary of Scottish Church History and Theology* (Edinburgh: T. and T. Clark, 1993).

Campbell, I. (ed.), *Nineteenth Century Scottish Fiction: Critical Essays* (Manchester: Carcanet New Press, 1979).

Campbell, T., *Standing Witnesses: An Illustrated Guide to the Scottish Covenanters* (Edinburgh: Saltire Society, 1996).

Cavallo G. and R. Chartier (eds), *A History of Reading in the West*, trans. L. G. Cochrane (Oxford: Polity Press, 1999).

Certeau, M. de, *The Practice of Everyday Life*, trans. S. Rendall (Berkeley and Los Angeles: University of California Press, 1984; 1988).

—— *The Writing of History*, trans. T. Conley (New York: Columbia University Press, 1988).

Chambers, R., *History of the Rebellions in Scotland under the Viscount of Dundee and the Earl of Mar in 1689 and 1715* (Edinburgh and London: Constable and Co.; Hurst, Chance and Co., 1829).

Chartier, R., *Forms and Meanings: Texts, Performances, and Audiences from Codex to Computer* (Philadelphia: University of Pennsylvania Press, 1995).

Clunas, A., 'R. L. Stevenson: Precursor of the Post-moderns', *Cencrastus*, 6 (1981), 9–11.

—— '"A Double Word": Writing and Justice in *The Master of Ballantrae*', *Studies in Scottish Literature*, 28 (1993), 55–74.

Colley, A. C., '"Writing Towards Home": The Landscape of *A Child's Garden of Verses*', *Victorian Poetry*, 35:3 (1997), 303–18.

Connell, J., *W. E. Henley* (London: Constable, 1949).

Court, F. E., *Institutionalizing English Literature: The Culture and Politics of Literary Study 1750–1900* (Stanford: Stanford University Press, 1992).

Cowan, E. and D. Gifford (eds), *The Polar Twins* (Edinburgh: John Donald, 1999.

Cowan, I. B., *The Scottish Covenanters 1660–1688* (London: Victor Gollancz, 1976).

Craig, C., *Out of History: Narrative Paradigms in Scottish and English Culture* (Edinburgh: Polygon, 1996).

—— *The Modern Scottish Novel: Narrative and the National Imagination* (Edinburgh: Edinburgh University Press, 1999).

Crawford, R. (ed.), *The Scottish Invention of English Literature* (Cambridge: Cambridge University Press, 1998).

Cross, N., *The Common Writer: Life in Nineteenth-century Grub Street* (Cambridge: Cambridge University Press, 1985).

Cunningham W., *Theological Lectures on subjects connected with natural theology and evidences of Christianity, the canon and inspiration of scripture* (London: James Nisbet and Co., 1878).

Currie, J., *History, Hagiography, and Fakestory: Representations of the Scottish Covenanters in Non-Fictional and Fictional Texts from 1638 to 1835*, PhD thesis, University of Stirling, 1999.

Daiches, D., *Stevenson and the Art of Fiction* (New York: privately printed, 1951).

Daly, N., *Modernism, Romance and the Fin de Siècle: Popular Fiction and British Culture 1880–1914* (Cambridge: Cambridge University Press, 1999).

Darnton, R., *The Kiss of Lamourette: Reflections in Cultural History* (London: Faber and Faber, 1990).

Davie, G. E., *The Democratic Intellect: Scotland and Her Universities in the Nineteenth Century* (Edinburgh: Edinburgh University Press, 1961).

Devine T. (ed.), *Scotland's Shame?: Bigotry and Sectarianism in Modern Scotland* (Edinburgh and London: Mainstream, 2000).

Dickson, B., 'The Gospel and Scottish Fiction', *Scottish Bulletin of Evangelical Theology*, 14:1 (1996), 51–64.

Donnachie, I. and C. Whatley, *The Manufacture of Scottish History* (Edinburgh: Polygon, 1992).

Donnelly, W. J., *Religion and the Poetic Imagination*, PhD thesis, University of Edinburgh, 1981.

Doyle, A. C., *The Refugees: A Tale of Two Continents* (London: Longmans, 1893).

Drummond, A. L. and J. Bulloch, *The Scottish Church 1688–1843: The Age of the Moderate* (Edinburgh: The Saint Andrew Press, 1973).

—— *The Church in Victorian Scotland 1843–1874* (Edinburgh: The Saint Andrew Press, 1975).

—— *The Church in Late Victorian Scotland 1874–1900* (Edinburgh: The Saint Andrew Press, 1978).

Dumas, A., *The Three Musketeers*; *Twenty Years After*; *The Vicomte de Brageleonne*; *Louise de la Vallière*; *The Man in the Iron Mask* (World Classics edition, ed. David Coward, following 1857 Routledge English translations) (Oxford: Oxford University Press, 1991–5).

Eigner, E., *Robert Louis Stevenson and Romantic Tradition* (Princeton: Princeton University Press, 1966).

Engelsing, R., "Die Perioden der Lesergeschichte in der Neuzeit: Das statistische Ausmass und die soziokulturelle Bedeutung der Lektüre', *Archiv für Geschichte des Buchwesens*, 10 (1970), 944–1002.

Farr, L. *Robert Louis Stevenson's Essays: Aesthetics, Masculinity and the Literary Marketplace*, PhD thesis, Birkbeck College, University of London, 2003.

—— 'Surpassing the Love of Women: Robert Louis Stevenson and the Pleasures of Boy-loving', *Journal of Stevenson Studies*, 2 (2005), 140–60.

Feltes, N. N., *Literary Capital and the Late Victorian Novel* (Madison: University of Wisconsin Press, 1993).

Ferguson, W., *Scotland 1689 to the Present* (Oliver and Boyd, London, 1968).

—— *The Identity of the Scottish Nation: An Historic Quest* (Edinburgh: Edinburgh University Press, 1998).

Fiedler, L. A., *No! in Thunder: The Collected Essays of Leslie Fiedler* (New York: Stein and Day, 1971).

Fielding, P., *Writing and Orality: Nationality, Culture and Nineteenth-century Scottish Fiction* (Oxford: Clarendon Press, 1996).

Flint, K., *The Woman Reader 1837–1914* (Oxford: Clarendon Press, 1993).

Fraser, R., *Victorian Quest Romance: Stevenson, Haggard, Kipling and Conan Doyle* (London: Northcote House/British Council, 1998).

Freedman, J., *Professions of Taste: Henry James, British Aestheticism, and Commodity Culture* (Stanford: Stanford University Press, 1990).

Freud, S., *Standard Edition of the Complete Psychological Works of Sigmund Freud*, vol. IX (1906–1908), trans. under the General Editorship of James Strachey in collaboration with Anna Freud, assisted by Alix Strachey and Alan Tyson (London: The Hogarth Press and the Institute of Psycho-analysis, 1959) (London: Vintage Press, 2001).

Frow, J., *Cultural Studies and Cultural Value* (Oxford: Clarendon Press, 1995).

Frye, N., *Anatomy of Criticism: Four Essays* (Princeton: Princeton University Press, 1957; 1971).

Furnas, J. C., *Voyage to Windward: The Life of Robert Louis Stevenson* (New York: William Sloane Associates, 1951).

Gadamer, H., *Truth and Method*, trans. J. Weinsheimer and D. G. Marshall; second, revised edition (London: Continuum 1975; 1989; 2004).

Goffman, E., *Frame Analysis: An Essay on the Organisation of Experience* (Harmondsworth: Penguin, 1975).

Graham, K., *English Criticism of the Novel 1865–1900* (Oxford: Clarendon Press, 1965).

Gray, W., 'Stevenson's "Auld Alliance": France, Art Theory and the Breath of Money in *The Wrecker*', *Scottish Studies Review*, 3:2 (2002), 54–65.

Gregerson, L., *The Reformation of the Subject: Spenser, Milton and the English Protestant Epic* (Cambridge; New York: Cambridge University Press, 1995).

Gribben, C., *The Puritan Millennium: Literature and Theology, 1550–1682* (Dublin: Four Courts Press, 2000).

—— 'James Hogg, Scottish Calvinism and Literary Theory', *Scottish Studies Review*, 5:2 (2004), 9–26.

Gross, J., *The Rise and Fall of the Man of Letters: English Literary Life Since 1800* (Harmondsworth: Penguin, 1969).

Habermas, J., *The Structural Transformation of the Public Sphere* (London: Polity Press, 1989)

Hadley, T., *Henry James and the Imagination of Pleasure* (New York: Cambridge University Press, 2002).

Hall, S., 'Notes on Deconstructing "the Popular"', in R. Samuel (ed.), *People's History and Socialist Theory* (London: Routledge, 1991), pp. 227–40.

Hamilton, I., *Keepers of the Flame: Literary Estates and the Rise of Biography* (London: Hutchinson, 1992).

Harvie, C., *Scotland and Nationalism: Scottish Society and Politics 1707–1977* (London: Allen and Unwin, 1977).

Hawthorne, N., *The Scarlet Letter* (1850), ed. R. Butterfield (London: Dent, 1971).

Hayward, W. S., *Tom Holt's Log: A Tale of the Deep Sea* (London: C. H. Clarke, 1868).

Henderson, G. D., *Religious Life in Seventeenth-century Scotland* (Cambridge: Cambridge University Press, 1937).

Hewison, J. K., *The Covenanters: A History of the Church in Scotland from the Reformation to the Revolution*, 2 vols, rev. edn (Glasgow: John Smith, 1913).

Hilgard, J. R., *Personality and Hypnosis: A Study of Imaginative Involvement* (Chicago: University of Chicago Press 1970).

Hirsch, G., 'The Commercial World of *The Wrecker*', *Journal of Stevenson Studies*, 2 (2005), 70–97.

Holland N., *The Dynamics of Literary Response* (New York: Oxford University Press, 1968).

Howard, D., J. Lucas and J. Goode, *Tradition and Tolerance in Nineteenth-century Fiction: Critical Essays on Some English and American Novels* (London: Routledge and Kegan Paul, 1966).

Howie, J., *Faithful Contendings Display'd: Being an historical relation of the state and actings of the suffering remnant in the Church of Scotland, who subsisted in select societies, and were united in general correspondence during the hottest time of the late persecution from the year 1681 to 1691* (Glasgow: John Bryce, 1780).

—— *Biographia Scoticana* (Glasgow: John Bryce, 1779).

—— *The Scots Worthies: Volume First Containing a Brief Historical Account of the most Eminent Noblemen, Gentlemen, Ministers and Others who testified or suffered for the cause of Reformation in Scotland, from the beginning of the sixteenth century to the year 1688 originally compiled by John Howie of Lochgoin, Now revised, corrected and enlarged by A Clergyman of the Church of Scotland and enriched with a preface and notes by William M'Gavin esquire* (Glasgow: McPhun, 1829).

Hubbard, T., *Seeking Mr Hyde: Studies in Robert Louis Stevenson, Symbolism, Myth and the Pre-modern* (Frankfurt am Main: Peter Lang, 1995).

Huey, E. B., *The Psychology and Pedagogy of Reading: With a Review of the History of Reading and Writing and of Methods, Texts and Hygiene in Reading* (London: Macmillan, 1908; Cambridge, MA and London: The MIT Press, 1968).

Hunt, L. (ed.), *The New Cultural History* (Berkeley, Los Angles and London: University of California Press, 1989).

Ingarden, R., *The Cognition of the Literary Work of Art* (Evanston, IL: Northwestern University Press, 1973).

Iser, W., *The Act of Reading: A Theory of Aesthetic Response* (London: Routledge and Kegan Paul, 1987).

James, H., *Notes on Novelists* (London: J. M. Dent, 1914).

James, W., *Principles of Psychology*, vol. 2 (New York: Dover, 1950).

Jameson, F., *The Political Unconscious: Narrative as a Socially Symbolic Act* (London: Methuen, 1981).

—— 'Science Fiction as a Spatial Genre: Generic Discontinuities and the Problem of Figuration in Vonda McIntyre's *The Exile Waiting*', *Science Fiction Studies*, 14 (1987), 44–59.

Japp, A., *Robert Louis Stevenson, a Record, an Estimate and a Memorial* (London: T. Werner Laurie, 1905).

Jauss, H. R., 'New Literary History as a Challenge to Literary Theory', *New Literary History*, 11:1 (1970), 7–37.

Johnstone, W. (ed.), *William Robert Smith: Essays in Reassessment* (Sheffield: Sheffield Academic Press, 1995).

Jolly, R., *Henry James: History, Narrative, Fiction* (Oxford: Clarendon Press, 1993).

—— 'Stevenson's "Sterling Domestic Fiction", "The Beach of Falesá"', *Review of English Studies* 50:200 (1999), 463–82.

Jones, W. B. (ed.), *Robert Louis Stevenson Reconsidered: New Critical Perspectives* (Jefferson, NC, and London: McFarland, 2003).

Jordan, J. O. and R. L. Patten (eds), *Literature in the Marketplace: Nineteenth-century British Publishing and Reading Practices* (Cambridge: Cambridge University Press, 1995).

Katz, W. R., *Rider Haggard and the Fiction of Empire: A Critical Study of British Imperial Fiction* (Cambridge: Cambridge University Press, 1987).

Keating, P., *The Haunted Study: A Social History of the English Novel 1875–1914* (London: Secker and Warburg, 1989; Fontana, 1991).

Kelman, J., *The Faith of Robert Louis Stevenson* (Edinburgh and London: Oliphant, Anderson and Ferrier, 1907).

Kernohan, R. D. (ed.), *The Realm of Reform: Presbyterianism and Calvinism in a Changing Scotland* (Edinburgh: The Handsel Press, 1999).

Kiely, R., *Robert Louis Stevenson and the Fiction of* Adventure (Cambridge, MA: Harvard University Press, 1964).

Kingston, W. H. G., *Peter the Whaler* (1851; London: Grant and Griffith, 1853).

Kirkton J., *The Secret and True History of the Church of Scotland from the Restoration to the Year 1678 by the Rev James Kirkton, to which is added an account of the murder of Archbishop Sharp by James Russell, an actor therein, edited from the mss by Charles Kirkpatrick Sharpe esq.* (Edinburgh: Longman, Hurst, Rees, Orme and Brown, 1817).

Klancher, J. P., *The Making of English Reading Audiences 1790–1832* (London and Madison: University of Wisconsin Press, 1987).

Lang, A., *Adventures among Books* (London: Longman, 1905).

Lascelles, M., *The Story-teller Retrieves the Past: Historical Fiction and Fictitious History in the Art of Scott, Stevenson, Kipling and Some Others* (Oxford: Clarendon Press, 1980).

Low, W. H., *A Chronicle of Friendships 1873–1900* (London: Hodder and Stoughton, 1908).

Lubbock, Sir J., *The Pleasures of Life: Part 1* (London: Macmillan, 1899).

Lund, M., *Reading Thackeray* (Detroit: Wayne State University Press, 1988).

MacColla, F., *At the Sign of the Clenched Fist* (Edinburgh: MacDonald, 1967).

MacCracken, S., *Pulp: Reading Popular Fiction* (Manchester: Manchester University Press, 1998).

Mackenzie, Sister M. L., *Experiments in Romance: Theory and Practice in the Fiction of Robert Louis Stevenson*, PhD thesis, University of Toronto, 1974.

Macksey R. A. and E. Donato (eds), *The Structuralist Controversy: The Language of Criticism and the Sciences of Man* (Baltimore and London: Johns Hopkins University Press, 1972).

MacLeod, D., 'Scottish Calvinism: A Dark, Repressive Force?', *Scottish Bulletin of Evangelical Theology*, 19:2 (2001), 195–225.

Mailloux, S., *Interpretive Conventions: The Reader in the Study of American Fiction* (Ithaca: Cornell University Press, 1982).

—— *Rhetorical Power* (Ithaca: Cornell University Press, 1989).

Manguel, A., *A History of Reading* (London: HarperCollins, 1996).

Margolis, A. T., *Henry James and the Problem of Audience: An International Act* (Ann Arbor, MI: UMI Research Press, 1985).

Marshall, G., *Presbyteries and Profits: Calvinism and the Development of Capitalism in Scotland 1560–1707* (Oxford: Clarendon Press, 1980).

Masson, R., *I Can Remember Robert Louis Stevenson* (Edinburgh and London: W. and R. Chambers, 1922).

Maxwell, Sir H., *Scottish Land Names: Their Origin and Meaning* (Edinburgh: William Blackwood and Sons, 1894).

McCulloch, F., '"The Broken Telescope": Misrepresentation in *The Coral Island*', *Children's Literature Association Quarterly*, 25:3 (2000), 137–45.

McDonald, P. D., *British Literary Culture and Publishing Practice 1880–1914* (Cambridge: Cambridge University Press, 1997).

McLaughlin, K., 'The Financial Imp: Ethics and Finance in Nineteenth Century Fiction', *Novel*, 29:2 (1996), 165–83.

McLynn, F., *Robert Louis Stevenson: A Biography* (London: Hutchinson, 1993).

Menikoff, B., *Robert Louis Stevenson and 'The Beach of Falesá': A Study in Victorian Publishing* (Edinburgh: Edinburgh University Press, 1984).

—— *Narrating Scotland: The Imagination of Robert Louis Stevenson* (Columbia: University of South Carolina Press, 2005).

Miller, K. (ed.), *Memoirs of a Modern Scotland* (London: Faber and Faber, 1970).

Moors, H. J., *With Stevenson in Samoa* (London and Leipsic: T. Fisher Unwin, 1911).

Muir, E., 'Robert Louis Stevenson', *The Modern Scot*, II: 3 (1931), 196–204.

—— *Scott and Scotland: The Predicament of the Scottish Writer* (London: George Routledge, 1936).

Nadel, I. B. (ed.), *Victorian Fiction: A Collection of Essays from the Period* (New York and London: Garland, 1986).

Nash, A., 'Two Unpublished Letters of Robert Louis Stevenson', *Notes and Queries*, 245:3 (2000), 334–6.

Nell, V., *Lost in a Book: The Psychology of Reading for Pleasure* (New Haven and London: Yale University Press, 1988).

Noble A. (ed.), *Robert Louis Stevenson* (London and Totowa, NJ: Vision Press and Barnes and Noble, 1983).

Norquay, G., *Challenges to Realism: Moral Absolutism in the Novels of Robert Louis Stevenson, Robin Jenkins and Muriel Spark*, PhD thesis, University of Edinburgh, 1985.

Olmsted, J. C., *A Victorian Art of Fiction: Essays on the Novel in British Periodicals 1870–1900* (New York and London: Garland, 1979).

Ong, W., 'The Writer's Audience Is Always a Fiction', *PMLA*, 90 (1975), 9–21.

Orel, H., *Victorian Literary Critics* (London: Macmillan, 1984).

Palmer, D. J., *The Rise of English Studies: An Account of the Study of English Language and Literature from its Origins to the Making of the Oxford English School* (London, New York, Toronto: Oxford University Press (for University of Hull), 1965).

Parfect, R., *Hell's Dexterities: The Violent Art of Robert Louis Stevenson*, PhD thesis, University of London, 2003.

Parrinder, P. and R. M. Philmus, *H. G. Wells's Literary Criticism* (Brighton: Harvester Press, 1980).

Phelps, W. L., *The Advance of the English Novel* (London: John Murray, 1919).

Pierce, J. A., 'The Belle Lettrist and the People's Publisher; or, the Context of *Treasure Island's* First-form Publication', *Victorian Periodicals Review*, 31:4 (1998), 356–68.

Polhemus, R. M and R. B. Henkle (eds), *Critical Reconstructions: The Relationship Between Fiction and Life* (Stanford: Stanford University Press, 1994).

Pope Hennessy, J., *Robert Louis Stevenson* (London: Cape, 1974).

Power, W., *Literature and Oatmeal: What Literature Has Meant to Scotland* (London: George Routledge, 1935).

Priestman, D. G., 'Old Battles Fought Anew', *Wordsworth Circle*, 12:2 (Spring 1981), 117–21.

Ramsay, M. P., *Calvin and Art: Considered in Relation to Scotland* (Edinburgh: Moray Press, 1938).

Reid, D. (ed.), *The Party-coloured Mind: Prose Relating to the Conflict of Church and State in Seventeenth-Century Scotland* (Edinburgh: Scottish Academic Press, 1982).

Reid, I., *Narrative Exchanges* (Routledge: London and New York, 1992).

Ricoeur, P., *Hermeneutics and the Human Sciences*, ed. and trans. J. B. Thompson (Cambridge: Cambridge University Press, 1981).

Riffaterre, M., *The Semiotics of Poetry* (London: Methuen, 1978).

Rose, J., *The Intellectual Life of the British Working Classes* (New Haven and London: Yale University Press, 2001).

Royle T. (ed.), *Jock Tamson's Bairns: Essays on a Scots Childhood* (London: Hamish Hamilton, 1977).

Saintsbury, G., *Essays in English Literature 1780–1860* (London: Percival and Co., 1890).

—— *Essays in English Literature 1780–1860 Second Series* (London: J. M. Dent and Co., 1893).

Sandison, A., *Robert Louis Stevenson and the Appearance of Modernism: A Future Feeling* (London: Macmillan, 1996).

Scott, Sir W., *Old Mortality*, ed. A. Calder (Harmondsworth: Penguin, 1975).

—— *The Tale of Old Mortality*, ed. D. Mack (Edinburgh: Edinburgh University Press, 1993).

Sharratt, B., *Reading Relations: Structures of Literary Production: A Dialectical Text/Book* (Brighton: Harvester Press, 1982).

Shaw, G. B., *Cashel Bryon's Profession*, rev. edn (London: Constable and Co. Ltd, 1932).

Simpson, K. G., 'Realism and Romance: Stevenson's Scottish Values', *Studies in Scottish Literature*, 20 (1985), 231–47.

Smellie, A., *Men of the Covenant* (1903; London, The Banner of Truth Trust, 1960).

Smith, G. S., *The Seeds of Secularization: Calvinism, Culture and Pluralism in America, 1870–1915* (Grand Rapids, Michigan: W. B. Eerdmans, 1985).

Smith, J. A., *Henry James and Robert Louis Stevenson: A Record of Friendship and Criticism* (London: Rupert Hart-Davis, 1948).

Smith, V., *Literary Culture and the Pacific: Nineteenth-century Textual Encounters* (Cambridge: Cambridge University Press, 1998).

Smout, T. C., *A History of the Scottish People 1560–1830* (1969: London, Fontana Press, 1998).

Stewart, G., *Dear Reader: The Conscripted Audience in Nineteenth-century British Fiction* (Baltimore and London: Johns Hopkins University Press, 1996).

Suleiman, S. R. and I. Crosman (eds), *The Reader in the Text: Essays on Audience and Interpretation* (Princeton: Princeton University Press, 1980).

Summers, M., *A Gothic Bibliography* (London: The Fortune Press, 1941).

Sutherland, J., *Victorian Fiction: Writers, Publishers, Readers* (London: Macmillan, 1995).

Taylor, J. T., *Early Opposition to the English Novel: The Popular Reaction from 1760 to 1830* (New York: King's Crown Press, 1943).

Tellegen, A. and G. Atkinson, 'Openness to Absorbing Self-altering Experiences (absorption), a Trait Related to Hypnotic Susceptibility', *Journal of Abnormal Psychology*, 83 (1974), 268–77.

Thwaite, A. (ed.), *Portraits from Life by Edmund Gosse* (London: Scolar Press, 1991).

Tickner, L., *Modern Life and Modern Subjects: British Art in the Early Twentieth Century* (New Haven and London: Yale University Press, 2000).

Tompkins, J. P. (ed.), *Reader Response Criticism: From Formalism to Post-structuralism* (Baltimore and London: Johns Hopkins University Press, 1980).

Treglown, J. and B. Bennett, *Grub Street and the Ivory Tower: Literary Journalism and Literary Scholarship from Fielding to the Internet* (Oxford: Clarendon Press, 1998).

Veeder, W. and G. Hirsch (eds), *Dr Jekyll and Mr Hyde after One Hundred Years* (Chicago: University of Chicago Press, 1988).

Walker, P., *Biographia Presbyteriana including Some Remarkable Passages in the Life and Death of Mr Alexander Peden* (1728), 2 vols (Edinburgh: D. Speare and J. Stevenson, 1827).

Warren, A., *The New England Conscience* (Ann Arbor: University of Michigan Press, 1966).

Weber, M., *The Protestant Ethic and the Spirit Of Capitalism*, trans. T. Parsons (London: Allen and Unwin, 1930).

Webster, A., *R. L. Stevenson and Henry Drummond* (London: The Lindsey Press, 1912).

Wendel, F., *Calvin: The Origins and Development of His Religious*

Thought, trans. P. Mairet (London: Collins, 1963).

Weyman, S. J. *The New Rector* (Leipzig: Heinemann and Balesteir, 1891).

—— *My Lady Rotha: A Romance* (Leipzig: Bernard Tauchnitz, 1894).

—— *Under the Red Robe* (Leipzig: Bernard Tauchnitz, 1894).

Whyte, C., *Modern Scottish Poetry* (Edinburgh: Edinburgh University Press, 2004).

Wilt, J., *The Readable People of George Meredith* (Princeton: Princeton University Press, 1975).

Wodrow, R., *The History of the Suffering of the Church of Scotland from the Restoration to the Revolution: collected from the public records, original manuscripts of that time, and other well-attested narratives*, 2 vols (Edinburgh: James Watson, 1721 and 1722; reprinted *With an original memoir of the author, extracts from his correspondence, a preliminary dissertation and notes by the Rev Robert Burns, Minister of St. George's Paisley*, 4 vols (Glasgow: Blackie and Son, 1836).

Yonge, C. M., *The Young Stepmother* (1857–60; Leipzig, 1861).

Index